Palgrave Studies in Nineteenth-Century
Writing and Culture

Series Editor
Joseph Bristow
Department of English
University of California – Los Angeles
Los Angeles, California
USA

*Palgrave Studies in Nineteenth-Century Writing and Culture* is a new monograph series that aims to represent the most innovative research on literary works that were produced in the English-speaking world from the time of the Napoleonic Wars to the fin de siècle. Attentive to the historical continuities between 'Romantic' and 'Victorian', the series will feature studies that help scholarship to reassess the meaning of these terms during a century marked by diverse cultural, literary, and political movements. The main aim of the series is to look at the increasing influence of types of historicism on our understanding of literary forms and genres. It reflects the shift from critical theory to cultural history that has affected not only the period 1800–1900 but also every field within the discipline of English literature. All titles in the series seek to offer fresh critical perspectives and challenging readings of both canonical and non-canonical writings of this era.

More information about this series at
http://www.springer.com/series/14607

Alan McNee

# The New Mountaineer in Late Victorian Britain

## Materiality, Modernity, and the Haptic Sublime

Alan McNee
London, UK

Palgrave Studies in Nineteenth-Century Writing and Culture
ISBN 978-3-319-33439-4      ISBN 978-3-319-33440-0 (eBook)
DOI 10.1007/978-3-319-33440-0

Library of Congress Control Number: 2016949043

© The Editor(s) (if applicable) and The Author(s) 2016
This work is subject to copyright. All rights are solely and exclusively licensed by the Publisher, whether the whole or part of the material is concerned, specifically the rights of translation, reprinting, reuse of illustrations, recitation, broadcasting, reproduction on microfilms or in any other physical way, and transmission or information storage and retrieval, electronic adaptation, computer software, or by similar or dissimilar methodology now known or hereafter developed.
The use of general descriptive names, registered names, trademarks, service marks, etc. in this publication does not imply, even in the absence of a specific statement, that such names are exempt from the relevant protective laws and regulations and therefore free for general use. The publisher, the authors and the editors are safe to assume that the advice and information in this book are believed to be true and accurate at the date of publication. Neither the publisher nor the authors or the editors give a warranty, express or implied, with respect to the material contained herein or for any errors or omissions that may have been made. The publisher remains neutral with regard to jurisdictional claims in published maps and institutional affiliations.

Cover illustration: © SOTK2011/Alamy Stock Photo

Printed on acid-free paper

This Palgrave Macmillan imprint is published by Springer Nature
The registered company is Springer International Publishing AG
The registered company address is: Gewerbestrasse 11, 6330 Cham, Switzerland

# Acknowledgements

I would like to thank a number of people who helped in the research, writing, and production of this book. Special thanks are due to Dr. Ana Parejo Vadillo, Dr. Luisa Calè, and Professor Hilary Fraser of Birkbeck College, and Dr. Stefano Evangelista of Trinity College, Oxford.

Tadeusz Hudowski, Librarian of the Alpine Club, and Glyn Hughes, Hon. Archivist of the Alpine Club, were extremely helpful in tracking down material and putting me in touch with other historians of mountaineering. Robin N. Campbell, Hon. Archivist of the Scottish Mountaineering Club, and David Medcalf, Hon. Archivist of the Climbers' Club, were also most helpful and supportive.

I would like to thank Nick and Rupert Pullee of the Pen-y-Gwryd Hotel in Snowdonia, for kindly allowing me access to the hotel's 'Locked Book'. I am also grateful to the staff of the National Library of Scotland in Edinburgh and the Cumbria County Archive in Kendal for their assistance in finding logbooks and other archive material, and to the staff of the British Library and the London Library. Excerpts from Wasdale Head visitors' books are by kind permission of the Fell and Rock Climbing Club Archives.

I would like to thank Benjamin Doyle and Tomas René of Palgrave Macmillan for their support with the editorial process, and Professor Joseph Bristow of UCLA for his very helpful and thoughtful comments on the manuscript. Thanks also to Dr. John Cooper of Exeter University, Dr. David Gillott of Birkbeck, and Ann Colley, Distinguished Professor at

Buffalo State College, SUNY, for their help and advice, and to Dr. Tanya Izzard for her advice on indexing. I am grateful to the editorial staff of Victorian Review and 19: Interdisciplinary Studies in the Long Nineteenth Century for their permission to use material that originally appeared in those journals.

# Contents

| | | |
|---|---|---|
| 1 | Introduction | 1 |
| 2 | The Rise of the New Mountaineer | 31 |
| 3 | Resisting the New Mountaineer | 73 |
| 4 | The Climbing Body | 109 |
| 5 | The Haptic Sublime | 149 |
| 6 | 'Trippers' and the New Mountain Landscape | 189 |
| 7 | Conclusion | 219 |
| Glossary | | 225 |
| Bibliography | | 227 |
| Index | | 247 |

# List of Figures

| | | |
|---|---|---|
| Fig. 2.1 | The Beispielspitz, from the *Badminton* guide. An example of the close attention given to route finding and identifying features | 34 |
| Fig. 2.2 | Photograph of Mt. Elias amended to show the route, from *Alpine Journal* 19 (1898) | 49 |
| Fig. 2.3 | Adverts for climbing and camping equipment, from *Alpine Journal* 11 (1884) | 57 |
| Fig. 4.1 | 'British Hill Weather', from the *Badminton* guide | 113 |
| Fig. 4.2 | Grim pleasure and black humour: 'Serves Him Right', from the *Badminton* guide | 131 |

CHAPTER 1

# Introduction

In 1898 the Scottish mountaineer John Norman Collie coined the term from which this book takes its title. 'The progressive, democratic finger of the "New Mountaineer" is laid with equal irreverence and mockery on Sgurr nan Gillean and Cir Mhor', Collie wrote.[1]

The details of Collie's protest (in essence, that contemporary climbers were dismissive of the challenges and charms of the Cuillin mountains on the Isle of Skye) are obscure now, but his use of the term 'New Mountaineer' remains significant. The New Mountaineer may never have joined the New Woman or the New Journalism in the lexicon of *fin-de-siècle* Britain, but Collie's belief that a paradigm shift had taken place in the culture of British mountaineering, and that climbers were approaching their activity in a new spirit, was shared by a number of influential writers. This book is about that shift. It examines the profound changes that took place in British mountaineering in the latter part of the nineteenth century, exemplified by the figure of the New Mountaineer, and discusses how attitudes to mountains in this period were transformed by developments both within the recreation of mountaineering and in the wider culture.

Perhaps the most important of the former was the emergence of the new genre of mountaineering literature, which helped to create a self-conscious community of climbers with broadly shared values and attitudes. Meanwhile various cultural and scientific trends influenced the direction of mountaineering. These included a growing preoccupation with the physical basis of aesthetic sensation, and with physicality and materiality in general; a new interest in the physiology of effort and fatigue; and a characteristically Victorian drive to enumerate, codify, and classify.

This book attempts to trace these developments, and to show how they affected the direction of mountaineering. In the pages that follow, I examine a wide range of literature, including a number of sources that have been ignored in most previous studies of the topic. These include the journals of British mountaineering clubs established several decades after the better-known Alpine Club, and visitors' books from hotels and inns where climbers stayed in Scotland, the English Lake District, and Wales. Through these and many other texts, including memoirs, diaries, and guidebooks, I show how a new approach to mountain climbing emerged in the period from around 1870, and how this was represented in contemporary accounts. I also question to what degree the New Mountaineer represented a real change in the practice of climbing and to what extent he was a product of mountaineering literature itself. I examine critiques and defences of the New Mountaineer, discuss the terms in which mountain experiences were represented, and suggest that an emphasis on physical contact with the quiddity of mountain landscapes became the dominant mode of discussing climbing in late-Victorian Britain. I also argue that, as Romantic discourses about mountains became marginalized, so the physicality and athleticism that replaced them gave rise to a new version of the sublime.

Mountaineering in late-Victorian Britain was one of the characteristic hobbies of the intellectual and commercial elite. This new recreation had a cultural significance that was disproportionate to the relatively small number of people who pursued it actively, and as we shall see writing about mountaineering has a history almost as old as the activity itself. However it is only since the middle of the twentieth century that writers on the sport's history have begun to analyze the causes or wider significance of the growth of mountaineering. Historians have generally interpreted climbing in one of several ways: as a manifestation of a new approach to risk; as an expression of imperialism; as an instance of the importance of manliness; or in the light of changing class and gender relations.

These are all legitimate and productive lines of enquiry. My own starting point, however, has been to question the very notion of a typical, representative Victorian mountaineer. Many previous accounts of nineteenth-century climbing have tended to elide the differences between the generations of climber who began the sport in the 1850s and those who were climbing towards the end of the century. Instead of assuming that mountaineers were a single group with a coherent, consistent set of values and attitudes, it is more helpful to talk of a multiplicity of narratives and a variety of different Victorian climbers with different attitudes and stated reasons for climbing.

A discernible shift in approach began around 1870, and continued to the end of the century. The climbers of this period had a distinct identity quite different from that of their predecessors in the fifties and sixties. One of my aims in this study has been to look closely at how accounts by mountaineers change over the course of the period from around 1870 to the end of the century, and how they differ from earlier climbing narratives, and to rethink the language of mountaineering. I have been careful to distinguish between the experiences of mountaineers and more general tourist accounts of mountain travel, and I have identified some of the contradictions and paradoxes in mountaineering literature and the different approaches taken by a range of writers. I have also investigated to what degree mountaineering was affected by the wider culture in which climbers operated, and to what extent it constituted a hermetically sealed subculture of its own.

I explore the New Mountaineer and his world over five chapters. Chapters 2 and 3 discusses the sporting, recreational approach that characterized the New Mountaineer, involving disciplines such as mapping and navigation, physical training, photography, and the specialized use of ropes and ice axes. I show how contemporaries regarded this as qualitatively different from the values of the early days of mountaineering, when recreational climbers had supposedly been heavily influenced by the legacy of Romantic writing. I then show another side of this picture by suggesting that these differences were often exaggerated or simplified by late nineteenth-century mountaineering writers. Many mountaineers from the 1850s and even earlier were in fact climbing with a similar attitude to that of the New Mountaineers. For the first generation of British mountaineers, adventure had often been just as powerful a motive as romantic transcendence. Conversely, many climbers in the late nineteenth century were still deeply influenced by Romantic attitudes. I suggest the New Mountaineer was as much a product of the narrative of mountaineering literature as of the praxis of mountain climbing. At the same time, I show that climbers in the late nineteenth century were increasingly confident in claiming that their direct physical engagement with mountains gave them a privileged experience of wild nature not available to the more casual mountain tourist or other observer.

Chapter 4, 'The Climbing Body', is concerned with physicality, and connects the New Mountaineer to the wider scientific, medical, and cultural preoccupations of late-Victorian society. I discuss the arguably unprecedented pleasure that climbers were able to take in sensations traditionally considered undesirable, including fatigue, cold, exposure to danger, and discomfort, and I suggest that these are linked to an idea of embodied perception that is central to the ethos of mountaineering at this time. Chapter 5, 'The Haptic Sublime', shows how this new approach leads, paradoxically, to a resurgence of the aesthetic of the sublime. However, this new, reinvigorated sublime is qualitatively different from eighteenth-century and Romantic discourses about wild nature. The haptic sublime involves an emphasis on direct physical experience and embodied understanding of mountain landscapes. The mountaineers of this period insisted on the greater intensity and precision of their experience of mountains, which was closely related to the physical nature of their encounters with rock face, glacier, and snow slope.

In Chapter 6, I examine how these new values and beliefs were potentially threatened by the phenomenon of mass tourism to mountain regions, and the strategies – both in the practice of mountaineering and its literature – that were adopted to deal with the threat. Mountaineers looked down on and resented the figure of the cockney tourist or tripper, but they also saw him as subversive of some of their most cherished values. Tourism altered both the physical and psychological landscape in which climbers pursued their hobby.

Before examining these topics, it will be helpful to set out the pre-history of the New Mountaineer. By the time Collie coined the term, mountaineering was already well established as a leisure activity. Eminent Victorians including Leslie Stephen, John Tyndall, Herbert Spencer, John Ruskin, and Martin Conway all contributed to the debate about the purpose and direction of mountaineering. However their prominence and the high level of public interest in mountaineering in this period make it easy to forget just how new this activity was, and how different the Victorian approach to mountains was to that of previous ages. In order to understand how radically different the activity of climbing became from the 1870s, we need to be familiar first with mountaineering's relatively short history, and secondly with its literature. These will be summarized in the next two sections.

## Victorian Mountaineering Historicized

Mountaineering as a recognized leisure activity, undertaken from sporting rather than from scientific motives, really only began in earnest in the middle of the nineteenth century. The formation of the Alpine Club in London in 1857, and the journals it started to publish from the end of that decade, gave shape to this new activity and propelled it into the wider public consciousness. Prior to this period, mountaineering had scarcely existed other than as the preserve of specialist scientists and a few adventurous travellers. Most recreational ascents of mountains in the early nineteenth century were limited to Mont Blanc (climbed because it was the highest summit in the Alps), Snowdon, Ben Nevis, and a few Lakeland peaks. To put the increase in climbing activity in the nineteenth century into perspective: by 1800, only about twenty-two major Alpine peaks had been scaled, a figure which rose to ninety-seven by the middle of the century.[2] By 1865, at the end of what became known as the Alpine Golden Age, climbers had made first ascents of 140 Alpine summits.[3]

Prior to this explosion of activity, there had been isolated ascents of mountains dating back several centuries; among the most commonly cited are climbs undertaken by the humanist scholar and poet Francesco Petrarca (Petrarch) in 1355 and the Swiss naturalist Conrad Gesner in 1543.[4] Such ascents were the exception to the rule that for most of human history people did not actively seek out the potential danger and discomfort of climbing mountains. It was not until the eighteenth century that mountain ascents became more common, with scientific or financial motives stimulating most efforts.[5] In 1760 the geologist Gottlieb Gruner published his study of Swiss glaciers, *Die Eisgebirge des Schweiserlandes*, based on research carried out in the field, then in 1783 Swiss scientist Horace Benedict de Saussure offered a cash prize to the first person to ascend Mont Blanc. Three years later, Michel-Gabriel Paccard and Jacques Balmat reached the summit and claimed the reward.[6] Saussure made his own ascent to carry out scientific observations the following year and between 1779 and 1796 published his four-volume *Voyages dans les Alpes* in which he propounded his theories on the origin and movement of glaciers, a topic that would continue to dominate scientific investigations in the Alps up to the middle of the nineteenth century.[7] Mont Blanc continued to be the focus of most mountaineering activity into the nineteenth century, with a total of thirteen ascents being made by 1819 – far more than for any other Alpine peak.[8] As a biographer of one of its most famous climbers later noted, those who climbed Mont Blanc in the late eighteenth and early nineteenth century were 'not mountaineers in the modern sense of the word, for they climbed no other mountains. They climbed Mont Blanc because it was the highest mountain in Europe; they saw no point in climbing anything smaller.'[9]

The combination of scientific and pecuniary motives that had conquered Mont Blanc persisted into the first half of the nineteenth century, with scientists assisted in travelling through the mountains by paid local guides, usually chamois hunters or herders – an arrangement that would eventually form the basis of the formal mountain guide system, with the formation of the Compagnie des Guides de Chamonix in 1821.[10] A number of British and Continental European scientists, including the Swiss biologist Louis Agassiz and Scottish physicist James David Forbes, carried out field work on glaciation, geology, and other aspects of Alpine science in the late eighteenth and early nineteenth centuries. By the 1830s Agassiz, examining the composition and movement of glaciers, had deduced that erratic rocks – large boulders that clearly came from a different region to where they were found – had been carried to their present position by glacial action.[11] Forbes made his first visit to the Alps in 1826 but began serious investigation into the structure of glaciers in the late 1830s and published his influential *Travels Through the Alps of Savoy* in 1843. In it he propounded his theory that the entire structure of a glacier was a viscous body that moved in much the same manner as a fluid, a theory which proved to be broadly correct but led to a bitter controversy between Forbes and Agassiz, and later between Forbes and the physicist and mountaineer John Tyndall. Forbes was effectively accused of plagiarizing the work of others, a charge that seriously damaged his reputation.[12]

The glacier controversies of the 1840s suggest the centrality of scientific research to the development of interest in mountains and mountaineering. Yet the intense publicity generated by this quarrel tends to obscure the existence of a concurrent strain in the history of mountain travel which owed much more to a thirst for adventure and to the legacy of Romantic discourses about mountains than to scientific research. Even by the early years of the nineteenth century some visitors to the Alps found, as Walt Unsworth puts it, 'science taking second place to the thrill of climbing'.[13] Meanwhile, the disparate group of writers and artists that would retroactively come to be known as the Romantic movement was depicting mountain landscapes in ways that celebrated rugged, irregular nature and often emphasized the subjective experience of the human visitor to the mountains. Thomas West's *A Guide to the Lakes* (1778), William Wordsworth's 1790 visit to the Alps, later recorded in his *Descriptive Sketches* (1793), in the sixth book of *The Prelude* (1805, 1850), and in *Memorials of a Tour of the Continent* (1822), Walter Scott's depiction of Highland scenery in his poetry and in novels including *Waverley* (1814) and *Rob Roy* (1817), the Shelleys' *The History of a Six Weeks' Tour* (1817), and George Gordon, Lord Byron's *Childe Harold's Pilgrimage* (published between 1812 and 1818) all contributed to a growing interest in mountains both at home and abroad, while the end of the Napoleonic wars, the introduction of regular cross-Channel steamers, and improved rail networks in Britain and on Continental Europe allowed more visitors to travel to mountainous areas.[14]

It is at this juncture of science, Romantic literary convention, and adventurous exploration that Victorian mountaineering begins to take shape, as these three motives for visiting mountains become intertwined, only to disentangle later in the century. There was no precise moment at which scientific motives ceased to be the main factor in mountain climbing, and fieldwork continued into the second half of the nineteenth century; Tyndall, for example, continued to investigate glaciers up to 1864, and published his *Forms of Water in Clouds, Rivers, Ice and Glaciers* in 1872. But by the middle of the century nearly all the important fieldwork in mountain science had been done. Meanwhile the practice of science itself had become more specialized and professionalized, with little scope for enthusiastic amateurs to make significant discoveries and few incentives for them to take along barometers and other technical equipment on their ascents.[15] Tyndall, a professional scientist who also happened to be a climber and sometime member of the Alpine Club, was an exceptional rather than a representative figure among Victorian mountaineers, and by the 1850s, as the mountaineering historian William Augustus Brevoort Coolidge put it, 'Englishmen were waking up to the fact that "mountaineering" is a pastime that combines many advantages, and is worth pursuing as an end in itself, without any regard to any thought of the advancement of natural science'.[16]

The downplaying of scientific motives and the ascendancy of adventure as a reason for climbing mountains was perhaps most clearly illustrated by two seminal events in the 1850s: Albert Smith's 1851 ascent of Mont Blanc (and subsequent London show about the climb) and Alfred Wills' 1854 ascent of the Wetterhorn, often described as the start of Alpine mountaineering's Golden Age. Smith was arguably the individual who did most to popularize mountaineering among Britons. Mont Blanc had been climbed just forty times before his visit, an average of less than once a year since Paccard and Balmat in 1786, and ascents were still rare enough that cannon were fired in Chamonix to hail successful climbers. In the five years following Smith's ascent, by contrast, Mont Blanc was climbed eighty-eight times, a rise in popularity which owed a good deal to Smith's considerable talents as a self-publicist.[17] The book he wrote about the climb, *The Story of Mont Blanc* (1853), and the phenomenally successful London stage show in which he recounted his adventures, were arguably the most important factors in popularizing mountaineering beyond the small coterie of scientists and adventurers who had climbed Mont Blanc in the preceding decades.[18]

Smith was not the only British climber to write about his adventures – John Auldjo's 1827 account of climbing Mont Blanc, for example, had been a powerful early influence on Smith's own ambition to scale the mountain – but the sheer scale and bravura nature of his show meant he influenced a wide swathe of the British public, notably the middle classes who would prove to be so crucial in the development of mountaineering. 'The Ascent of Mont Blanc', which Smith performed at the Egyptian Hall in Piccadilly between 1852 and 1858, played to packed houses throughout its two thousand performances. Writing about the history of mountaineering at the end of the century, Charles Edward Mathews (himself an important figure in the Golden Age and a founding member of the Alpine Club) was to claim that 'scores of men who afterwards distinguished themselves in the exploration of the great Alps first had their imagination fired by listening to the interesting story told at the Egyptian Hall'.[19]

'The Ascent of Mont Blanc' took the form of an illustrated lecture accompanied by a diorama – a moving panorama painted with scenes of the ascent, as well as of Smith's journey from London to the Alps, and of his escapades in Paris on the return journey. The format combined educative content with amusing spectacle, and proved a huge hit with mid-Victorian audiences: the phenomenon of 'Mont Blanc mania' was widely commented upon at the time. Smith's irreverent, humorous tone had the effect of debunking both the scientific approach and the traditional Romantic conceptions of the Alps.

His written account of his Mont Blanc adventure was similarly dismissive of both Romantic and scientific conventions of mountain literature, preferring instead a breathless tone of adventure and excitement. This description of the 'all but perpendicular iceberg' of the Mur de la Côte gives a taste of Smith's prose style:

> Should the foot slip, or the baton give way, there is no chance for life – you would glide like lightning from one frozen crag to another, and finally be dashed to pieces, hundreds of feet below in the horrible depths of the glacier.[20]

Clearly there is little room for either calm scientific enquiry or Romantic transcendence here. In places he even seems to be deliberately undermining the scientific approach to mountains. Upon arriving on the summit, he reported,

> We made no 'scientific observations' – the acute and honest de Saussure had done everything that was wanted by the world of that kind; and those who have since worried themselves during the ascent about 'elevations' and 'temperatures' have added nothing to what he told us sixty years ago.[21]

Smith betrayed an attitude of mind that was determined to bypass the scientific justification for Alpine travel in favour of adventure and sensation. His approach to climbing turned out to be prescient: in the decades to come, the last vestiges of scientific motives for mountaineering would disappear, as would any pretence at a quest for the sublime inspired by the values that Romantic poets and artists had located in the mountains. The new generation of Victorian middle-class men would approach the Alps, and increasingly the mountains of their own islands, with the same hearty sporting zeal that characterized participants in the Oxford and Cambridge boat race or public school cricket matches. While Smith may not have single-handedly caused this change in the British attitude towards mountains and mountain climbing, he was both an important catalyst for it and an early proponent of it.

Alfred Wills was a very different figure to Albert Smith, but his legacy would prove equally influential. Wills – who in later life as a high court judge would preside over Oscar Wilde's 1895 trial for gross indecency – reached the summit of the Wetterhorn in September 1854, inaugurating the Golden Age of British Alpinism. His climb has often been held up as the first ascent of an Alpine mountain other than Mont Blanc made for purely 'sporting' reasons, a claim that ignores the Continental European climbers who had made recreational ascents of numerous other mountains in the years before Wills first visited the Alps.[22] Wills was not even the first to climb the Wetterhorn: his was probably the fifth ascent of it.[23] But it was 'the first climb to which predominantly sporting motives were attributed at the time'.[24] By choosing a mountain other than Mont Blanc he set a precedent other British visitors would soon follow, and the publicity surrounding Wills' achievement stimulated a public imagination that was already primed by Albert Smith's show and book. Wills wrote about his experience in *Wanderings Among the High Alps* (1856), a book whose moments of high drama echo the adventurous tone of Smith's descriptions and set the tone for subsequent descriptions of mountain experiences in journals and books. Writing of the moments before he and his guide, Auguste Balmat, reached the summit, Wills' normally restrained and rather dry prose style gives way to excitement and tension:

> As I took the last step, Balmat disappeared from my sight; my left shoulder grazed against the angle of the icy embrasure, while, on the right, the glacier fell away abruptly beneath me, towards an unknown and awful abyss: a hand from an invisible person grasped mine; I stepped across, and had passed the ridge of the Wetterhorn![25]

Wills has been described as 'the first person to advocate mountaineering as a pursuit worthwhile in itself'.[26] In this respect he was as important as Albert Smith as a propagandist for the non-scientific approach to mountains. After Wills and Smith the stated reasons for climbing mountains had permanently changed. What might be termed Romantic motives for mountain climbing had also been influential for at least some visitors in the late eighteenth and early nineteenth century, but these too eroded in the years following Smith's success. Romantic literature had clearly been an influence on how mountain landscapes were viewed, although it is less clear to what degree it ever influenced mountaineering practices: as Robert H. Bates points out, a considerable proportion of Romantic poetry about mountains either deals with the valleys or lower slopes, or describes mountains viewed from a distance.[27] Experiencing mountains close up, with direct physical contact and consequent knowledge of what Martin Conway would call the 'cold stony reality' of their materiality, soon became central to the ethos of late-Victorian climbers.[28]

The Alpine Club was formed in 1857, and quickly established itself as the driving force of this new British pastime. Its membership list included both the intellectual aristocracy of mid-Victorian Britain – Stephen, Tyndall, Thomas Huxley, and Matthew Arnold were among its more prominent members – and the climbers who would create the Golden Age by conquering new peaks in a surge of mountaineering activity in the years leading up to the Matterhorn tragedy of 1865. This latter group included John Ball, Edward Shirley Kennedy, Thomas Hinchcliff, and the brothers Charles Edward Mathews and George Spencer Mathews. The Club's publications, *Peaks, Passes, and Glaciers* (1859–1862) and then the *Alpine Journal* (1863 onwards), were read and discussed well beyond its relatively exclusive membership, keeping mountaineering in the public eye where Albert Smith and Alfred Wills had already lodged it.[29] By 1862, the *Cornhill Magazine* could begin an article on 'The Art of Alpine Travel' by asserting that mountaineering was now 'firmly established as one of our national sports', a claim that could not have been made even a decade earlier.[30]

From its inception, the Alpine Club was in a rather paradoxical position with regards to the tradition of scientific mountaineering. Originally conceived as simply a dining club, it quickly changed into a more serious organization, holding monthly meetings where members read papers about their mountaineering exploits.[31] Although the *Alpine Journal* was subtitled 'A Record of Mountain Adventures and Scientific Observations by Members of the Alpine Club', the linkage of adventure and scientific observation this implied proved short-lived, and most of the papers and articles continued to de-emphasize science, as Wills and Smith had done. The Club's early publications did contain a considerable number of papers on scientific topics: the second volume of *Peaks, Passes, and Glaciers*, for example, carried an article on the 'Amount of Ozone at Different Altitudes' by Francis Fox Tuckett.[32] However, the very first article in the first edition of the *Alpine Journal*, an account of 'The Ascent of Monte della Disgrazia' by the Club's then president, Edward Shirley Kennedy, indicates how ready mountaineers were to jettison the scientific justification for climbing mountains by the early 1860s. Kennedy opens with a description that would not seem out of place in a Gothic novel: 'As the strokes of midnight were clanging from the Campanile of Sondrio, a carriage rolled heavily into the court-yard of the Hotel della Maddalena'.[33] He continues in this vein for several paragraphs:

> How free and exultant is the true mountaineer, when he exchanges the warmly-glowing atmosphere of the south for the cold and invigorating

blasts of the mountain; when he leaves behind him the gentle beauty of the lakes, and glories in the savage grandeur of riven rock and contorted glacier.[34]

Having settled into a prose style that seems heavily influenced by Romantic literary conventions (with stock assumptions about the characteristics of Mediterranean countries, phrases like 'savage grandeur', and notions of the liberating and spiritually elevating qualities of mountain landscapes), Kennedy then introduces two competing elements, which could broadly be termed the scientific and the athletic:

> Our energies [in the Italian Alps] were partly devoted to the elucidation of matters of antiquarian and geological interest; but while ethnology and physical science claimed their due, another and a mightier attraction existed; we had an unascended peak in contemplation, and what mountaineer can resist the charms which such an object presents?[35]

With its uncomfortable attempts to accommodate different priorities and its explicit admission that mountain adventure will always take precedence over scientific observation, this first *Journal* article sets the tone for much subsequent mountaineering prose. Later in the same article, after describing his party reaching the summit, Kennedy asks rhetorically, 'What was our first thought?', and supplies a range of possible answers from the aesthetic and the scientific to the purely phlegmatic. Appreciation of the magnificent view is one option, as is recourse to scientific measurement ('where is the barometer and the boiling-water apparatus?'). 'What have we to eat and drink?' is another possibility, along with 'How shall we get down again?' Instead, Kennedy concludes: 'Each and every one of these sources of gratification sink into insignificance when compared to the exhilarating consciousness of difficulty overcome, and of success attained by perseverance'.[36]

Despite this acknowledgement that the triumphant overcoming of physical challenges would now take precedence over scientific or aesthetic considerations, subsequent volumes of the *Alpine Journal* did attempt to shoehorn scientific and adventure discourses into the same publication. So, for example, a technical article on 'The Sympiezometer and Aneroid Barometer' sits rather incongruously in Volume 2 next to an account of 'Excursions in the Graian Alps' in which the writer, R.C. Nichols, recalls how he had 'hoped to make a fair bag of new peaks and passes'.[37]

The adventurous, athletic discourse represented by the latter article soon prevailed, and the number of scientific articles decreased. The first volume of the *Journal* had its own scientific index, listing short articles on 'Phosphorescent Snow', 'Electricity in the Pyrenees', and 'Minimum Thermometers', but by the third volume there were scarcely any such articles outside the brief 'Miscellanea' section at the end. By 1865 Leslie Stephen could confidently mock what he regarded as the pretensions of scientific mountaineers in a speech to members about his ascent of the Rothhorn:

> 'And what philosophical observations did you make?' will be the enquiry of one of those fanatics who, by a reasoning process to me utterly inscrutable, have somehow irrevocably associated Alpine travelling with science. To them I answer, that the temperature was approximately (I had no thermometer) 212 degrees (Farenheit) below freezing point. As for ozone, if any existed in the atmosphere, it was a greater fool than I take it for.[38]

The notoriously thin-skinned John Tyndall regarded Stephen's speech as such a direct attack that he resigned from the Club in protest (Tyndall was prone to take offence, having fallen out over the years not only with Forbes but with other scientists including James and William Thomson and Peter Guthrie Tait, and with the equally argumentative Edward Whymper).[39] Stephen's comments, however, were remarkable only for their degree of levity and irreverence: he was simply reflecting an attitude that was increasingly common among British mountaineers. After all, even Tyndall himself had ruefully admitted in 1860 that the contribution of his fellow mountaineers to science had been '*nil*' and that instead, 'Their pleasure is that of overcoming acknowledged difficulties, and of witnessing natural grandeur'.[40]

Nonetheless, a scientific *sensibility* did continue to inform and influence the way mountaineers thought and wrote about their recreation, and it is worth noting that Stephen's article in this volume of the *Journal* came immediately after a complex technical article on the determination of altitude.[41] A scientific cast of mind allied to a professional, technically-skilled approach adopted by the middle-class men who dominated the culture of mountaineering would soon give rise to narratives of adventure and athleticism recounted in a register which maintained the scientific and classificatory conventions and assumptions of mid- to late-Victorian Britain. Thus, while the ethos of adventure in late-Victorian climbing in some respects undermined and supplanted the practice of climbing for scientific motives, the continuing influence of what David Robbins calls 'scientism' would remain a pervasive and important element of how mountaineers thought and wrote about their sport.[42] Rather than being a specific, avowed motive, Robbins sees scientism as a lingering attachment to the traditions and conventions of science, and to a scientific cast of mind.

The period after the Golden Age witnessed the paradoxical spectacle of a diminution of actual science accompanied by the continuation of Robbins' 'scientism'. As the century wore on, this made climbers increasingly prone to claim, not so much superior scientific knowledge as a kind of heightened or sharpened awareness of their environment. Bruce Hevly suggests that, even as early as the glacier controversies of the 1840s, the 'rhetoric of adventure' had become an important element in the culture of science itself, at least as carried out in the field by men like Forbes and Tyndall. Scientists, Hevly argues, tended to claim 'reliable perception on the basis of authentic, rigorous, manly experience', and he contends that scientific mountaineers claimed what he called 'The Authority of Adventurous Observation'.[43] Hevly's argument that British scientists 'acted as part of a culture that celebrated sport as one of the distinguishing marks of gentlemen and a route to a disciplined perception of the world' may be relevant to the question of how and why science was ultimately eclipsed by adventure as a motive for mountain climbing in the second half of the century.[44] He shows how Tyndall, for example, presented the phenomenon of regelation (the fusing together of pieces of ice which have previously melted under pressure, once the pressure is removed) in terms not so much of conventional science but of mountain adventure. Tyndall, Hevly suggests, represented regelation as 'the property of glacial ice that allowed intrepid climbers to carefully edge their way over deep crevasses'.[45] This is the passage that Hevly refers to, from Tyndall's *The Glaciers of the Alps*:

> It is this same principle of regelation which enables men to cross snow bridges in safety. By gentle cautious pressure the loose granules of the substance are cemented into a continuous mass, all sudden shocks which might cause the frozen surfaces to snap asunder being avoided. In this way an arch of snow fifteen or twenty inches in thickness may be rendered so firm that a man will cross it, although it may span a chasm one hundred feet in depth.[46]

Thus, suggests Hevly, 'the physical properties of ice become simultaneously the stuff of science and the stuff of adventure'.[47] In other words, the scientists themselves were at least partly responsible for the ascendancy of narratives of sport and adventure that came to displace scientific discourses in the second part of the century. Science and scientists thus helped create the conditions that brought about their own marginalization from the culture of mountaineering.

If scientists themselves became marginal, the 'Authority of Adventurous Observation' continued to be a central element in the claims made by mountaineers in the latter part of the century. Just as Hevly suggests both Forbes and Tyndall 'argued that their research on the causes of glacial motion were rendered reliable by the purposeful action each expended in the Alps', so later generations of climbers, from Stephen onwards, would argue that their own purposeful action in the mountains gave rise to a greater degree of accurate, intimate understanding of the true nature of mountain landscapes than the passive observer could hope for.[48] This claim to authority – an authority based not just on visual evidence but on direct physical experience – was very important to Victorian climbers, and was frequently and insistently made in climbing literature long after the practical pursuit of science had ceased to be a feature of mountaineering.

The Alpine Golden Age ended abruptly and violently in July 1865. The English mountaineer Edward Whymper and six companions had just completed the first ascent of the Matterhorn and were descending when one of them slipped. The rope broke and Roger Hadow, Chamonix mountain guide Michel Croz, Lord Francis Douglas, and the Reverend Charles Hudson all fell to their deaths. Whymper and his two surviving guides, the elder and the younger Peter Taugwalder, made their way down to Zermatt to break the news.[49] Recriminations began almost immediately, and soon a backlash against the very idea of mountaineering had begun. An outraged editorial in *The Times* asked, 'Is it life? Is it duty? Is it common sense? Is it allowable? Is it not wrong?'[50] and Charles Dickens denounced the 'foolhardihood' and 'contempt for and waste of human life' involved in the activity.[51] Mountaineering briefly lost its prestige and was seen by many as unjustifiably dangerous, even disreputable.

In retrospect the impact of the Matterhorn disaster appears as a brief interlude in the broader story of mountaineering's growth as a sport, but that was certainly not how it seemed to its adherents at the time. Looking back at this period from the vantage point of the early twentieth century, Coolidge recalled how mountaineers felt themselves a beleaguered minority in the wake of the accident and the public opprobrium it engendered:

> Few in number, all knowing each other personally, shunning the public gaze so far as possible (and in those days it *was* possible to do so), they went about under a sort of dark shade, looked on with scarcely disguised contempt by the world of ordinary travellers. They, so to speak, climbed on sufferance, enjoying themselves much, it is true, but keeping all expression of that joy to themselves in order not to excite derision.[52]

This atmosphere was not to last long. Instead, the Golden Age gave way to another period of intense activity, during which the route to the summit and the technique used to scale it became the most important factors in the prestige and attraction of a climb, and British climbers also turned their attention to the mountains of the Lake District, north Wales, and Scotland. After the brief period of disapproval that followed the Matterhorn tragedy, climbing became more popular than ever.

## The Literature of Mountaineering

The year 1871 proved to be an *annus mirabilis* for mountaineering literature, with the publication of three classic works: Leslie Stephen's *The Playground of Europe*, John Tyndall's *Hours of Exercise in the Alps*, and Edward Whymper's *Scrambles Amongst the Alps in the Years 1860–1869*. All three caught the public imagination, although perhaps for different reasons. Whymper's book was of interest in part because he used it to make public his own version of the events on the Matterhorn six years earlier. Stephen's was marked by what Jim Ring calls his 'combination of adventure with wit, charm and intelligence'.[53] Tyndall described his book as 'for the most part a record of bodily action', and recounted exciting descriptions of assaults on the Matterhorn, Bel Alp, and Weisshorn, among other Alpine peaks, but he also revealed an unexpectedly poetic, even spiritual sensibility on the part of this seemingly dry man of science.[54] All three, though, have in common an unashamed celebration of adventure, physical challenge, and the measured but unflinching acceptance of an element of risk. None of their authors would have been characterized as New Mountaineers – instead, they were of the generation responsible for the Golden Age.[55] But the sensibility of these books seems to usher in a new era, in which the changes discussed in this book become manifest and are increasingly the subject of discussion and debate. From the early 1870s onwards, a distinct new era in British mountain climbing had begun, and the characteristic figure of the New Mountaineer was starting to emerge.

Within a few years of the Alpine Club's establishment, articles began to appear in the *Alpine Journal* describing early ascents of mountains, and by the end of the century it was common for mountaineers to write about the history of their sport.[56] By the late nineteenth century, mountaineering had found its first dedicated historian in W.A.B. Coolidge. Coolidge, who edited the *Alpine Journal* from 1880 to 1889, wrote numerous detailed articles about historical Alpine ascents, and later published *The Alps in Nature and History* (1908), a comprehensive study of the history of Alpine mountaineering, as well as of the geography, politics, and natural history of the region. Around the same time, Francis Gribble was publishing his account of early mountain ascents, including those of Petrarch and Gesner as well as the first recorded ascent of Mont Aiguille near Grenoble in 1492.[57]

Coolidge and Gribble, like many subsequent historians of mountaineering, mostly restricted themselves to straightforward factual accounts of the sport's history with little analysis of the causes or wider significance of the growth of climbing. It was not until Marjorie Hope Nicolson's *Mountain Gloom and Mountain Glory* (1959) that a serious interpretation of the historical background to the new interest in mountain landscapes was attempted. Some nineteenth-century mountaineers had noted in their speeches and publications how novel their sport was, but Nicolson was the first to analyze in detail the historical shift in human attitudes to mountains, from viewing them with fear and repugnance to seeing them as beautiful, fascinating, and in some respects as the repository of natural virtue. Nicolson argued that the change from 'Mountain Gloom' to 'Mountain Glory' (phrases borrowed from John Ruskin) was the result of a fundamental shift in the way humans viewed wild nature, itself the result of profound changes in beliefs about the structure of the universe and about humanity's relationship to its natural environment.[58] Nicolson did not discuss mountain climbing itself but her book effectively constitutes a prehistory of mountaineering, tracing the new set of attitudes and conditions that made it possible for people to contemplate climbing mountains for recreation.

Until the late twentieth century, writing about mountaineering tended to fall broadly into one of two categories: narrative history recounting the dates when individual peaks were first climbed, subsequent ascents by different routes, and the development of techniques and equipment; or more general surveys of the development of attitudes to mountains, and in particular of the influence of Romantic literature and art on attitudes to mountain landscapes. Narrative histories of climbing include Ronald Clark's *The Victorian Mountaineers* (1953), R.L.G. Irving's *A History of British Mountaineering* (1955), Unsworth's *Hold the Heights* (1993), and Simon Thompson's *Unjustifiable Risk* (2010). Others focus on particular mountain regions. Alan Hankinson's *The First Tigers* (1972) covers the early days of rock climbing in the Lake District and his *The Mountain Men* (1977) does the same for north Wales. Scotland's mountain climbing history has been described by Campbell Steven in *The Story of Scotland's Hills* (1975) and its prehistory in Ian Mitchell's *Scotland's Mountains Before the Mountaineers* (1998), while particular regions and even individual mountains have also been the subject of detailed histories.[59] Jim Ring's *How the English Made the Alps* (2000), Fergus Fleming's *Killing Dragons* (2001), and Trevor Braham's *When the Alps Cast Their Spell* (2004) focus on how late eighteenth and nineteenth-century Britons moved from regarding the Alps as a remote, inhospitable region that had to be crossed to reach southern Europe on the Grand Tour to viewing them as a venue for recreational activities.

As well as these broad historical surveys, the rise of mountaineering has more recently been the subject of more detailed analysis. In *Landscape and Memory* (1995), Simon Schama, following Nicolson's example, puts Victorian mountaineering into the broader history of shifting attitudes to nature, while Robert Macfarlane's *Mountains of the Mind* (2003) explains the appeal of climbing with reference to developments in geology, aesthetics, literature, cartography, and popular culture. Others view the rise of mountaineering through the prism of class, imperialism, gender, and other aspects of wider Victorian society. David Robertson discusses Alpine climbing as an expression of Victorian masculinity, with its stress on games and sportsmanship, arguing that what was important to mountaineers was 'right-minded management of the stout-hearted effort'.[60] Peter Hansen emphasizes the importance of mountaineering in the construction of a specifically upper middle-class masculine identity in the mid- to late nineteenth century, suggesting that mountaineering was 'one of the cultural responses of the middle class to the historical experiences of industry and empire, class formation and self-definition, prosperity and the accelerating circulation of wealth itself.'[61] Hansen also explicitly links mountain climbing to imperial expansion, claiming that from the early days of the Alpine

Club mountaineers 'institutionalized [mountaineering] as a form of imperial exploration'.[62] More recently, in his 2013 book *The Summits of Modern Man: Mountaineering After the Enlightenment,* Hansen has examined what he calls 'the summit position' – the preoccupation with who was the first person to reach a mountain's summit, and the domination of the natural world that this position implies. He traces the post-Enlightenment milieu in which this approach to mountains arose, concentrating especially on the intellectual and cultural tumult of eighteenth-century Geneva, and proposes mountain climbing as inextricably tied up with modernity.[63]

Reuben Ellis, too, links mountaineering to empire in his study of how the expanding discipline of geography intersected with imperial expansion through exploration. Ellis notes that the era 'during which geography developed as a formal category of academic investigation in Britain is also the era of Europe's most pronounced imperial expansion', and suggests that by the late nineteenth century mountains 'increasingly came to embody a sense of "lateness", representing the last places left for Western explorers to discover and traffic'.[64]

Conversely, other historians, notably Robbins and Hevly, have concentrated on the legacy of scientific research and its effect on the practice of mountaineering. Robbins's 'scientism' is, he posits, just one of three 'different and potentially conflicting discourses' in the culture of Victorian mountaineering, stemming from the Alpine Club's structure 'in the image of a learned society' in the Enlightenment tradition.[65] The other two competing discourses Robbins suggests are athleticism and romanticism, and he argues that 'all three typically coexist within the consciousness of the individuals and the culture of the group' well into the 1880s.[66] Hevly, as we have seen, stresses the authority that mountaineering borrowed from its scientific background and from the scientific credentials of its practitioners, while suggesting that, paradoxically, this led to an undermining of the importance of science in later years. Theodore Hoppen sees the role of mountaineering as partly to do with establishing networks of like-minded individuals, especially scientists. He describes the Alps as the 'characteristic venue' of the upper middle-class intelligentsia of the mid-Victorian years, and attributes this group's love of mountaineering to a variety of factors: 'a new attitude to nature, a love of physical exertion, a search for the transcendental beyond orthodox religion, even a quest of scientific discovery'.[67]

Elaine Freedgood, Jonathan Simon, and Roger Eaton have all written on the centrality of risk-taking to the pursuit of mountaineering. Freedgood sees mountain climbing in the Victorian period as 'a collective means of pre-emptively expressing and relieving anxiety' by the 'voluntary and knowing embrace of danger'.[68] This embrace of risk, she argues, was a new way of coping with the anxiety that capitalist society (and the risks it engendered) created. Climbing allowed its participants to remove the heightened risks of modern life to the mountains, where they could be taken on voluntarily and at leisure rather than encountered at some unknown or unexpected moment.[69] Simon (writing primarily about its role in advanced post-industrial societies rather than in Victorian Britain) theorizes mountaineering and other forms of extreme sport both as a way of coping with the particular demands that modern society generates and as a way of building communities of interest.[70] He sees the deliberate embrace of risk through such activities as both a reaction to what he calls the move to 'disaggregate risk' from society back to individuals in modern liberal states,[71] and as a way of providing 'practical experiences, ideas, and narratives around which new kinds of subjectivity are being created and popularized'.[72] Eaton, on the other hand, concentrates his discussion of risk on the figure of Tyndall, who, he argues, saw the dangers of Alpine climbing as a 'professional, moral, and emotional challenge [ . . . ] he was utterly and explicitly unable to resolve'.[73] Rather than viewing mountaineering as a way of coping with increased societal risk, Eaton suggests that Tyndall's very specific experience of climbing in dangerous mountain regions with primarily scientific motives created an irreconcilable tension between, on the one hand, his scientific rationalism and desire for self-control, and on the other, his fascination with the 'vast domain' whose 'attractive power he could not name or define, and whose value he could not fathom'.[74] Eaton extrapolates from Tyndall's situation to suggest that up to the end of the 1860s, British mountaineers 'maintained alpinism as an ideally risk-free pastime, a monument to English nerve, control, common-sense, and a very qualified sense of responsibility'.[75]

This relatively extensive literature on the topic of risk contrasts with a paucity of historical work on the individual disciplinary strands of climbing. Climbers in the latter part of the century were increasingly preoccupied with the mastery of various technical disciplines and skills, yet few historians have singled out these individual areas for close attention. Rachel Hewitt's history of the British Ordnance Survey is a rare exception. Although not specifically concerned with maps for mountaineers, Hewitt describes the combination of Enlightenment and military motives that led to the detailed mapping of the British Isles in the eighteenth and nineteenth centuries, and points out the ambivalent reaction of Romantic writers to this project of creating comprehensive knowledge about the landscape – an ambivalence that would disappear later in the century as British mountaineers increasingly placed mapping and navigation high on the list of skills they valued.[76]

The visual culture of mountaineering has also attracted attention. Joe Kember links it to Victorian exhibition culture, demonstrating how the presentation of panoramic views in Albert Smith's show, for example, was part of a commodification of mountain landscapes through their capture and presentation in a 'familiar and comfortable' setting.[77] Ann C. Colley also focuses on 'the aesthetic dimensions of the Victorian mountain experience', recording the experiences and perceptions not only of mountaineers but also tourists, artists, and writers who visited the Alps.[78] Colley examines the complex and shifting understanding of the sublime in the Victorian period, and suggests that by the middle of the nineteenth century the fact that spectators in the valley could use telescopes to follow climbing expeditions had turned mountaineering into a visual spectacle, replacing the 'lingering ideals of Romanticism' with the theatricality of 'a spectator sport, complete with parades and celebrations'.[79] Colley also writes about Ruskin's mountain aesthetic, arguing that his visual theories are informed and influenced by his experience of mountain climbing to a much greater degree than has traditionally been recognized.[80] Like two earlier historians of female mountaineers, Cicely Williams and Rebecca A. Brown, she also attempts to redress the widespread assumption that women climbers in the Victorian period were a rarity, and questions the notion that they were constantly marginalized or disapproved of by the male mountaineering establishment.[81]

Other writers have concentrated on individual mountaineers. As well as Eaton's work on Tyndall, Francis O'Gorman has written about what he terms Tyndall's 'muscular agnosticism', suggesting that Tyndall's writing about the Alps constitutes both a space 'for the construction of particular forms of masculine identity' and a site for the 'fashioning of specifically agnostic responses to the Alpine landscape in the face of a considerable tradition of writing which had privileged the Alps as the locus of Christian or theist spiritual experience'.[82]

Leslie Stephen is the subject of Catherine W. Hollis's *Leslie Stephen as Mountaineer*, in which she proposes that his philosophy of mountaineering constitutes what she calls the 'Empirical Sublime'.[83] Hollis argues that the 'perceptual experience of Alpine mountaineering also fed Stephen's emerging intellectual fascination with problems of knowledge and perspective', which he later explored in his Introduction to *English Thought in the Eighteenth Century* (1876) and in the essay 'What is Materialism?' (1886). Other major biographies of important Victorian climbers include Simon Thompson's *A Long Walk with Lord Conway* (2013), about Martin Conway, and Ian Smith's life of Edward Whymper, *Shadow of the Matterhorn* (2011).[84]

Anne D. Wallace's work on the cultural significance of what she terms 'the peripatetic' is not directly about mountaineering but about changes in the practice and meaning of walking. Wallace, too, discusses Leslie Stephen as one of several writers who argue that 'the natural, primitive quality of the physical act of walking restores the natural proportions of our perceptions, reconnecting us with both the physical world and the moral order inherent in it'.[85] Kevin Morrison, in a paper on Stephen's 'theory of embodied perception', contrasts Stephen's writings both with the Romantic stress on the importance of the imagination and with Ruskin's insistence on visual clarity.[86] Darren Bevin, meanwhile, examines the contrasting influences of Albert Smith and Ruskin on changing attitudes to mountains, and suggests that while Ruskin's legacy is better known, it may have been Smith, with his 'aggressive and populist approach', who actually had the most lasting effect on how people perceived and responded to mountain landscapes by the end of the nineteenth century.[87]

## Complicating the New Mountaineer

Many of these accounts have been immensely valuable in my own work, and I quote from a number of them in the chapters that follow. In particular, my work draws on Hansen's analysis of the role mountaineering played in the definition of middle-class masculinity, on Colley's iconoclastic approach to traditional assumptions about the role of women, and on Schama's subtle analysis of the very specific class-consciousness of the Alpine Club's members. I also incorporate and add to Hewitt's explication of the background to British map-making efforts; I describe, for example, the considerable efforts made by British mountaineers to supplement the official Ordnance Survey maps. However, I have also drawn from a range of critical work beyond the scope of mountaineering history. In particular, I have tried to move beyond the conventional view that mountain climbing was largely influenced and motivated by the impulse for imperial conquest.

Imperialism, of course, permeated late nineteenth-century culture, with almost every type of activity both influenced by and making its contribution to a culture of imperial expansion and colonialism.[88] Mountaineering, involving as it did the physical exploration of formerly untrodden areas and the constant need to find new ground to conquer, was by its nature implicated in the imperial project. Yet it is worth asking to what degree mountaineers were also influenced by other less obvious factors, including subtle shifts in modes of perception in the late nineteenth century, and the growth of a culture of classification, codification, specialist knowledge, and technical skill connected to the rise of the professional middle classes.[89] With these questions in mind, I have taken the approach outlined at the start of this Introduction: examining in detail the material culture of late-Victorian climbing, with its preoccupation with equipment, maps, specialist clothing, and technical disciplines; examining the emerging genre of climbing literature as a way of creating a self-conscious mountaineering community, with a shared body of knowledge and a culture that valued professional skill and technical competence;[90] analyzing the changing understanding of the relationship between the physical and the visual during this period in question, and how this affected climbers' perceptions of their own experiences; and taking a fresh look at the aesthetics of the Victorian mountaineers, to discover whether the common perception that aesthetic concerns were diminished by mountaineering culture actually hides a more complex reality.

My analysis of physicality, and of the way that mountaineers insisted upon visual evidence being supplemented and verified by physical experience, takes into account a more general cultural shift in this period towards allocating greater importance to touch and physical sensation. The need to supplement visual sensations with tactile or haptic evidence became important to mountaineers around the same time that comparable developments were taking place across a range of fields, from physiology to aesthetics. In this respect, I have found Jonathan Crary's *Techniques of the Observer* (1992) and *Suspensions of Perception* (2001) invaluable, tracing as they do the development of a new understanding of the embodied nature of vision over the course of the nineteenth century.[91] The work of David Parisi on the growing importance of touch in the nineteenth century and Anson Rabinbach on the notion of the 'human motor' have also been helpful in my understanding of the intellectual and cultural environment in which late nineteenth-century climbers operated.[92] In examining how class boundaries were tested as well as undermined by developments in mountain transport and tourism, and exploring the tensions between mountaineers and other visitors to the mountains, the insights of James Buzard and John K. Walton on travel literature – and particularly the perceived distinction between travel and tourism that was so important to mountaineering writers – have proven invaluable.[93]

The story of mountaineering in the late nineteenth century was marked by a tension between agency and exigency: the agency of liberal subjects making choices, and not necessarily being at the mercy of ideologies such as imperialism, while at the same time still being contingently affected by, for example, the cultural, scientific, and political changes that were taking place in wider society. Each stage in the development of British mountaineering involved a range of different and sometimes conflicting and overlapping approaches, as the controversy over the rise of the New Mountaineer will demonstrate. Nonetheless, there is sufficient evidence to argue that a broadly shared set of attitudes, motives, and beliefs did emerge in the last three decades of the nineteenth century, and that the late-Victorian mountaineers were in some respects qualitatively distinct from their predecessors. The motives of the early pioneers were fragmented and heterogeneous: they did not have a coherently expressed set of motives and a consistent ethos, nor was there an institutional framework within which climbing took place and accounts were published. All this changed in the last few decades of the nineteenth century, as a self-conscious community of mountaineers emerged.

## Notes

1. John Norman Collie, 'A Reverie', *Scottish Mountaineering Club Journal*, 5 (1898–99), 93–102 (p. 98). Cir Mhor is a mountain on the Isle of Arran, while Sgurr nan Gillean is one of the Cuillin mountains on the Isle of Skye.
2. Walt Unsworth, *Hold the Heights: The Foundations of Mountaineering* (London: Hodder & Stoughton, 1993), p. 24.
3. Unsworth, *Hold the Heights*, p. 70.
4. Francis Gribble, *The Early Mountaineers* (London: T. Fisher Unwin, 1899), pp. 18–21.
5. Exceptions include the visit by Richard Pococke and William Windham to one of Mont Blanc's glaciers in 1741 and the ascent of the peak by Captain Mark Beaufoy in 1787. All three Englishmen attributed their activities to patriotism and a thirst for adventure rather than scientific curiosity. See Simon Thompson, *Unjustifiable Risk: The Story of British Climbing* (Milnthorpe, Cumbria: Cicerone, 2010), p. 17.

6. See W.A.B. Coolidge, *The Alps in Nature and History* (London: Methuen, 1908), p. 210; Simon Schama, *Landscape and Memory* (New York: Alfred A. Knopf, 1995), p. 491; Gavin de Beer, *Early Travellers in the Alps* (New York: October House, 1930), p. 180.
7. Trevor Braham, *When the Alps Cast Their Spell: Mountaineers of the Alpine Golden Age* (Glasgow: Neil Wilson, 2004), p. 8.
8. Walt Unsworth, *Savage Snows: The Story of Mont Blanc* (London: Hodder & Stoughton, 1986), p. 37. The nine peaks on the Italian-Swiss border that form the Monte Rosa massif, the second-highest in the Alps, were also the object of various attempts from the early nineteenth century but Mont Blanc remained the main goal for the few visitors who chose to climb. See Braham, *Alps Cast Their Spell*, p. 14; Gribble, *Early Mountaineers*, p. 188.
9. Raymund Fitzsimons, *The Baron of Piccadilly: The Travels and Entertainments of Albert Smith, 1816–1860* (London: Geoffrey Bles, 1967), p. 32.
10. Jim Ring, *How the English Made the Alps* (London: John Murray, 2000), p. 41.
11. Kate Flint, *The Victorians and the Visual Imagination* (Cambridge: Cambridge University Press, 2000), p. 130.
12. Frank F. Cunningham, *James David Forbes: Pioneer Scottish Glaciologist* (Edinburgh: Scottish Academic Press, 1990), pp. 95–109.
13. Unsworth, *Hold the Heights*, p. 53.
14. Ring, *English Made the Alps*, p. 24. I discuss the impact of improved transport links and other infrastructure in Chapter 6. For a thoughtful discussion of Romantic mountain climbing, see Simon Bainbridge, 'Romantic Writers and Mountaineering', *Romanticism*, 18 (2012), 1–15.
15. Richard Yeo and J.D. Bernal, for example, point to the growth of specialist scientific institutions and journals that had taken place in the first part of the nineteenth century: Richard Yeo, *Defining Science: William Whewell, Natural Knowledge, and Public Debate in Early Victorian Britain* (Cambridge: Cambridge University Press, 1993), p. 35; J.D. Bernal, *Science and Industry in the Nineteenth Century* (New York: Routledge, 1953), p. 5.
16. Coolidge, *Alps in Nature and History*, p. 231.
17. Peter Hansen, 'Albert Smith, The Alpine Club, and the Invention of Mountaineering in Mid-Victorian Britain', *Journal of British Studies*, 34 (1995), 300–24 (p. 300).
18. See Alan McNee, *The Cockney Who Sold the Alps: Albert Smith and the Ascent of Mont Blanc* (Brighton: Victorian Secrets, 2015). Earlier biographies of Smith were Fitzsimons' *The Baron of Piccadilly* and J. Monroe Thorington's *Mont Blanc Sideshow: The Life and Times of Albert Smith* (Philadelphia: John C. Winston Company, 1934).
19. Charles Edward Mathews, *The Annals of Mont Blanc* (London: T. Fisher Unwin, 1898), p. 196.

20. Albert Smith, *The Story of Mont Blanc* (London: David Bogue, 1853), p. 199.
21. Smith, *Story of Mont Blanc*, p. 206.
22. Arnold Lunn, *A Century of Mountaineering, 1857–1897* (London: George Allen & Unwin, 1957), p. 29.
23. Unsworth, *Hold the Heights*, p. 61.
24. Ring, *English Made the Alps*, p. 56.
25. Alfred Wills, *Wanderings Among the High Alps* (London: Richard Bentley, 1856), p. 217.
26. Fergus Fleming, *Killing Dragons: The Conquest of the Alps* (London: Granta, 2001), p. 170.
27. Robert H. Bates, *Mystery, Beauty, and Danger: The Literature of the Mountains and Mountain Climbing Published in English Before 1946* (Portsmouth, NH: Peter E. Randall, 2000), pp. 13–22.
28. Martin Conway, *The Alps from End to End* (London: Archibald Constable, 1895), p. 174.
29. *Peaks, Passes, and Glaciers*, for example, went into a second edition just six weeks after publication. See Fleming, *Killing Dragons*, p. 175.
30. 'The Art of Alpine Travel', *Cornhill Magazine*, July–Dec 1862, pp. 206–16 (p. 206).
31. Unsworth, *Hold the Heights*, p. 68. Theodore Hoppen notes how many members of the Alpine Club were also members of the X Club (a dining club for supporters of the theory of natural selection founded by Huxley in 1864) and of the older group known as 'The Club': K. Theodore Hoppen, *The Mid-Victorian Generation, 1846–1886* (Oxford: Clarendon Press, 1998), p. 488.
32. Francis Fox Tuckett, 'Amounts of Ozone at Different Altitudes', *Peaks, Passes, and Glaciers*, 2 (1862), 445–54.
33. Edward Shirley Kennedy, 'The Ascent of Monte della Disgrazia', *Alpine Journal*, 1 (1863–64), 3–20 (p. 3).
34. Kennedy, 'Monte della Disgrazia', p. 3.
35. Kennedy, 'Monte della Disgrazia', p. 3.
36. Kennedy, 'Monte della Disgrazia', p. 19.
37. R. C. Nichols, 'Excursions in the Graian Alps: The Ascent of the Ste. Helene', *Alpine Journal*, 2 (1865–66), 387–97 (p. 387); William Mathews, 'The Sympiezometer and Aneroid Barometer', *Alpine Journal*, 2 (1865–66), 397–404.
38. Leslie Stephen, 'Ascent of the Rothhorn', *Alpine Journal*, 2 (1865–66), 67–79 (p. 76).
39. Cunningham, *James David Forbes*, p. 256.
40. John Tyndall, *Glaciers of the Alps* (London: John Murray, 1860), p. 168, emphasis in original.

41. William Mathews, 'On the Determination of Heights by Means of the Barometer', *Alpine Journal*, 2 (1865–66), Part 2, 63–67.
42. David Robbins, 'Sport, Hegemony and the Middle Class: The Victorian Mountaineers', *Theory, Culture and Society*, 4 (1987) 579–601 (p. 586).
43. Bruce Hevly, 'The Heroic Science of Glacier Motion', *Osiris*, 2 (1996), 66–86 (p. 68).
44. Hevly, 'Heroic Science', p. 66.
45. Hevly, 'Heroic Science', p. 78.
46. Tyndall, *Glaciers of the Alps*, p. 48.
47. Hevly, 'Heroic Science', p. 78.
48. Hevly, 'Heroic Science', p. 66.
49. Guido Rey, *The Matterhorn*, trans. by J.E.C. Eaton (London: T. Fisher Unwin, 1907) p. 108.
50. Editorial, *The Times*, 27 July 1865, p. 8.
51. Charles Dickens, 'Hardihood and Foolhardihood', *All the Year Round*, August 1865 (p. 86).
52. Coolidge, *Alps in Nature*, p. 239, emphasis in original.
53. Ring, *English Made the Alps*, p. 98.
54. John Tyndall, *Hours of Exercise in the Alps* (London: Longman, Green, 1871), p. vi.
55. Stephen, for example, made first ascents of a number of Alpine peaks between 1859 and the late 1860s, including the Schreckhorn, Monte della Disgrazia, and Mont Blanc by the St Gervais route: Frederic William Maitland, *Life and Letters of Leslie Stephen* (London: Duckworth, 1906), pp. 83–87.
56. See, for example, Clinton T. Dent, 'Alpine Climbing—Past, Present, and Future', *Alpine Journal*, 9 (1878–80), 65–72; Alexander Nicolson, 'Skye and Sgur-nan-Gillean in 1865', *Scottish Mountaineering Club Journal*, 2 (1892–93), 99–108.
57. Gribble, *Early Mountaineers*, p. 28.
58. Marjorie Hope Nicolson, *Mountain Gloom and Mountain Glory: The Development of the Aesthetics of the Infinite* (Seattle: University of Washington Press, 1959), p. 3. Ruskin had used the phrases in the fourth volume of *Modern Painters*, in which he discusses mountain aesthetics, to denote the differing effects of mountains on human beings throughout history: John Ruskin, *Modern Painters*, 5 vols (London: J. M. Dent, 1843–60), IV (1856), pp. 309–74.
59. See, for example, Ken Crocket and Simon Richardson, *Ben Nevis: Britain's Highest Mountain* ([n.p.]: Scottish Mountaineering Trust, 1986); Greg Strange, *The Cairngorms: 100 Years of Mountaineering* ([n.p.]: Scottish Mountaineering Trust, 2010).

60. David Robertson, 'Mid-Victorians Amongst the Alps', in *Nature and the Victorian Imagination*, ed. by U.C. Knoepflmacher and G.B. Tennyson (Berkeley: University of California Press, 1977), pp. 113–36 (p. 130).
61. Peter H. Hansen, 'British Mountaineering, 1850–1914' (unpublished doctoral dissertation, Harvard University, 1991), p. 440.
62. Hansen, 'Albert Smith, the Alpine Club', p. 304.
63. Peter Hansen, *The Summits of Modern Man: Mountaineering After the Enlightenment* (Cambridge, MA: Harvard University Press, 2013).
64. Reuben Ellis, *Vertical Margins: Mountaineering and the Landscapes of Neo-Imperialism* (Madison: University of Wisconsin Press, 2001), pp. 22–29.
65. Robbins, 'Victorian Mountaineers', p. 586.
66. Robbins, 'Victorian Mountaineers', p. 589.
67. Hoppen, *Mid-Victorian Generation*, p. 489.
68. Elaine Freedgood, *Victorian Writing About Risk: Imagining a Safe England in a Dangerous World* (Cambridge: Cambridge University Press, 2000), p. 105.
69. Freedgood, *Writing About Risk*, p. 122.
70. Jonathan Simon, 'Taking Risks: Extreme Sports and the Embrace of Risk in Advanced Liberal Societies', in *Embracing Risk: The Changing Culture of Insurance and Responsibility*, ed. by Tom Baker and Jonathan Simon (Chicago and London: University of Chicago Press, 2002), pp. 177–208 (p. 203).
71. Simon, 'Taking Risks', p. 178.
72. Simon, 'Taking Risks', p. 180.
73. R.D. Eaton, 'In the "World of Death and Beauty": Risk, Control, and John Tyndall as Alpinist', *Victorian Literature and Culture*, 41 (2013), 55–73 (p. 55).
74. Eaton, 'Tyndall as Alpinist', p. 69.
75. Eaton, 'Tyndall as Alpinist', p. 70.
76. Rachel Hewitt, *Map of a Nation: A Biography of the Ordnance Survey* (London: Granta, 2010), p. 207.
77. Joe Kember, 'The View from the Top of Mont Blanc: The Alpine Entertainment in Victorian Britain', *Living Pictures*, 2 (2003), 21–45 (p. 30).
78. Ann C. Colley, *Victorians in the Mountains: Sinking the Sublime* (Farnham, Surrey: Ashgate, 2010), p. 3.
79. Colley, *Victorians in the Mountains*, p. 5.
80. Ann C. Colley, 'John Ruskin: Climbing and the Vulnerable Eye', *Victorian Literature and Culture*, 37 (2009), 43–66 (p. 43).
81. Colley, *Victorians in the Mountains*, pp. 101–41. See also Rebecca A. Brown, *Women on High: Pioneers of Mountaineering* (Boston: Appalachian Mountain Club Books, 2002); Cicely Williams, *Women on the Rope: The*

*Feminine Share in Mountain Adventure* (London: George Allen and Unwin, 1973).
82. Francis O'Gorman, '"The Mightiest Evangel of the Alpine Club": Masculinity and Agnosticism in the Alpine Writing of John Tyndall', in *Masculinity and Spirituality in Victorian Culture*, ed. by Andrew Bradstock, Sean Gill, Anne Hogan, and Sue Morgan (Basingstoke: Macmillan, 2000), pp. 134–48 (p. 134).
83. Catherine W. Hollis, *Leslie Stephen as Mountaineer: 'Where Does Mont Blanc End, and Where Do I Begin?'*, The Bloomsbury Heritage Series (London: Cecil Woolf, 2010), p. 35.
84. Ian Smith, *Shadow of the Matterhorn: The Life of Edward Whymper* (Ross-on-Wye: Carreg, 2011); Simon Thompson, *A Long Walk with Lord Conway: An Exploration of the Alps and an English Adventurer* (Oxford: Signal Books, 2013).
85. Anne D. Wallace, *Walking, Literature and English Culture: The Origins and Uses of the Peripatetic in the Nineteenth Century* (Oxford: Clarendon Press, 1993), p. 13.
86. Kevin A. Morrison, 'Embodiment and Modernity: Ruskin, Stephen, Merleau-Ponty and the Alps', *Comparative Literature Studies*, 46 (2009), 498–511 (p. 500).
87. Darren Bevin, *Cultural Climbs: John Ruskin, Albert Smith and the Alpine Aesthetic* (Berlin: VDM Verlag, 2010), p. 176.
88. Ross Forman, for example, has demonstrated how imperial assumptions influenced a wide variety of phenomena, from cookery books to travel guides, adventure fiction to exhibitions, and even pornography, in the 1880s and 1890s: Ross Forman, 'Empire', in *The Cambridge Companion to the* Fin de Siècle, ed. by Gail Marshall (Cambridge: Cambridge University Press, 2007), pp. 91–111.
89. In this respect, I have found the work of Richard Yeo, Kate Flint, and Paul Young on the classificatory culture of the period helpful: Richard Yeo, 'Natural Philosophy', in *An Oxford Companion to the Romantic Age: British Culture, 1776–1832*, ed. by Ian McCalman and others (Oxford: Oxford University Press, 1999), pp. 320–28; Flint, *Victorians and Visual Imagination*; Paul Young, *Globalization and the Great Exhibition: The Victorian New World Order* (Basingstoke: Palgrave Macmillan, 2009).
90. Discussions of masculinity and sporting culture by Norman Vance, Robert J. Park, Richard Holt, and James Eli Adams have been useful in this respect, elucidating how concerns about 'manliness' and the professional ideals of middle-class men informed their leisure activities: Norman Vance, *The Sinews of the Spirit: The Ideal of Christian Manliness in Victorian Literature and Religious Thought* (Cambridge: Cambridge University Press, 1985); Roberta J. Park, 'Biological Thought, Athletics and the Formation of a

"Man of Character", 1800–1900', in *Manliness and Morality—Middle-Class Masculinity in Britain and America, 1800–1914*, ed. by J.A. Mangan and James Walvin (Manchester: Manchester University Press, 1987), pp. 7–34; Richard Holt, *Sport and the British: A Modern History* (Oxford: Clarendon Press, 1989); James Eli Adams, *Dandies and Desert Saints: Styles of Victorian Masculinity* (Ithaca and London: Cornell University Press, 1995).

91. Jonathan Crary, *Techniques of the Observer: On Vision and Modernity in the Nineteenth Century* (Cambridge, MA: MIT Press, 1992); *Suspensions of Perception: Attention, Spectacle, and Modern Culture* (Cambridge, MA: MIT Press, 2001).

92. David Parisi, 'Tactile Modernity: On the Rationalisation of Touch in the Nineteenth Century', in *Media, Technology and Literature*, ed. by Collette Colligan and Margaret Linley (Farnham, Surrey: Ashgate, 2011), pp. 189–214; Anson Rabinbach, *The Human Motor: Energy, Fatigue and the Origins of Modernity* (Berkeley and Los Angeles: University of California Press, 1992).

93. James Buzard, *The Beaten Track: European Tourism, Literature, and the Ways to Culture, 1800–1918* (Oxford: Clarendon Press, 1993); John K. Walton, 'British Tourism Between Industrialisation and Globalization', in *The Making of Modern Tourism: The Cultural History of the British Experience, 1600–2000*, ed. by Hartmut Berghoff, Barbara Korte, Ralf Schneider, and Christopher Harvie (Basingstoke: Palgrave, 2002), pp. 109–31.

CHAPTER 2

# The Rise of the New Mountaineer

## Introduction

By the end of the Golden Age, mountaineering was a firmly established, if still sometimes controversial hobby among the British middle classes, and mountaineering literature was increasingly important in promulgating the values and beliefs of its participants. From around 1870 onwards, a new figure began to appear in the literature. The term 'New Mountaineer' may not have been coined until 1898, but the kind of climber John Norman Collie was referring to had been discussed and criticized well before this date. I have chosen to use Collie's phrase as a convenient shorthand, as it was the strongest and most succinct attempt made in this period to define this new, paradigmatic figure.

The New Mountaineer (invariably portrayed as a male figure) was physically tough, daring, and technically competent. His approach was organized and systematic, and he embraced a variety of new disciplines. He enjoyed an athletic challenge, was enthusiastic about modernity, and saw no contradiction in using the latest equipment and techniques to help him scale summits.

Although the New Mountaineer shared many characteristics with earlier generations who had climbed during the Golden Age of mountaineering and before, contemporaries often regarded him as a distinctively modern creature. This modernity was apparent both in the way he carried out the physical act of climbing and in the attitudes and values he brought to the mountains. It seemed to many commentators that the approaches associated with Romantic mountain travellers or with the more recent mountaineers of the 1850s and 1860s had been supplanted by something quite different. By some accounts, the New Mountaineer was deficient in spirituality or sensitivity to natural beauty, more concerned with 'bagging' peaks and testing himself against nature than with the aesthetics of mountain landscapes. His values were expressed, communicated, and sometimes criticized in the pages of mountaineering texts, a genre that would prove crucial in forging the identity of the Victorian mountaineers. They were also embodied in the emphatically modern accoutrements of climbing that came increasingly to mediate the physical relationship between the New Mountaineer and the mountain.

## Manliness and Modernity

'What was formerly done casually and instinctively', wrote the pioneering rock climber Walter Parry Haskett Smith in 1894, 'has for the last dozen years or so been done systematically and of set purpose.'[1] Smith's remark identified a significant shift that had taken place in the culture of British climbing, though in fact it had been underway since the early 1870s. This shift encompassed nearly every aspect of mountaineering culture. Mountain climbing had become systematic, organized, and codified. A new preoccupation with measurement and quantification held sway.

Increasingly quantification – looking at the precise height, the exact distance, the specific location, the number of mountains above a certain height or in a particular range – came to be seen not just as a useful adjunct to the activity of mountaineering, but as something absolutely central to the activity itself. This new approach was part of a shift away from both Romantic approaches to mountain landscapes and the relatively desultory, apparently casual attitude of the adventurous eccentrics of the Alpine Golden Age. Mountains, precisely measured and categorized, became the location for physical challenge and the testing of oneself. This was the result, or so it was believed, of the ascendancy of the group that would come to be dubbed the New Mountaineers.

The Alpine Club, the first great institution of British climbing, had been founded in 1857, but the growth of mountaineering as a sport in the 1880s and 1890s saw the formation of new clubs focused largely on climbing in the British Isles: the Cairngorm Club in Aberdeen in 1887, followed in 1889 by the Glasgow-based Scottish Mountaineering Club, and then in 1898 by the Climbers' Club, associated with climbing in north Wales. Mountaineering club journals became a key component of the growing body of mountaineering literature. *Peaks, Passes, and Glaciers*, the forerunner of the *Alpine Journal*, had begun publication in 1859 and proved an instant success with the British public. By the late nineteenth century, however, the new clubs had established their own journals, which were concerned less to communicate the experience of climbers to the wider public than to speak climber to climber. The *Scottish Mountaineering Club Journal*, first published in 1890, the *Cairngorm Club Journal*, from 1893, and the *Climbers' Club Journal*, which began in 1898, were soon publishing not only accounts of mountaineering expeditions but also practical tips for training and preparation. The *Alpine Journal*, too, increasingly spoke to a self-conscious community of British climbers with common values and a dynamic, modern approach to their hobby.

Mountaineering, like most other areas of life in late Victorian Britain, was characterized by a profound concern with the nature of modernity, and this is reflected in the pages of the club journals and in other mountaineering texts. The New Mountaineer was unapologetic about his modernity, and happy to use technology when it assisted his climbing. He developed specialist equipment such as ice axes and crampons, allowing him to climb harder routes on steep snow and ice. The design and strength of climbing ropes became standardized and increasingly reliable, and climbers devised new techniques for using the rope to move safely over exposed ground and protect the leader on a climb. Outdoor clothing was still rudimentary, but mountaineers were learning to adapt everything – from the buttons and pocket flaps on their Norfolk jackets to the pattern of nails on their boots – to the specific demands of mountain conditions. Nutritional and training regimes for the mountaineer were proposed. Rapid advances in the portability of photographic equipment allowed the New Mountaineer to carry a hand-held camera on his trips to the mountains, in turn influencing the way mountaineering was represented in books, journals, and exhibitions. Mountaineers built up an impressive range of skills in mapping and navigation, often supplementing the work of the official cartographers of the Ordnance Survey. They reported on, analyzed, and tabulated everything from the heights of mountains to the nature and causes of mountaineering accidents (see Fig. 2.1).

In all these areas, the New Mountaineers of the late nineteenth century were building on the experience and accrued knowledge of their

**Fig. 2.1** The Beispielspitz, from the *Badminton* guide. An example of the close attention given to route finding and identifying features

predecessors, but they approached their climbing in a wholly new way. Their adoption of technology, their passion for tabulation and codification, and the professionalization of their approach suggested a fascination with the materiality of climbing, both in its effects on the body and in the objects that were used by climbers. Whether boasting that the introduction of electric lighting at an exhibition of Alpine pictures meant that for the first time 'the works exhibited were fairly seen, and the lady-guests of the [Alpine] Club were able to inspect them closely without fear of being set fire to',[2] or extolling the benefits of a self-heating tin which could 'furnish a hot meal in about ten minutes, without the necessity of making any fire',[3] the mountaineers of the late nineteenth century regarded modern technology as an ally, and not something that was out of place in the mountain environment. Much as they prized the ruggedness and remoteness of the mountains they climbed, the New Mountaineers brought to these places a quintessentially modern sensibility.

An 1893 article in the *Manchester City News* attempted to capture the atmosphere of the Sligachan Hotel on Skye, one of the main climbing centres in Britain in the late nineteenth century. The paper's correspondent described a milieu where the culture of mountaineering coexisted quite unashamedly with that of modernity, mass communication, and commerce:

> Sitting out here in the open, with shaggy Highland cattle eyeing you suspiciously, with a noisy stream racing a few yards distant, and the dark granite precipices of the Coolins [*sic*] only three miles away, rising boldly above the crimson heathery foreground, you may get news of the stock exchange and contrive an operation without inconvenience. It is a strange concatenation of interests. But it is life as it is lived nowadays, and therefore must not be accounted incongruous.[4]

The writer noted that the Hotel also served as 'a post office and telegraph office'. The presence of a telegraph, an important symbol of modernity, is especially significant. The telegraph, as Stephen Kern notes, made it possible 'to experience many distant events at the same time', a phenomenon he describes as 'part of a major change in the experience of the present'.[5] It was, in other words, characteristic of a modernized, rational, and scientifically ordered world. The New Mountaineer, his modernity unquestionable even when climbing in one of the remotest parts of the country, was the characteristic denizen of this world.

One aspect of modernity that directly influenced climbing in this period was the rise of professionalization. Climbing remained an amateur sport, but its ethos was changing in line with a wider set of social and cultural changes in the late nineteenth century, perhaps the most powerful being the rise of the middle classes and the related ascendancy of the professional man. The mid-Victorian period had seen a massive expansion of the middle classes, with newly established professionals – teachers, doctors, and civil servants – joining the more traditional clergymen, lawyers, and academics in the ranks of the upper middle classes.[6] Stefan Collini suggests that one of the key changes in this period was that 'many of the social connotations of the old "status professionalism" were transferred to the new "occupational professionalism" '.[7] In other words, social status and respectability were increasingly dependent upon the nature of one's profession, rather than the ownership of land and title that had traditionally conferred these attributes. Collini notes:

> The ethic of work and the ethos of strenuousness which were making their mark on even the upper reaches of English society by the mid-nineteenth century endowed the energetic pursuit of a profession with added respectability without forfeiting its traditional genteel status.[8]

The professionalized nature of mountaineering in the late Victorian period was manifested not in the sense that it was carried out by professional mountaineers, but rather in the attitudes of those who undertook it, and in the particular social status they held. The new professions had been well represented in the ranks of the Alpine Club since its formation in 1857. An analysis by Hansen of the Club's membership rolls, *The Alpine Club Register*, shows that membership 'was drawn overwhelmingly from the professional middle classes', particularly in the 'genteel professions, including bankers, civil servants, clergymen, country gentlemen, university dons and public schoolmasters', while confirming 'the absence of all but a handful of aristocratic or working class members'.[9] The membership records of the newer Scottish Mountaineering Club and Cairngorm Club show that mountaineering continued to be primarily a hobby of the professional classes. The Cairngorm Club, in particular, counted a number of medical doctors, Justices of the Peace, the Lord Provost of Aberdeen, and the Sheriff of Ross, Cromarty and Sutherland among its members in 1893, when the first volume of its *Journal* listed its 'ordinary' members.[10] The Climbers' Club continued this tradition: 70 of its 200 members were also Alpine Club members, and 'almost all members were in the professions, the Bar or Universities, or were schoolmasters or solicitors'.[11]

The middle classes, and middle-class values, were thus in the ascendant in this period. Among other things, these values included a high regard for a rational, scientific approach to problems, and for the virtues of competence; accurate record keeping; the purposeful and rational use of leisure time; and for a professional ideal based, as Harold Perkin points out, 'on trained expertise and selection by merit, a selection made not by the open market but by the judgement of similarly educated experts'.[12] Perkin notes that this professional ideal came to supplant the entrepreneurial ideal that had flourished earlier in the century. This ideal was understood as emphatically masculine, and contemporary writing about mountaineering almost invariably assumed that climbers were male.

Mountaineering shared with other sports and games in the late Victorian period a preoccupation with the idea of manliness, which Richard Holt describes as residing in 'the harmonious growth of the physique and character side by side'.[13] Mountaineering writers regularly expressed this preoccupation, from the early days of the Golden Age through to the era of the New Mountaineer. Edward Whymper stated:

> We glory in the physical regeneration which is the product of our exertions; we exult over the grandeur of the scenes that are brought before our eyes [ ... ] but we value more highly the development of manliness, and the evolution, under combat with difficulties, of those noble qualities of human nature – courage, patience, endurance and fortitude.[14]

There is a good deal of consistency between this 1871 claim by Whymper and comparable remarks by late-Victorian climbers. William Naismith, a prominent Glaswegian climber and founder of the Scottish Mountaineering Club, claimed in 1893 that climbing in Britain without guides 'is a grand school for prudence, self-reliance, endurance and other qualities that make up manliness'.[15]

Climbing was seen as the quintessential 'manly' activity of the new professional classes. What Norman Vance calls the 'slightly raffish outdoor atmosphere of the English tradition of physical manliness',[16] which had traditionally involved hunting and shooting followed by heavy drinking, was giving way to a more genteel form of manly outdoor activity, but one which still retained an element of physical danger. The bluff, prosaic tone of the New Mountaineers also fitted with what James Eli Adams describes as 'a norm of "manliness" identified above all with honest, straightforward speech and action, shorn of any hint of subtlety or equivocation'.[17] Even when manliness was not specifically referred to, it was implicitly assumed to be a central part of the climber's ethos in a great deal of mountaineering literature. Models of stoicism allied to sensitivity, physical prowess combined with aesthetic appreciation, and natural tendency to command coupled with native humility and good manners all recur throughout the period and combine to form what J.A. Mangan and James Walvin call 'a neo-Spartan ideal of masculinity'. This ideal, they suggest, 'was diffused throughout the English-speaking world with the unreflecting and ethnocentric confidence of an imperial race'.[18] Even if the New Mountaineer was sometimes criticized for being rather deficient in aesthetic appreciation, his essential manliness was never in doubt.

Alongside the ideal of manliness was a belief – again, implicit in many if not most mountaineering texts – that, as Roberta J. Park puts it, 'the "new gentleman" was "an aristocrat of character" not an aristocrat by birth'.[19] Schama notes that in spite of the relative social exclusiveness of the Alpine Club, its members were not 'snobs in the technical sense of pure social contempt' but 'nonetheless did think of themselves as a caste apart, a Spartan phalanx tough with virtue, spare with speech, seeking the chill clarity of the mountains'.[20] This idea of a new type of aristocracy, broadly analogous to the shift from 'status professionalism' to 'occupational professionalism', was clearly appealing to a class whose increasing confidence had allowed it to move away from traditional aristocratic modes of behaviour and pastimes. A shift away from hunting and shooting towards more genteel but still physically challenging and potentially dangerous activities like mountaineering was just one aspect of this redefinition.[21]

This neo-Spartan ideal and concern with manliness inevitably meant that women were often written out of contemporary accounts of mountaineering. Women had, in fact, been climbing since the earliest days of mountaineering, even before it came to be recognized as a sport. The first woman to ascend Mont Blanc, Marie Paradis, did so as early as 1808,[22] with another more famous ascent by Henriette d'Angeville in 1835.[23] Once mountaineering grew in popularity, women quickly became active climbers, despite their exclusion from the Alpine Club and the frequent disapproval of male relatives. Lucy Walker climbed in the Alps with her father and brother from 1858, reaching the summit of the Matterhorn in 1871 and ticking off a total of ninety-five summits and passes over the course of her career.[24] Walker retired from serious climbing in 1879, but was later involved in setting up the Ladies' Alpine Club.[25] *Alpine Journal* editor Coolidge was frequently accompanied by his aunt, Meta Brevoort, who pioneered winter climbing and often camped at high altitude in order to climb multiple peaks.[26]

Other women were prepared to climb without male relatives; Anna and Ellen Pigeon climbed together in the Alps between 1869 and 1876, chalking up a total of sixty-three major ascents.[27] Elizabeth Le Blond, a pioneering mountain photographer and another founder member of the Ladies' Alpine Club, specialized in winter ascents of Alpine peaks and published a book of her experiences in 1883 (under her married name, Mrs. Fred Burnaby),[28] while Kathleen Richards achieved six first Alpine ascents during the 1870s and 1880s.[29] By 1887, George Meredith, writing to Leslie Stephen's wife, would ask her to mention to her husband that 'a lady told me last week of her intention to scale the Matterhorn, had she not been obliged to nurse her husband. It has become "quite a woman's mountain", she said.'[30]

The conventional view of historians has been that these achievements were either ignored or patronized by the *Alpine Journal* and other climbing publications, and the review in the *Journal* of Le Blond's book seems to bear this out. Having previously praised the 'remarkable' series of climbs she achieved during the winter of 1882/83, and predicted that they would 'form one of the most brilliant chapters in the history of winter mountaineering',[31] the *Alpine Journal* published a patronizing and dismissive review of her book. Its reviewer, 'after searching in vain for more satisfying matter, has to remind himself that he is dealing with a lady's book, and the book of a lady who has written to amuse an idle hour'.[32] Having acknowledged that Le Blond had accomplished some impressive winter ascents, he went on to assign most of the credit for this to her guides, stating that the fact 'that [the climbs] were carried through without serious mishap suggests much for the judgement and skill of Mrs Burnaby's guides, as well as for her own perseverance.'[33]

The typical attitude towards women climbers has been assumed to be summed up in Leslie Stephen's 1866 remark that assessments of a mountain's difficulty generally pass through five stages: 'inaccessible – the most difficult point in the Alps – a good hard climb, but nothing out of the way – a perfectly straightforward bit of work – and finally, an easy day for a lady'.[34] Certainly, the Alpine Club, in common with other gentlemen's clubs of the time, did not admit female members and would rarely if ever publish accounts of climbs written by women.[35] So, for example, an account by Meta Brevoort of her and her nephew's 1871 ascent of the Bietschhorn had to be submitted to the *Alpine Journal* under Coolidge's name to be accepted.[36] The *Journal* did report in 1872 on the Pigeon sisters' crossing of the Sesia-Joch pass from Zermatt to Alagna four years previously, but even this was put together by combining notes supplied by the Pigeons with an account in an Italian newspaper, rather than being published under the sisters' own names.[37] In a rare exception, the *Journal* published an article by Mrs. E.P. Jackson under the author's name in 1889, in which she described a winter season climbing in the Alps.[38]

More recently, Ann Colley has challenged this view of a consistently dismissive attitude to women climbers, suggesting that women were not as widely discriminated against as has been assumed. 'Although prejudice existed, it functioned alongside an active participation in mountaineering – so active, indeed, that the sheer number of women climbers is extraordinary',[39] argues Colley, who claims that 'women were not summarily discouraged from participating in what most recent commentators assume was solely a male-centred sport based on power and privilege'.[40] Colley does not deny that gender was an issue in mountaineering, but believes that 'gender did not, as a rule, matter in the overwhelmingly debilitating way commentators have claimed'.[41] As well as the sheer numbers of women who climbed, she points to relatively supportive utterances by male climbers, such as an 1887 address to the Alpine Club by its then (male) president, Florence Craufurd Grove. 'With women, as with men, it has been found the best of the sex take naturally to mountaineering', claimed Craufurd Grove, 'and if they come in increased numbers to the snow-line their presence will, I am sure, be welcomed by all whose welcome they will care for'.[42] Hansen, in turn, has challenged Colley's relatively sanguine analysis of the position of women climbers, arguing that gender is 'constitutive of configurations of power and culture', and that a precise delineation of changing gender relations over the period would show significant differences between the mid- and late century.[43] Clare Roche, meanwhile, has demonstrated how a substantial minority of the numerous female visitors to the Alps in the second half of the nineteenth century participated in climbing, despite the prevailing medical advice against strenuous exercise for women. Roche argues that the activities of female climbers in this period 'contest the notion that mountaineering was a uniquely male activity and demonstrate a blurring of the concept of separate spheres'.[44]

The complexities of gender in Victorian mountaineering are too extensive to do justice to in this book, and the subject deserves far more extensive research than has so far been published. What is clear, however, is that women were not simply passive recipients of the attitudes of male climbers; they demonstrated a great deal of agency themselves, but ultimately had little control over the *discourse* of mountaineering, given their exclusion from official accounts in climbing club journals. Denied membership of the Alpine Club, female climbers formed their own organization, the Ladies' Alpine Club, in 1907, but even before that there is clear evidence of women mountaineers expressing resentment and resistance to entrenched attitudes – among them, Mary Mummery, wife of the distinguished British climber Albert Mummery. Mary contributed a chapter to her husband's 1895 memoir *My Climbs in the Alps and Caucasus*, in which she turns Stephen's notorious 'easy day for a lady' remark on its head. Using the phrase ironically, given its context in a chapter about a difficult ascent, she criticizes what she calls the 'strong prejudices [which] are apt to be aroused the moment a woman attempts any more formidable sort of mountaineering'.[45] She mocks the attitudes of male climbers who believe that women 'should be satisfied with watching through a telescope some weedy and invertebrate masher being hauled up a steep peak by a couple of burly guides'.[46] Of course, the fact that Mary Mummery felt the need to condemn such attitudes suggests they were still current and widespread by the 1890s. The phrase 'easy day for a lady' was used, for example, in the publicity for the Cairngorm Club's 1890 Easter meeting, and the idea that a climb capable of being undertaken by a woman was necessarily less difficult seemed to persist in the face of all evidence to the contrary.[47]

Such comments indicate that even if the physical practice of mountain climbing was open to women, the literature of mountaineering tended to assume that climbers were male. Mountaineering existed within a profoundly male-dominated culture while at the same time contributing – indirectly, and in some cases probably even unintentionally – to the growth of that culture, with its emphasis on manliness and Spartan ideals.

## 'Special Knowledge': The Importance of Expertise

If manliness was one important aspect of the middle-class professional's world-view, it was by no means the only one to influence the culture of late-Victorian mountaineering. The rational, scientific approach and the notion of professional expertise were arguably just as important to the New Mountaineers. Although they were no more likely than their predecessors in the early days of the Alpine Club to carry out original scientific research, they continued to prize a scientific turn of mind which could turn its attention to the phenomena encountered in the mountains with a cool, objective gaze.

Here, for example, is Owen Glynne Jones, a pioneer of British rock climbing and a physicist by training, in the introduction to his 1897 climbing guide to the English Lake District:

> Probably the scientific mountaineer gains most. He is certain to acquire rare and valuable knowledge of facts in zoology, botany, or geology, if he starts with the necessary intellectual equipment. The physicist's mind is perpetually exercised by the natural phenomena he witnesses; mist bows, Brocken spectres, frost haloes, electrical discharges of the queerest description, mirages, all these offer him problems of the most interesting kind.[48]

Jones goes on to say that in fact the climber is generally so busy with the business of climbing that, 'the natural sciences are usually left to themselves, and their consideration reserved for special expeditions', but the impression nonetheless remains of a trained individual who comes to the mountains with a specific body of knowledge and expertise, and a professional and scientific cast of mind. Educated in the sciences, trained in the rudiments of first aid, physically fit and well nourished, this new breed of mountaineers reflects the modern, professional, and multidisciplinary spirit of the age, in contrast to the relatively desultory training and varied motives of the early pioneers. The antics of the 1850s, with Albert Smith being virtually dragged up Mont Blanc by his guides or Wills climbing the Wetterhorn as a diversion from his Alpine honeymoon, seem very far removed from this new ethos.

The new, specialist approach dovetailed neatly with another phenomenon of the period: the well-established Victorian drive to classify, enumerate, codify, and create lists and tables of information. So when Coolidge, who became editor of the *Alpine Journal* in 1879, began his life's work of compiling a detailed history of Alpine mountaineering he approached the topic by 'giving all that related to the Alps the same careful scrutiny that scholars had previously devoted only to weightier subjects', as his biographer puts it.[49] 'Never before was such an excessive accumulation of Alpine knowledge made available, acquired by a man to whom its dissemination was the main task of life.'[50] Coolidge was regarded even by his contemporaries as a single-minded obsessive, but his project – the tireless and seemingly endless accumulation of facts, figures, and details – was entirely in keeping with the prevailing ethos in mountaineering and in wider Victorian society.[51]

Kate Flint has proposed a Foucauldian reading of the nineteenth century, which emphasizes 'the fact that practices of surveillance, or bringing material to the surface, worked in collaboration with practices of codification and classification'.[52] Flint's emphasis on the widespread use of 'classificatory procedures' ('from the growth in statistical societies to the establishment of the British Museum catalogue; from cartography to the work of natural historians; from graphology manuals to dictionaries of plants and of dreams') is helpful in putting this new preoccupation of the Victorian mountaineers into the context of wider Victorian society.[53] Science became accepted as a worthy pursuit during the earlier part of the century, following what Richard Yeo describes as the 'division of intellectual labour' that took place in the late eighteenth and early nineteenth centuries, with the appearance of scientific societies devoted to a single subject and the 'crystallization into disciplines with separate research agendas, technical apparatuses, methods and concepts'.[54]

This specialization and professionalization of science meant that it was no longer practical for enthusiastic amateurs to carry out original scientific research in the mountains. It did, however, create an environment in which mountaineers, like other members of the professional classes, were aware of the latest developments in scientific research and had a sense that the world around them was being analyzed and investigated. The legacy of such public spectacles as the Great Exhibition of 1851 and James Wyld's Great Globe (displayed in Leicester Square in the same year, allowing audiences to view a giant scale model of the earth) had helped to create what Paul Young, referring to the Great Exhibition, calls a 'systematic world picture' – a sense that everything that could be known about the world was gradually being collected, classified, and displayed for the edification and education of the Victorian public.[55]

For the Victorian mountaineers, a comprehensive and detailed understanding of mountains was part of this 'systematic world picture'. Mapping and navigation were key to acquiring this knowledge and were among the most important of the technical skills associated with mountaineering in the latter part of the century. The New Mountaineers were both the beneficiaries and to some degree the instigators of a period of intense activity in the mapping of mountain regions.

Maps had, of course, been important since the early days of mountaineering; indeed many of the pioneering climbers in the Alps had been the first people accurately to map the various Alpine regions. But a number of factors led to the increased centrality of mapping and navigation to the culture of the New Mountaineer, including the rise of guideless climbing and the extension of climbing to mountainous areas of the British Isles. Climbing without local guides necessitated greater attention to route finding and the use of a map and compass as first rather than last resort, while many of Britain's mountainous areas, particularly in the Scottish Highlands, remained inadequately mapped until the latter part of the century.

The New Mountaineers of the 70s, 80s, and 90s were admittedly working with much better basic materials than their predecessors. Travelling in the Alps in 1862, Francis Fox Tuckett, one of the stalwarts of the Golden Age of mountaineering, had to rely on an unpublished French War Office map acquired in Paris en route to the mountains. He quickly found that even this official document had major omissions and errors, and set about correcting it from his own observations in the field.[56] The situation in Britain around the same time was little better. On a walking holiday in Scotland in 1863, the philosopher Herbert Spencer was misled by a map showing only one range of mountains between Glen Quoich and Glen Shiel, getting lost before realizing there were in fact two ranges to be negotiated. 'I was impressed with the heavy responsibility which rests on the makers and publishers of guidebooks', he later wrote. 'I suspect that from time to time lives are lost, and every year many illnesses caused, in consequence of their misdirection'.[57]

The situation gradually improved in the latter decades of the century, in part due to the work of such official government surveys as the Ordnance Survey in Britain and the Federal Office of Topography in Switzerland, but also because the mountaineers themselves supplied information and observations to improve the quality of mountain maps. The Alpine Club had its own collection of maps, which included copies of large scale government surveys of the various Alpine states as well as maps created and published by its members.[58] Writing about the recently published 'Alpine Club Map of Switzerland' in 1875, the geologist Thomas George Bonney stressed the degree of care that had been taken in producing it:

> Only those who have tried the task can have any idea of the infinite pains, patience, and skill required in the construction of a map which rises above the level of an ordinary sketch route [...]. Differences and discrepancies have to be reconciled, lacunae filled up, redundancies, where there is a

reduction of scale, put away, endless questions of nomenclature and orthography settled, and a keen watch kept against personal errors.[59]

Despite the efforts of the mountaineers and official government surveyors, the quality of Alpine maps remained variable. As late as 1879, Coolidge recalled, a visitor to the Italian Alps had to rely on a one-to-fifty-thousand scale map 'which was notoriously very vague above the snow-line'.[60] The *Alpine Journal* was fastidious in reporting to members on the publication of new maps, announcing for example that a new map of the Adamello and Presanella ranges (then in the Austrian Alps, although now in Italian territory) had been issued by the Austrian military in 1875.[61] It also took a keen interest in the mapping of mountain ranges beyond the Alps. The *Journal* reported on the work of Russian Caucasian Survey that was attempting to create a new, more precise set of maps of the Caucasus during the 1880s.[62] It was also increasingly interested in the maps being produced in India and neighbouring states by the Great Trigonometrical Survey, which began its work in 1819 and continued throughout the nineteenth century.[63] The Survey was an amalgamation of science and imperialism, not only mapping the boundaries of British India (as well as some states that remained outside the Empire) but also establishing in 1852 the height of the world's tallest mountain.[64]

In Britain, the Ordnance Survey was extending its coverage of domestic mountain ranges, but both the *Alpine Journal* and the journals of domestic climbing clubs regularly pointed out shortcomings in its work, especially in Scotland. The Survey, which officially came into existence in 1791, had its origins in the pacification of the Highlands after the 1745 Jacobite rebellion, but its focus had quickly shifted to mapping the coast of England in preparation for a feared French invasion by sea during the Seven Years War. It did not complete the First Series of maps of the British Isles until 1870, and would not produce cheap folding maps suitable for use by hikers and climbers until the early twentieth century.[65]

British mountaineers were increasingly active in supplementing the Survey's work with their own observations of domestic mountain ranges. An 1890 article on Skye by William Naismith in the *Scottish Mountaineering Club Journal* points out that the Ordnance's surveyors appear to have 'funked' the passage of a particular couloir when carrying out their work,[66] while a review of a new series of 'Reduced Ordnance Survey

Maps' published by John Bartholomew and Company in the same year is critical of the 'inaccuracy with which it has been carried out' and gives an extensive list of errors in altitudes and other details.[67] Clinton Dent, writing in the *Alpine Journal* in 1891, also points out the shortcomings of the Ordnance Survey's mapping of the Cuillins. 'The Ordnance map is a little uncertain in the nomenclature of the group of peaks known as Alaisdair, and the name Sgumain is applied to them collectively', notes Dent, adding that a sketch map recently created and published by Charles Pilkington still needs corrections but does at least give the correct nomenclature and thereby improves on the Ordnance map.[68] Pilkington, later to be president of the Alpine Club, had his map reproduced by a Manchester publisher and in the same issue of the *Journal* let it be known that he would supply it, post free, to any mountaineer prepared to undertake further corrections from their own observations – a good example of how climbers in this period were building up their collective knowledge, creating a community of common interest through the pages of mountaineering journals.[69]

The initiative shown by this generation of mountaineers in mapmaking was evident in other topographic and navigational disciplines. The drive to map, measure, and record mountain facts found perhaps its most influential outlet in the compilation and publication of Munro's Tables – the list of 283 Scottish mountains above three thousand feet in altitude, created by Sir Hugh Munro in 1891. Some earlier publications, such as Robert Hall's *The Highland Sportsman* (1882), had included rudimentary lists of Scotland's highest peaks, but these tended to be incomplete and inaccurate. Munro, who in 1894 would become the Scottish Mountaineering Club's third president, created the first comprehensive list and published it in the *Scottish Mountaineering Club Journal*.[70]

The response to the publication of Munro's Tables is instructive. In 1901, the Reverend Archibald Eneas Robertson reached the summit of Meall Dearg, one of the peaks that make up the formidable Aonach Eagach ridge above Glencoe, and in doing so became the first man to climb all the Munros.[71] Robertson's achievement in becoming 'the first Munroist', as his biographer calls him, had taken ten years but it was the logical conclusion of a process that had begun almost as soon as the tables were published. Munro's Tables quickly became a touchstone for value among mountaineers and hill walkers: if a mountain reached Munro's magical three thousand feet, its ascent was somehow considered to have more intrinsic value than that of a lesser peak. Thus, writing in 1894 in the

*Scottish Mountaineering Club Journal* about the Scottish mountain Beinn Mhic Mhonaidh, Francis J. Dewar could remark:

> Beinn Mhic Mhonaidh lies on the south-eastern side of Glenstrae, and although under 3,000 feet, and therefore unclassed as a 'Ben', is worth a visit from members of the Club who may be at Dalmally and have exhausted the 3,000 feet hills in the neighbourhood.[72]

This assumption that a mountain below Munro's arbitrary three thousand feet is only 'worth a visit' when other, higher mountains have been ticked off the list became increasingly prevalent in the writing of the period. Herbert Boyd, writing about 'Ben A'an' in the *Scottish Mountaineering Club Journal* in 1896, noted that the eponymous mountain falls short 'of the dignity of a Munro – that mystic, but occasionally fallacious, patent of nobility to which every ambitious Scottish mountain is now supposed to aspire'.[73] Munro's Tables implicitly encouraged both a hierarchy of mountains and an approach to mountain climbing that elevated a particular category of mountains to importance. Having been listed and tabulated, these mountains could then be climbed and ticked off a list, and the ascent of these specific mountains would confer greater prestige, and be considered intrinsically more important, than that of lesser peaks.

The publication of Munro's Tables, and their enthusiastic response from the mountaineering community, was just one example of the drive towards measurement, tabulation, and quantification and the application of these procedures to the disciplines of mapping and navigation. In 1892 Naismith formulated his rule of thumb for calculating how long a journey over mountainous terrain should take. Naismith's Rule specified that a walker should allow one hour for every three miles plus half an hour for each thousand feet of ascent.[74] Munro's Tables and Naismith's Rule came into existence in an environment where increasingly accurate topographical information was being supplied by mountaineers themselves. In this environment it was assumed that the average mountaineer would acquire the skills necessary to contribute to the sport's growing body of knowledge. For example, writing in the influential *Badminton* guide to mountaineering in 1892, Clinton Dent recommended carrying a prismatic compass and clinometer, although he noted that the latter was no longer strictly necessary in the Alps, 'where the mountain regions have been most minutely surveyed'.[75] In less thoroughly surveyed regions, however, Dent warned: 'the mountaineer who is unable to give, with some approach to accuracy, the heights of new mountains which he has ascended will be little thought of'.[76] In such areas, he added, the mountaineer should even consider the use of a mercury barometer, a more accurate alternative to the better-known aneroid barometer.[77]

Dent's belief that the mountaineer should have the requisite technical skills to make such measurements was widespread among climbing writers. C.G. Cash, for example, writing in the *Cairngorm Club Journal* in 1900, recommended that Club members approach Ordnance Survey field teams and offer to 'place their special knowledge at their service'.[78] He took issue with the Ordnance Survey's six-inch maps of the Cairngorms, which he described as:

> deplorably deceptive for all the higher ground; they show no contours; they give a very inadequate and often misleading selection of heights [ ... ] they are decidedly lacking in place-names; and generally speaking, they are quite disappointing to the mountaineer.[79]

Cash urged his readers to bring pressure on their MPs to vote for more funding for the Ordnance Survey, 'and demand and insist that all our land should be adequately and beautifully mapped'.[80] He himself spent a day with the Ordnance surveyors in the Highlands and 'had the satisfaction of helping to ensure a number of corrections and improvements in the map of that one district'.[81]

In effectively proposing that mountaineers could supervise the work of the Ordnance Survey, Cash assumed that his fellow mountaineers had the expertise and quasi-professional confidence to offer advice to government surveyors. This suggests that he saw them as participating in a professional discipline. This level of confidence, and indeed this degree of geographical precision, was something quite new among visitors to the mountains. The publications of the Scottish Mountaineering Club, Cairngorm Club, and Climbers' Club, as well as late century volumes of the *Alpine Journal*, are illustrated with detailed maps and with photos which have been amended to show precise features of routes, in contrast to the much more impressionistic line drawings in early numbers of the *Alpine Journal* (see Fig. 2.2).

The recognition of the growing importance of precise mapping and navigational skill brought with it a new style of writing about the practice of mountaineering. This is discernible not only in club journals but in the other new mountaineering texts of the late nineteenth century – the

**Fig. 2.2** Photograph of Mt. Elias amended to show the route, from *Alpine Journal* 19 (1898)

visitors' books of popular mountaineering hotels. As well as the Sligachan on Skye, the main British hotels used by climbers in the late nineteenth century were the Clachaig in Glencoe, the Wasdale Head Inn in the Lake District, and the Pen-y-Gwryd in Snowdonia.

The Sligachan visitors' book, which opens in 1885, is packed with terse commentaries in which timing, altitude, and technical climbing issues are recorded in a workmanlike and unemotional tone: 'Up Sgurr Nan Gillean by the Pinnacles and down by the West (Bhaslin) Ridge, with John Mackenzie as guide. A grand rock scramble. Rope necessary.' Thus wrote Arthur H. Henderson in August 1894.[82] Other comments indicate a new interest in the precise amount of ground that can be covered in a particular period of time: 'Went straight to Camasunary, then round by Loch Scavaig, Bad Step, Loch Coruisk, Loch Dhu, down that way to Glen Sligachan and the Hotel; all this in ten hours and with my wife: rather a feat for a lady!'[83] As the century drew to a close, more and more guests felt compelled to share detailed timings for their ascents of the various peaks on a particular route, and to compare their own navigational notes with the heights listed in Munro's Tables, in the *Scottish Mountaineering Club Journal*, or on the Ordnance Survey maps. An entry in the Sligachan visitors' book for 17 July 1896 by R.G. Napier and J.H. Bull notes:

> Our aneroid readings on the summits of two peaks of Alasdair agreed exactly with the heights given in *SMC Journal*, volume 2, page 171, viz. Alasdair 3,275 feet, NE Alasdair 3,203 feet – but we found the height of the col to be 3,150 feet, not as given 3,050 feet.[84]

The level of temporal and geographical detail demonstrated here – cross-checking the details already published in a mountaineering club publication with the use of scientific instruments such as an aneroid barometer, which would normally be associated with professional surveyors – is a long way from the sentiments expressed in Byron's *Childe Harold's Pilgrimage* (1812–1818), where high mountains are described as 'a feeling',[85] or Wordsworth's claim in *The Prelude* that mountains provide 'a never-failing principle of joy,/ And purest passion'.[86] Hewitt, writing about the development of the Ordnance Survey in the eighteenth and nineteenth centuries, notes the deep ambivalence that many Romantic writers had displayed towards the very concept of mapping, an extension of their broader scepticism towards Enlightenment notions.[87] Such ambivalence about the benefits of mapping had entirely vanished from the attitude of late nineteenth-century mountaineers. Instead, mapping and navigation, along with other forms of specialist knowledge, were central to their activities, part of an approach to mountains that saw competence as essential. As Dent put it in the *Badminton* guide:

> Mountaineering is, beyond all other sports, one that it is imperative to take up, to a certain extent, seriously. If a man intends to climb high, it is his bounden duty to acquire all the proficiency he can develop in himself, for the sake of his companions.[88]

This is clearly quite different to what was perceived as the Romantic tradition of mountain travel. Coleridge's haphazard method of descending mountains, for instance, was in no way influenced by notions of proficiency or competence – indeed, by the standards of the later Victorian mountaineers it was recklessly incompetent. Coleridge's habit of ascending and then descending mountains by the most direct route, regardless of steepness or difficulty and without attempting even the most basic route finding, resulted in 1802 in his unplanned and very nearly fatal descent of Broad Stand on Scafell – sometimes described as the first recorded rock climb.[89] As Carl Thompson points out, Coleridge's approach was characterized by 'an emphasis on chance, and on travel experiences that are supposedly unscripted'.[90] This is qualitatively different from the late nineteenth-century approach of the New Mountaineers, in which competence, planning, and technique are used to mitigate danger, even if they cannot fully remove it, and in which the mountaineer is forearmed with the trinity of Naismith's Rule (to ensure he is off the mountains before darkness falls), a copy of an Ordnance Survey map (which has been rendered more accurate by Cash's painstaking professionalism), and Munro's Tables (to guarantee he is climbing a mountain significant enough to be worth the effort).

All this new efficiency led to significant improvements in navigation, safety, and the ability to plan routes, and made climbing mountains a less spontaneous and more technically complex and codified activity. From an experience of mountain climbing seemingly characterized by deliberately random wandering, the mountain climbers of the Victorian period increasingly participated in an activity in which training, topographical skill, and scientific measurement allowed them to exercise greater control. An internal, emotional engagement with mountain landscapes was supplanted by a highly specific, physical, and tactile experience, in which the knowledge and agency of the climber was crucial.

## THE NEW MATERIAL CULTURE: EQUIPMENT AND TRAINING

Climbing, announced Scottish Mountaineering Club president George Gilbert Ramsay in 1889, was now 'a science of a highly complex character, cultivated by trained experts, with a vocabulary, an artillery, and rigorous methods of its own'.[91] Ramsay's characterization of mountaineering was by no means confined to the disciplines of mapping and navigation. It also reflected, for example, the greater importance attached to the equipment and techniques of mountaineering. A new array of climbing gear, specialist clothing, and such accoutrements as tents, sleeping bags, and cooking stoves formed part of the 'artillery' of the late-Victorian mountaineer, who had access to products unheard of by earlier generations of climbers. Everything from the technical specifications of rope to the optimum diet for the mountaineer was incorporated into a new material culture that emphasized the practical and physical nature of the climber's contact with the mountain landscape.

While the New Mountaineer was concerned with the details of navigation and mapping, he was also preoccupied with the physical nature of maps, guidebooks, and other navigation equipment. The type of material maps were printed on, the best size for their use in the field, and methods for keeping them dry in poor weather conditions were all discussed at club meetings and in the pages of club journals and other mountaineering texts. So, for example, Edward Downes Law read a paper to the Alpine Club in 1880 on the possible use of India rubber as a better material for maps than paper, noting that German army officers were already using such maps on field exercises.[92] The following month, he gave another talk on the use of cotton as a material for maps, illustrating this lecture with cotton maps of Afghanistan printed by the Great Trigonometrical Survey.[93]

Such detailed interest in the materiality of maps, guidebooks, and other equipment would become increasingly prevalent. A reviewer noted approvingly in 1883, for example, that the latest volume of Baedeker's guide to the Eastern Alps 'may be divided into eleven separately sewn parts, which are guaranteed to keep together and are specially convenient for those climbers who indulge in the luxury of carrying their own knapsack'.[94] A short *Alpine Journal* article in 1889 noted that up to this point the Swiss Federal Office of Topography's official map of Switzerland had been 'divided most inconveniently, and that the only way out of the difficulty hitherto has been to have the sheets specially cut, joined and mounted'.[95] Dent, in the *Badminton* guide, recommended that maps should be cut up into sections and mounted, and that

> These should fold up into a size that can be conveniently carried in the pocket. When engaged in exploring minutely a limited district, it is a good plan to have all the sections separate, each being the size of a sheet of notepaper; these can be numbered, and then stored in an oil-skin envelope like a pack of cards. The required sheet is placed uppermost, and in wet weather the climber can make out what he wants through the oil-skin without damaging his map.[96]

This level of detail in describing how to fold, mount, and carry a map is the corollary of the navigational and topographic minutiae recorded in club journals and visitors books. The texts of the New Mountaineers reflect a fascination with the detail of the material, physical experience of mountaineering which is substantively different from the much broader narratives in the age of *Peaks, Passes, and Glaciers* or the early volumes of the *Alpine Journal*.

Climbing equipment had become vastly more sophisticated since the days of the early pioneers. When Tuckett, for example, undertook his first Alpine climbing trip in 1856, one of his guides carried a ladder, and another had a woodcutter's axe slung across his shoulder. Their only concession to technical climbing equipment was to carry an alpenstock apiece.[97] The alpenstock was essentially a long walking pole, about six feet in length, with a metal spike on the end. Later in the century this was adapted by the addition of a pick and adze on the top to create the mountaineering ice axe. The pick allowed the climber to gain purchase on steep snow or ice slopes, and the adze was used to cut steps. The ice axe took some time to catch on, and as late as 1868 Hereford Brooke George, the first editor of the *Alpine Journal*, was introducing the question of 'Axe versus Alpenstock' as 'the most important topic which a mountaineer preparing for a Swiss tour has to consider – with what sort of weapon he is going to arm himself for the coming campaign'.[98] George came down firmly in favour of the axe.

By 1892 when Dent wrote about equipment in the *Badminton* guide he could report that the alpenstock was virtually obsolete since 'it is a fact that everything which can be done with the alpenstock can be done also and better with the axe'.[99] Dent spent five pages on the various designs, weights, and precise dimensions of the ice axe, with notes on care of the axe, material to be used, and how to carry it while rock climbing.

Naismith recalled that the use of the ice axe in Scotland had been virtually unknown until the early 1880s,[100] but by the late 1890s it had become so commonplace that a correspondent in the *Scottish Mountaineering Club Journal* reported that on arriving at the railway station at Tulloch in the Highlands, 'I was able to pass the porters, navvies &c., and they gave only a casual glance at my ice-axe'.[101] By the end of the century, climbers were starting to carry two axes, one long and one short, to deal with more technically difficult pitches. This became standard practice in the Alps and in winter conditions on British hills.[102]

The use and specifications of climbing ropes developed in a similar way. The early mountaineers and their guides often omitted to use ropes at all, and when guides did use them they were often carried casually in their hands. Some climbers even untied the rope in exposed places to avoid the whole party being pulled off if one person fell.[103] From around the late 1860s, articles in mountaineering journals regularly reiterated the importance of using the rope correctly and in the right situations – not only when scaling rocks but also when crossing glaciers and on steep snow.[104] A standard Alpine Club rope, based on the recommendation of a club committee in 1864, was manufactured for climbers by John Buckingham of Shaftesbury Avenue. One and a quarter inches in diameter and composed of Manila hemp, this rope had a distinguishing red mark between the strands to allow climbers to be confident they were buying the correct article.[105]

Such detailed concern with the technical specifications of climbing equipment would have been alien to most mountaineers of the Golden Age. The Matterhorn tragedy of 1865, for example, happened in part because the rope that snapped was made of sash cord, rather than the Manila fibre used later in the century.[106] By contrast, the New Mountaineers were almost obsessive about the equipment they took to the mountains. This applied not only to ropes and ice axes but to new consumer goods of all kinds. One of the exhibits at the Alpine Club's annual picture exhibition in 1890, for example, was 'a self-cooking soup tin, by Messrs. Silver and Co.', and the exhibition that year included not only pictures but 'a collection of Alpine appliances'.[107] The Alpine Club formed a special committee in 1891 to prepare a comprehensive report on equipment. The committee requested via the *Alpine Journal* that members send in their own notes on 'such *precise* information as you may have acquired from your own practical experience', including 'the name and address of the tradesman or firm from whom a particular object referred to can be purchased'.[108]

The committee's interest was not confined to technical climbing equipment but also covered clothing, rucksacks, tents, sleeping bags, food and cooking apparatus, and photographic instruments. This was typical of the New Mountaineers' keen interest both in equipment expressly designed for the mountains and also in developments that could be adopted by climbers. Prominent in this latter category was the new generation of compact cameras that became popular from the late 1880s. Even before this, photography had been a regular topic in the *Alpine Journal*, which carried articles by the renowned mountain photographer William Donkin up until his death on an expedition to the Caucasus in 1888. A brief survey of articles and speeches on photography by Donkin and other mountaineers between the late sixties and late nineties will serve to give an impression of how rapidly the techniques and technology of photography developed in this period, and how far this relatively new hobby was incorporated into the even newer pastime of mountaineering.

In a paper read to the Alpine Club in 1869, George noted that only in the past two to three years had it become possible to 'take photographs anywhere and everywhere that the climber chooses to go', attributing this to the relatively light equipment that had recently become available.[109] He recalled a trip to the Bernese Oberland in 1865 when his companion's photographic apparatus was 'a heavy load for the stoutest of Oberland porters', and contrasted this with a trip just four years later when 'the whole apparatus I carried during my tour of 1869 weighed rather less than four pounds, exclusive of the stand, which was fitted to the handle of my axe'.[110] He described his own invention of an ice axe that converted into a camera stand, and when the speech was printed in the *Alpine Journal* the following year the article was accompanied by illustrations of this device.

Thirteen years later, Donkin could point to further progress made in the portability of photographic equipment, and in particular to the development of dry plates which had obviated the traditional need for full processing in the field, as 'sensitive plates are prepared for you by the manufacturer at a few shillings per dozen, which will keep indefinitely if protected from light and damp, and are ready at any time to be put in the camera'.[111] Donkin described in considerable detail the equipment he took with him for mountain photography, including

> a new arrangement for carrying the sensitive plates, known as Hare's changing box; it holds twenty plates, any one of which can be transferred to a slide, exposed in the camera, and returned to the box without any possibility of extraneous light reaching it. The whole apparatus carried in a leather rucksack weighs about 18 lbs., and the tripod stand 3 lbs. more.[112]

Nonetheless, Elizabeth Le Blond described in her 1928 autobiography the sheer physical hardship involved in mountain photography as late as the 1880s. 'It was trying work setting up a camera with half-frozen hands, hiding one's head under a focusing cloth which kept blowing away, and adjusting innumerable screws in a temperature well below freezing point', she recalled.[113] The banker and classical scholar Walter Leaf shared his thoughts on recent developments in photography in 1891, noting 'the great advance which has been made towards the perfection of the photographer's last pet – the hand-held camera'.[114] He went into some detail about particular models, recommending in particular the 'Kodak No. 3 Junior' as 'best suited to the beginner who does not want the trouble of learning any technical processes whatever'.[115] A couple of years later, the first photo of Mont Blanc taken with the recently invented telephoto lens caused a ripple of excitement at the Alpine Club's annual picture exhibition, which by this stage regularly featured both paintings and photographs. The exhibition's reviewer predicted that the new lens would make it possible to photograph the inaccessible mountains of Nepal from the Sikkim frontier of India.[116] At the following year's exhibition, it was noted that the improved quality of enlargements, along with the new 'telephotographic' lens, would mean that 'the future mountaineer will soon no longer need to wait for the summer to find new routes up mountains'.[117]

The significance of these articles is twofold. First, they reflect the growing interest in photography as a medium for reproducing the sights that mountaineers experienced, and for allowing those experiences to be recollected or previewed at leisure. Photographs increasingly replaced line drawings in climbing club journals by the late nineteenth century, and the Alpine Club's annual picture exhibitions featured photographs as well as paintings, with reviewers frequently writing more about the photos than the paintings.[118] Second, the articles illustrate the fascination that specialist equipment (and the technical skills required to use it) held for the mountaineers of this period, who benefited both from the rapid technological progress that made equipment lighter and more portable and the increased commercial availability of these new products. Advertisements for camping and mountaineering products began to appear in the *Alpine Journal* with increasing frequency from the early 1880s onwards (see Fig. 2.3).

A preoccupation with the physical and the material was not confined to cameras, ropes, ice axes, and other manufactured objects. The New Mountaineers also took a keen interest in training their bodies for climbing, and especially in the correct nutrition for the mountaineer. In this, as in their interest in manufactured commodities, they demonstrated the characteristic modernity and seriousness of purpose of the late-Victorian professional. Gilbert Thomson wrote a guide in an 1892 issue of the *Scottish Mountaineering Club Journal* to training for the city-bound mountaineer who could not get to the mountains regularly, suggesting specific sites near Edinburgh and Glasgow of 'sufficient extent and variety to brace the muscles and try the skill of the mountaineer'.[119] The first issue of the *Climbers' Club Journal* carried articles on first aid for climbing accidents and on practice scrambling in Derbyshire. Neither topic would typically have been covered in the early years of the older *Alpine Journal*.[120] A subsequent issue discussed training, recommending the benefits of 'a hand traverse, well calculated to make one's fingers stiff for a week'

Fig. 2.3 Adverts for climbing and camping equipment, from *Alpine Journal* 11 (1884)

and even a 'course of boulder jumping on the shore' below Beachy Head to prepare for walking over glacial moraines.[121] The *Alpine Journal*, too, was taking seriously the idea that climbing was a sport requiring rigorous preparation, in contrast to the rather more casual approach that had characterized the mountaineering of the 1850s and early 1860s. An 1885 article by Craufurd Grove on the 'Alpine Training Diet', for instance, suggested a serious dietary regime for climbers readying themselves for an Alpine trip. Craufurd Grove contrasted the conventional dietary wisdom of the mid-1860s, 'when the Alpine Club was in the most glorious state of activity', with the current state of knowledge about nutrition.[122] The recommended regime for athletes in these earlier days had been a protein-heavy diet of beef or mutton, with few vegetables or carbohydrates, he recalled. By contrast, the modern climber had access to the latest nutritional science:

> During and after prolonged exertion nature cries aloud for heat-giving foods. The heat-giving foods are the starchy, the fatty, and notably the saccharine. These are precisely the foods which can be 'stored' in the body with the greatest ease, and used as a reserve force, and are at the same time the most valuable, because indirect sources of muscular energy.[123]

A comparison with the list of provisions that Albert Smith took on his 1851 Mont Blanc ascent is telling. Smith's inventory, reproduced in *The Story of Mont Blanc*, included approximately a hundred bottles of wine, champagne, and cognac, four legs of mutton, six pieces of veal, eleven large fowls, and some beef.[124] Later in the 1850s, on his first ascent of the Aletschhorn in the Swiss Alps, Tuckett had taken 'black bread, cheese, and wine' to sustain him.[125] Craufurd Grove, by contrast, reflected the latest thinking on the need to provide the correct fuel for the climbing body's optimum performance. By 1889, the *Alpine Journal* was reporting on a new kind of condensed food, a biscuit made with kola nuts ('a fruit which is employed by the warriors of the Soudan to sustain their strength through long marches') and suggested that these could usefully be adopted by climbers. It recommended that 'four should be eaten on rising, and three after lunch and dinner respectively'.[126]

The contrast between the New Mountaineer and his forebears is considerable. The New Mountaineer – his body trained and nourished according to modern scientific techniques, his rope, ice axe, and other technical gear manufactured to official specifications, his rucksack full of the fruits of late Victorian commodity capitalism – did not simply wander in the mountains in the manner of Romantic travellers. His preparation and equipment were considerably more professional and single-minded than that of even the most adventurous climbers of the Golden Age. Stephen, Wills, Tyndall, and Whymper achieved extraordinary feats in the fifties and sixties, but they were all the more impressive for having been done with relatively rudimentary equipment and desultory training. The New Mountaineer had the benefit of specialist equipment, greatly improved maps, and above all a body of knowledge built up over decades – and the most important medium for disseminating this knowledge throughout the mountaineering community was literature.

## Writing the New Mountaineer: The Birth of a Genre

The sport of mountaineering and the genre of mountaineering literature emerged almost contemporaneously, with the publishing success of the first volume of *Peaks, Passes, and Glaciers* in 1859. By the late nineteenth century, however, this new genre had flourished and diversified. In addition to the *Alpine Journal*, there were the journals of the various new mountaineering clubs, countless memoirs of Alpine and British climbing, guide books for mountaineers and later guides aimed specifically at rock climbers, climbing diaries, and the comments in the visitors' books of climbers' hotels.

These various types of climbing text contributed to the sense of an emerging community of mountaineers, while at the same time reflecting changes and developments in the actual practices of that community. The rise of the New Mountaineer was reflected but to some degree also created by the new genre of mountaineering literature. Rather than continuing to address the wider, non-climbing public who had devoured the early volumes of *Peaks, Passes, and Glaciers*, mountaineering literature became more specialized and more inward-looking as the century progressed, increasingly giving the impression of a community talking to itself.

One example of how this manifested itself can be found in the visitors' books of hotels popular with climbers. Up until the 1880s, both climbers and ordinary tourists would use the visitors' books to record their experiences, with entries varying from banal remarks about the food and beds through to detailed accounts of new routes or first winter ascents of particular gullies. In 1884, the Pen-y-Gwryd hotel in Snowdonia introduced a book with the telling title, 'Not the Visitors' Book', to be kept separate for accounts by climbers (and for some other edifying entries, such as remarks on natural history, geology and local history). A similarly elite book was proposed for the Wasdale Head Inn, although it was not introduced, while the Sligachan started a book marked 'For Climbing Entries Only' in 1893. The introduction of books kept for the exclusive use of climbers suggested that climbing narratives constituted a wholly distinct genre to the experiences of these hotels' other guests. As we have seen, these books were used to record detailed accounts of climbs, with notes on timing, navigational issues, and technical difficulty, all for the benefit of other mountaineers. They also constituted an informal and unofficial public record of what individual climbers had achieved. So David Hepburn used the Sligachan book in 1894 to record his exploits on the Pinnacle Ridge of Sgurr nan Gillean, giving detailed timings for the ascent of each of the five Pinnacles.[127] Similarly, in the visitors' book of the Clachaig Inn in Glencoe, the renowned Lake District climber George Abraham listed details of climbs he had undertaken while visiting,[128] and the mountaineering writer J. Lehmann Oppenheimer gave details of a new route he had forged on the Aonach Dubh.[129]

Similar accounts were written in the Pen-y-Gwryd visitors' book. As well as the usual accounts of climbs undertaken in the region, and suggestions for new climbing and scrambling routes, the Pen-y-Gwryd book also contains detailed accounts of fatal accidents and other mishaps, and the overall impression it gives is of a group creating its own history and lore through writing about its activities. So an account of an ascent of the North Gully of Tryfan, a mountain close to the hotel, signed by H.B. Dixon, A.S. Cornelius, H. Gamble, and A. Marshall and dated 1 April 1892, has had an asterisk added to Marshall's name with the following note: 'Killed in Deep Ghyll, Scafell, Dec, 1893'.[130] The book has become not just a record of activities undertaken around the neighbouring mountains of north Wales but one of the documents charting the fortunes of the wider community of British mountaineers in other climbing centres. As well as names familiar from the climbing club journals and other formal mountaineering texts of the period, including Owen Glynne Jones, James Merriman Archer Thomson, Oscar Eckenstein, and Ashley Abraham, the Pen-y-Gwryd book includes regular contributors from climbers W.E. Corlett and E. Kidson, who were less well known in wider climbing circles but mainstays of the group of mountaineers who regularly visited north Wales.

This sense of a discrete community writing its own history is reinforced by certain phrases that crop up repeatedly and which suggest that the writers have been prevailed upon by their peer group to record their experiences. 'I have been asked to insert our experience of a view of the "Brocken Spectre" from Snowdon', writes E. Cowrie of Eastbourne in May 1887,[131] while in July that year 'T. S.' (possibly T.V. Scully, another Pen-y-Gwryd regular) writes, 'It has been suggested that some account of a night ascent of Snowdon via Crib Goch and Crib y Ddygsl might interest sojourners at Pen-y-Gwryd'.[132] There are also occasional stringent criticisms of fellow climbers. For example, at the end of a long account of 'A Night on Cader Idris', in which three visitors detailed their uplanned night out on this mountain in southern Snowdonia in 1891, someone has written succinctly: 'Moral. Don't cross mountains without compass and ordnance map.'[133] Even more censorious was Oscar Eckenstein's debunking of a claim to have ascended Snowdon in winter conditions in January 1894. 'According to the statements of John Owen; and of two gentlemen who watched this party and subsequently examined the tracks, the party went nowhere near the top of Snowdon', wrote Eckenstein, who went on to accuse the group of writing 'a mendacious account'.[134]

Cumulatively, these entries create the impression of a community of broadly like-minded individuals speaking to each other about their common preoccupations, setting precedents, sharing advice and information with each other, and building up a picture of mountain landscapes through detailed observation and recording. They also suggest a medium in which climbers implicitly lay out their achievements for judgement and approval by their peer group, a practice that brings to mind Perkin's remarks on middle-class professionals of this period increasingly seeking 'the judgement of similarly educated experts'.[135]

More formal, published mountaineering literature increasingly displays this self-referential tone, too. While some late nineteenth-century mountaineering books (for example Mummery's *My Climbs in the Alps and Caucasus*) continued to be popular with the wider public, the journals of the Scottish Mountaineering Club and the Cairngorm Club were written very much with a climbing readership in mind, and their contributors made few if any concessions to the non-climbing reader. The *Alpine Journal*, too, had shifted tone from its early days, when it had seemed to be telling stories of mountain adventure to a wider Victorian public. Increasingly it concentrated instead on speaking to Alpine Club members, and by extension to the wider community of mountaineers. Articles in club journals were frequently based on papers that had been read to meetings of the club, giving the sense of collective wisdom being recycled and communicated to the wider group, and of the spoken word being given a material form.

The climbing club journals were central to the development of late-Victorian mountaineering's distinctive culture. They communicated information to their readers about new ascents, or ascents of mountains by new routes; about developments in equipment and clothing; about accidents that had taken place; and even about climbers who had discovered physical mementos left on summits by others.[136] They were written with a tone of voice which propagated the vernacular and climbing slang of the Alps, and in some cases transferred it to the mountains of Britain, while also reflecting the distinctive jargon of the New Mountaineer, with his talk of 'bagging' peaks and references to the use of a 'machine' (bicycle) to approach climbs.[137] They created a sense of common history and a consciousness of the rapid development of their own sport.[138] They often criticized the depredations of tourists and tourist infrastructure, reinforcing the mountaineers' sense of being set apart from the common herd.

Coverage of mountaineering accidents in climbing literature provides a useful case study in how the importance of the material and the tangible connected to the creation of a sense of common purpose, and how club journals allowed the mountaineers a virtual space in which to meet and exchange information and opinions. The *Alpine Journal* had recorded accidents on an ad hoc basis from its early editions, but it was not until the fourth volume, covering the period 1868–1870, that it started to write about them in a regular feature. This constituted a more formal, semi-official version of the accounts written in visitors' books. Stephen wrote the first such report in November 1869, on the death of the Reverend Julius Elliot on the Schreckhorn, and his account set the tone for coverage of accidents in subsequent volumes. Respectful and tactful, but unflinching in his description of what had occurred, Stephen noted that Elliot had fallen after refusing his guide's request to use the rope, and had 'glided rapidly down the steep snow-slopes of the northeast face of the mountain, rolling occasionally over until he disappeared from their sight some 1,000 ft. below, near the Lauter-Aar glacier'.[139] Stephen attempted to analyze why the accident happened and the lessons to be learnt from it – in this case, that the rope should always be worn in steep places and that the party should be sufficiently spaced that if one climber falls the others are in a position to arrest his fall with the rope.[140] Such analysis would become standard practice in later written accounts of climbing accidents.

## 2 THE RISE OF THE NEW MOUNTAINEER

Two years later, after a notorious episode in September 1870 in which eleven climbers died in bad weather on Mont Blanc, John Stogdon read a paper to the Club on the causes of the tragedy and the lessons to be drawn from it. He recalled an ascent of the same mountain a month before the accident, when he and his companions had set off in good conditions but quickly became disoriented in mist and battered by high winds. He pointed out that Mont Blanc – by this stage often regarded as a relatively safe and straightforward climb – could be extremely dangerous in bad weather: 'If Mont Blanc has been the scene of many successful expeditions, he has, on the other hand, more blood on those white snows of his than, I think we may say, all the other Alpine peaks put together.'[141]

As with many other papers read before members at club meetings, Stogdon's was published in the *Alpine Journal*. By 1882, the *Journal* was not only publishing regular accounts of accidents but also ran a lengthy article in which Charles Edward Mathews presented a tabulated list of fatal Alpine accidents from 1856 to date. The list ran over several pages, with the known causes of each of the forty-six incidents listed beside them. Mathews' accompanying text noted that while 'mountaineering is extremely dangerous in the case of incapable, of imprudent, of thoughtless men', accidents were not inevitable and were invariably caused by mistakes: 'I venture to state that of all the accidents in our sad obituary, there is hardly one which need have happened; there is hardly one which could not have been prevented by proper caution and proper care.'[142]

Accidents continued to occur, of course, and by 1888 the *Alpine Journal* would open its regular 'Alpine Accidents' feature by remarking: 'It is once more our sad duty to record the loss of many lives in the course of mountain excursions'.[143] But the coverage of accidents and fatalities clearly illustrates the nexus of various aspects of the New Mountaineers' approach. In the systematic reporting of accidents the various defining characteristics of the New Mountaineer seem to come together as a coherent whole. Their emphasis on the material and the physical is reflected in an interest in the details of precisely what caused each misadventure. Their penchant for recording facts and figures, and immersion in the classificatory culture of late-Victorian Britain is demonstrated by, for instance, the tabulation of accidents and their causes; danger, like other aspects of mountains and mountaineering, is being classified and categorized in these texts. Their assumption of professional competence and sense of their own skill and technical expertise is shown by the regular insistence in these articles that accidents do not simply happen but are caused by mistakes and inexperience.

It was also to a large extent in the mountaineering club journals that debates about the ethos and future direction of the sport took place. While it helped to construct a virtual community of like-minded individuals, the genre of mountaineering literature also brought out into the open the debates and tensions that were growing among the sport's participants. Among them in this period was a growing sense of unease about the direction of mountaineering – unease that found its focus in the figure of the New Mountaineer. There were also key debates about the role of guides, controversies between individual climbers, and criticisms of guidebooks and other texts that were considered to be less than accurate.

Some of the earliest debates in the period under discussion were about the propriety or otherwise of guideless climbing. Climbing with guides was virtually de rigeur until at least the late 1860s, and virtually all the first ascents of Alpine summits by British mountaineers were made in the company of local guides. The Reverend Arthur Gilbert Girdlestone published his book *The High Alps Without Guides* in 1870 with the express intention of pointing out 'the advantages of mountaineering as a means of recreation, and the possibility of indulging in it to a very great extent without the cost or the annoyances of professional assistance'.[144] His book was far from universally welcomed, and Craufurd Grove responded to it directly with a paper read to the *Alpine Club* (and later published in the *Journal*) on 'The Comparative Skill of Travellers and Guides', in he which attempted to refute the idea that the amateur mountaineer could ever emulate the skill and lifelong experience of the locally born guide.[145]

The controversy did not last long and guideless climbing later became widely accepted. By the mid-1880s, the *Alpine Journal* would report without adverse comment guideless ascents of a number of Alpine peaks,[146] although its editor, Coolidge, noted that 'while recording the exploits of adventurous climbers, we are bound once more to insist on the necessity of very great caution and constant self-control, without which guideless climbing is likely to fall into disrepute'.[147]

Climbing literature, then, gave expression to and in some respects helped drive the change in the ethos of mountaineering. The New Mountaineer was not only reflected in the journals, visitors' books and other mountaineering texts; to some degree, he was also created and nurtured by them. However, the New Mountaineer was not the only figure at large in the mountain landscape of the late nineteenth century. At the time when this new approach seemed to have achieved hegemony, there was a strong reaction against it and a nostalgic pull back towards what were perceived as older values.

## Notes

1. Walter Parry Haskett Smith, *Climbing in the British Isles*, 2 vols (London: Longmans, Green, 1894), I, vii.
2. 'Alpine Notes', *Alpine Journal*, 12 (1884–86), 462–71 (p. 462).
3. Clinton Dent, 'Equipment and Outfit', in *Badminton Library of Sports and Pastimes: Mountaineering*, ed. by Clinton Dent (London: Longmans, Green, 1892), pp. 39–76 (p. 60). The *Badminton Library* was a series of books published between 1885 and 1902 covering various sports and pastimes popular in Britain. Other contributors to the mountaineering volume included Martin Conway, Alfred Wills, Douglas Freshfield, and Charles Edward Mathews, and it was often referred to in other climbing texts as the standard work on mountaineering.
4. Edinburgh, National Library of Scotland (NLS), Acc. 11538, Item 16, Sligachan Hotel visitors' book, 1893–1921, untitled cutting, *Manchester City News*, 23 September 1893, p. 14.
5. Stephen Kern, *The Culture of Space and Time, 1880–1918* (London: Weidenfeld and Nicolson, 1983), p. 68.
6. Robbins, 'The Victorian Mountaineers', p. 584.
7. Stefan Collini, *Public Moralists: Political Thought and Intellectual Life in Britain, 1850–1930* (Oxford: Clarendon Press, 1991), p. 32.
8. Collini, *Public Moralists*, p. 32.
9. Hansen, 'Albert Smith, the Alpine Club', p. 310.
10. 'Ordinary Members of the Cairngorm Club', *Cairngorm Club Journal*, 1 (1893–96), unpaginated.
11. Douglas Milner, 'The Art and Sport of Rock Climbing in the English Lake District', in *The Lake District: A Sort of National Property* (London: Victoria and Albert Museum, 1984), pp. 105–15 (p. 109).
12. Harold Perkin, *The Rise of Professional Society: England Since 1880* (London: Routledge, 1989), p. xii.
13. Holt, *Sport and the British*, p. 91.
14. Edward Whymper, *Scrambles Amongst the Alps in the Years 1860–1869* (London: John Murray, 1871), p. 407.
15. William Naismith, 'Snowcraft in Scotland', *Scottish Mountaineering Club Journal*, 2 (1892–93), 157–67 (p. 158).
16. Vance, *Sinews of the Spirit*, p. 11.
17. Eli Adams, *Dandies and Desert Saints*, p. 14.

18. J.A. Mangan and James Walvin, eds., 'Introduction', in *Manliness and Morality*, (Manchester: Manchester University Press, 1987), pp. 1–6 (p. 3).
19. Roberta J. Park, 'Biological Thought, Athletics and the Formation of a "Man of Character", 1800–1900', in *Manliness and Morality*, ed. by Mangan and Walvin, p. 7.
20. Schama, *Landscape and Memory*, p. 502.
21. Mountaineering writers often noted that one of the advantages of their sport was the absence of cruelty to animals, or as Owen Glynne Jones put it, 'the joy of conquest without any woe to the conquered'. Jones went on to list as one of climbing's attractions the fact that it 'does not claim the sacrifice of beasts and fishes'. Owen Glynne Jones, *Rock Climbing in the English Lake District* (London: Longmans, Green, 1897), p. xlix.
22. Stefano Ardito, *Mont Blanc: Discovery and Conquest of the Giant of the Alps* (Shrewsbury: Swan Hill Press, 1996), p. 58.
23. Henriette d'Angeville, *My Ascent of Mont Blanc* (1838; London: Harper Collins, 1992).
24. Brown, *Women on High*, p. 48.
25. Brown, *Women on High*, p. 56.
26. Brown, *Women on High*, p. 61.
27. Jane Robinson, *Wayward Women: A Guide to Women Travellers* (Oxford: Oxford University Press, 1990), p. 72.
28. Mrs Fred Burnaby, *The High Alps in Winter: Or, Mountaineering in Search of Health* (London: Sampson Low, Marston, Searle, and Rivington, 1883).
29. Robinson, *Wayward Women*, p. 23.
30. *The Letters of George Meredith*, ed. by C.L. Cline, 2 vols (Oxford: Clarendon Press, 1970), I, 899.
31. 'Alpine Notes', *Alpine Journal*, 11 (1882–84), 238–43 (p. 243).
32. 'Reviews and Notices', *Alpine Journal*, 11 (1882–84), 305–07 (p. 306).
33. 'Reviews and Notices', *Alpine Journal*, 11, p. 307.
34. Leslie Stephen, 'Alpine Dangers', *Alpine Journal*, 2 (1865–66), 273–85 (p. 274).
35. Neither the Scottish Mountaineering Club nor the Climbers' Club admitted female members until well into the twentieth century. The Cairngorm Club, however, was open to women from the beginning, although it never had more than half a dozen female members at any stage up to 1914: Sheila Murray, *The Cairngorm Club, 1887–1987* (Aberdeen: The Cairngorm Club, 1987), p. 37.
36. Williams, *Women on the Rope*, p. 51.
37. 'The Passage of the Sesia-Joch from Zermatt to Alagna by English Ladies', *Alpine Journal*, 5 (1870–72), 367–72.
38. Mrs E.P. Jackson, 'A Winter Quartette', *Alpine Journal*, 14 (1888–89), 200–10.

39. Colley, *Victorians in the Mountains*, p. 102.
40. Colley, *Victorians in the Mountains*, p. 103.
41. Colley, *Victorians in the Mountains*, p. 102.
42. F. Craufurd Grove, 'Address to the Alpine Club', *Alpine Journal*, 13 (1886–88), 213–20 (p. 216).
43. Peter H. Hansen, 'Review', *Victorian Studies*, 54 (2012), 334–36 (p. 335).
44. Clare Roche, 'Women Climbers 1850–1900: A Challenge to Male Hegemony', *Sport in History* (2013), doi: 10.1080/17460263.2013.826437.
45. Mary Mummery, 'Der Teufelsgrat', in *My Climbs in the Alps and Caucasus*, ed. by Albert Mummery (London: T. Unwin Fisher, 1895), pp. 66–95 (p. 66).
46. Mary Mummery, 'Der Teufelsgrat', p. 68.
47. Murray, *Cairngorm Club*, p. 16. Conversely, a tricky climb in New Zealand was described by a correspondent in the *Alpine Journal* in 1894 as 'a nasty bit of work, especially for a lady': 'Alpine Notes', *Alpine Journal*, 17 (1894–95), 196–201 (p. 200).
48. Jones, *Rock Climbing*, p. li.
49. Ronald Clark, *An Eccentric in the Alps* (London: Museum Press, 1969), p. 32.
50. Clark, *Eccentric in the Alps*, p. 130.
51. In his 1895 presidential address to the Alpine Club, Douglas Freshfield pointedly described Coolidge as being 'engaged, with almost excessive care and conscientiousness' on his task: Douglas Freshfield, 'An Address to the Alpine Club', *Alpine Journal*, 18 (1896–97), 1–17 (p. 8).
52. Flint, *Visual Imagination*, p. 13.
53. Flint, *Visual Imagination*, p. 13.
54. Yeo, 'Natural Philosophy', in *Romantic Age*, ed. by McCalman and others, p. 326.
55. Paul Young, *Globalization and the Great Exhibition: The Victorian New World Order* (Basingstoke: Palgrave Macmillan, 2009), p. 71.
56. W.A.B. Coolidge and Eliot Howard, eds., *A Pioneer in the High Alps: Alpine Diaries and Letters of F. F. Tuckett, 1856–1874* (London: Edward Arnold, 1920), p. 128.
57. Herbert Spencer, *An Autobiography*, 2 vols (London: Williams and Norgate, 1904), II, 79.
58. Douglas Freshfield, 'The Club Map Cupboard', *Alpine Journal*, 10 (1880–82), 42–44; London, Alpine Club Archive, ACM7000 Book 2, 'Catalogue of Maps'.
59. T.G. Bonney, 'The Alpine Club Map of Switzerland', *Alpine Journal*, 7 (1874–76), 218–23 (p. 219).

60. W.A.B. Coolidge, *Alpine Studies* (London: Longmans, Green, 1912), p. 3.
61. 'A New Map of the Adamello', *Alpine Journal*, 7 (1874–76), 277–78.
62. 'New Maps of the Caucasus', *Alpine Journal*, 14 (1888–89), 57.
63. The survey grew out of earlier surveying work that began in the early nineteenth century. See John Keay, *The Great Arc: The Dramatic Tale of How India Was Mapped and Everest Was Named* (London: HarperCollins, 2000).
64. Richard Sale, *Mapping the Himalayas: Michael Ward and the Pandit Legacy* (Ross-on-Wye: Carreg, 2009), p. 41.
65. Hewitt, *Map of a Nation*, p. 176.
66. William Naismith, 'Three Days Among the Cuchulins', *Scottish Mountaineering Club Journal*, 1 (1890–91), 56–62 (p. 61).
67. Hugh Munro, 'Reduced Ordnance Survey Maps', *Scottish Mountaineering Club Journal*, 1 (1890–91), 180–83 (p. 181).
68. Clinton Dent, 'The Rocky Mountains of Skye', *Alpine Journal*, 15 (1890–91), 422–36 (p. 431).
69. 'Alpine Notes', *Alpine Journal*, 15 (1890–91), 440–48 (p. 447).
70. Andrew Dempster, *The Munro Phenomenon* (Edinburgh: Mainstream Publishing, 1995), p. 15.
71. Peter Drummond, *The First Munroist* (Glasgow: Ernest Press, 1993), p. 2.
72. Francis J. Dewar, 'Beinn Mhic Mhonaidh', *Scottish Mountaineering Club Journal*, 3 (1894–95), 70–72 (p. 70).
73. H.C. Boyd, 'Ben A'an', *Scottish Mountaineering Club Journal*, 4 (1896–97), 155–58 (p. 155).
74. Dempster, *Munro Phenomenon*, p. 36.
75. Dent, 'Equipment and Outfit', in *Badminton*, ed. by Dent, p. 65.
76. Dent, 'Equipment and Outfit', in *Badminton*, ed. by Dent, p. 66.
77. Dent, 'Equipment and Outfit', in *Badminton*, ed. by Dent, p. 66.
78. C.G. Cash, 'The Ordnance Survey and the Cairngorms', *Cairngorm Club Journal*, 3 (1899–1902), 85–88 (p. 88).
79. Cash, 'Ordnance Survey', p. 85.
80. Cash, 'Ordnance Survey', p. 86.
81. Cash, 'Ordnance Survey', p. 88.
82. NLS, Acc. 11538, Item 16, Sligachan Hotel visitors' book, 'For Climbing Remarks Only', 1893–1921, p. 20.
83. NLS, Acc. 11538, Item 16, 1894, p. 23.
84. NLS, Acc. 11538, Item 16, p. 52.
85. George Gordon, Lord Byron, *Childe Harold's Pilgrimage*, III. 682, in *Lord Byron: The Major Works*, ed. by Jerome J. McGann (Oxford: Oxford University Press, 2008), pp. 19–206.

86. William Wordsworth, 'The Prelude, II. 465–66', in The Prelude: The Four Texts, ed. by Jonathan Wordsworth (London: Penguin, 1995), pp. 75–101.
87. Hewitt, Map of a Nation, p. 207.
88. Clinton Dent, ed., 'Reconnoitring', in Badminton Library of Sports and Pastimes: Mountaineering (London: Longmans, Green, 1982), pp. 137–56 (p. 138).
89. Ian Thompson, The English Lakes: A History (London: Bloomsbury, 2010), p. 217.
90. Carl Thompson, The Suffering Traveller and the Romantic Imagination (Oxford: Clarendon Press, 2007), p. 20.
91. George Gilbert Ramsay, 'The President's Address to the First Annual Dinner, December 12, 1889', Scottish Mountaineering Club Journal, 1 (1890–91), 1–11 (p. 3).
92. Edward Downes Law, 'Alpine Notes: India Rubber Versus Paper as a Material for Alpine Maps', Alpine Journal, 10 (1880–82), 40–41.
93. Edward Downes Law, 'Alpine Notes: Cotton Versus India Rubber', Alpine Journal, 10 (1880–82), 41–42.
94. 'Reviews and Notices', Alpine Journal, 11 (1882–84), 183–91 (p. 190).
95. 'Reviews and Notices', Alpine Journal, 14 (1888–89), 255–74 (p. 273).
96. Dent, 'Equipment and Outfit, in Badminton, ed. by Dent, p. 67.
97. Coolidge and Howard, Pioneer in the High Alps, ed. by Howard and Coolidge, p. 2.
98. H.B. George, 'Axe Versus Alpenstock', Alpine Journal, 4 (1868–70), 126–29 (p. 126).
99. Dent, 'Equipment and Outfit', in Badminton, ed. by Dent, p. 73.
100. Naismith, 'Snowcraft', p. 158.
101. Edred M. Corner, 'The Loch Treig Hills and Ben Na Lap', Scottish Mountaineering Club Journal, 5 (1898–99), 66–69 (p. 66).
102. The correct use of the axe remained a subject of contention well into the 1890s. Naismith's 1893 article on 'Snowcraft in Scotland' triggered a debate over whether it was best to use the pick or spike of the axe while glissading. See Naismith, 'Snowcraft', p. 165; J.H. Gibson, 'Snowcraft in Scotland', Scottish Mountaineering Club Journal, 2 (1892–93), 322–24.
103. Lunn, A Century of Mountaineering, p. 49.
104. See, for example, Leslie Stephen, 'Recent Accidents in the Alps', Alpine Journal, 4 (1868–70), 373–79 (p. 373); and Charles Edward Mathews, 'The Alpine Obituary', Alpine Journal, 11 (1882–84), 78–89 (p. 85).
105. Dent, 'Equipment and Outfit, in Badminton, ed. by Dent, p. 73.
106. J.W.S. Hearle, H.A. McKenna, and N. O'Hear, Handbook of Fibre Rope Technology (Cambridge: Woodhead, 2004), p. 30. As late as 1876 a correspondent in the Alpine Journal warned readers that guides at Cogne, in the

Valle d'Aosta, were using 'the slender cords which generally serve to fasten hay-bundles, and are absolutely worthless for mountaineering purposes', and called upon the Italian Alpine Club to supply some proper rope to the inn there: 'New Expeditions in 1876', *Alpine Journal*, 8 (1876–78), 97–110 (p. 104).
107. P.W.T., 'Alpine Implements, etc', *Alpine Journal*, 15 (1890–91), 98.
108. 'Proceedings of the Alpine Club', *Alpine Journal*, 15 (1890–91), 457–60 (p. 459), emphasis in original.
109. H.B. George, 'Photography in the High Alps', *Alpine Journal*, 4 (1868–70), 402–10 (p. 402).
110. George, 'Photography in the High Alps', p. 403.
111. W.F. Donkin, 'Photography in the High Alps', *Alpine Journal*, 11 (1882–84), 63–71 (p. 67).
112. Donkin, 'Photography', p. 67.
113. Mrs. Aubrey (Elizabeth) Le Blond, *Day In, Day Out* (London: The Bodley Head, 1928), p. 129.
114. Walter Leaf, 'Climbing with a Hand-Camera', *Alpine Journal*, 15 (1890–91), 472–79 (p. 472).
115. Leaf, 'Climbing', p. 476.
116. 'The Alpine Club Exhibition of Pictures and Photographs', *Alpine Journal*, 16 (1892–93), 342–47 (p. 347).
117. 'The Winter Exhibition of the Alpine Club', *Alpine Journal*, 17 (1894–95), 78–85 (p. 84).
118. See, for example, 'Alpine Notes', *Alpine Journal*, 12 (1884–86), 167–78.
119. Gilbert Thomson, 'Practice Scrambles', *Scottish Mountaineering Club Journal*, 2 (1892–93), 8–12 (p. 12).
120. E.C. Daniel, 'First Aid to the Injured in Climbing Accidents', *Climbers' Club Journal*, 1 (1898–99), 43–49; Ernest A. Baker, 'Practice Scrambles in Derbyshire', *Climbers' Club Journal*, 1 (1898–99), 53–65.
121. H. Somerset Bullock, 'Chalk Climbing on Beachy Head', *Climbers' Club Journal*, 1 (1898–99), 91–97 (p. 97).
122. F. Craufurd Grove, 'Alpine Training Diet', *Alpine Journal*, 12 (1884–86), 149–56 (p. 152).
123. Craufurd Grove, 'Alpine Training Diet', p. 155.
124. Smith, *Story of Mont Blanc*, p. 159.
125. Coolidge and Howard, ed., *Pioneer in the High Alps*, p. 35.
126. 'Mountaineering Made Easy', *Alpine Journal*, 14 (1888–89), 326–27 (p. 327).
127. NLS, Acc. 11538, Item 16, p. 25.
128. NLS, Acc. 11538, Item 14, Clachaig Hotel, Glencoe logbook 1889–1904, 26 October–9 November 1900.
129. NLS, Acc. 11538, Item 14, 24–31 August 1901.

130. Pen-y-Gwryd Hotel, 'Not the Visitors' Book: Contributions on Mountain Rambles, Botany, Geology, and Other Subjects of Interest Connected with Pen-y-Gwryd', 1893, p. 56.
131. Pen-y-Gwryd, May 1887, p. 16.
132. Pen-y-Gwryd, 31 July 1887, p. 19.
133. Pen-y-Gwryd, 1891, p. 44.
134. Pen-y-Gwryd, 21 January 1894, p. 2. Eckenstein was an accomplished climber with a reputation for irascibility, who later climbed in the Himalayas with the notorious Aleister Crowley: see Alan Hankinson, *The Mountain Men: A History of Rock Climbing in North Wales—From Its Beginning to 1914* (Cheshire: Mara Books, 1977), p. 59; T.S. Blakeney and D.F.O. Dangar, 'Oscar Eckenstein', *Alpine Journal*, 65 (1960), 62–79; Aleister Crowley, *The Confessions of Aleister Crowley*, ed. by John Symonds and Kenneth Grant (London: Penguin, 1989), p. 151.
135. Perkin, *Professional Society*, p. xii.
136. It was common practice for the first climber to reach an Alpine summit to leave a card in a bottle, and the *Alpine Journal* often recorded the discovery of these cards by subsequent visitors. See, for example, 'Alpine Notes', *Alpine Journal*, 12 (1884–86), 462–71 (p. 467); 'Records Left on Mountain Tops', *Alpine Journal*, 14 (1888–89), 323; Hermann Woolley, 'The Ascent of Dych-tau', *Alpine Journal*, 15 (1890–91), 173–91 (p. 188); 'New Expeditions in 1894', *Alpine Journal*, 17 (1894–95), 250–66 (p. 260).
137. See, for example, Thomas Fraser S. Campbell's article in the first volume of the *Scottish Mountaineering Club Journal*, in which he applies the Alpine term 'mauvais pas' (meaning a particularly difficult point on a climb) to hills on the Scottish island of Arran: Thomas Fraser S. Campbell, 'The Glen Sannox Hills', *Scottish Mountaineering Club Journal*, 1 (1890–91), 31–36 (p. 34). For references to a 'machine', see Collie, 'A Reverie', p. 102; W. Brown, 'Ascent of Ben Nevis by the N.E. Buttress', *Scottish Mountaineering Club Journal*, 3 (1894–95), 323–31 (p. 325).
138. See, for example, Naismith's article on his two very different experiences of visiting Ben Nevis at the start and end of the 1880s, in which he recalls that his 1880 ascent was still rare enough to be heralded by a local newspaper as 'the first ascent of Ben Nevis without guides': W.W. Naismith, 'Ben Nevis in 1880 and 1889', *Scottish Mountaineering Club Journal*, 1 (1890–91), 215–21 (p. 218).
139. Leslie Stephen, 'Recent Accidents in the Alps', *Alpine Journal*, 4 (1868–70), 373–79 (p. 373).
140. Stephen, 'Recent Accidents', p. 377.
141. J. Stogdon, 'The Late Accident on Mont Blanc', *Alpine Journal*, 5 (1870–72), 194–99 (p. 199).

142. Mathews, 'The Alpine Obituary', p. 85.
143. 'Alpine Accidents', *Alpine Journal*, 14 (1888–89), 136–43 (p. 136).
144. A.G. Girdlestone, *The High Alps Without Guides, Being a Narrative of Adventures in Switzerland* (London: Longmans, Green, 1870), p. v.
145. F. Craufurd Grove, 'The Comparative Skill of Travellers and Guides', *Alpine Journal*, 5 (1870–72), 87–96.
146. 'Alpine Notes', *Alpine Journal*, 12 (1884–86), 128–29.
147. 'Alpine Notes', *Alpine Journal*, 12 (1884–86), 423–24 (p. 423).

CHAPTER 3

# Resisting the New Mountaineer

## Introduction

The New Mountaineers were not the only people writing about mountains. It might appear that the new approach to mountaineering had achieved hegemony by the late nineteenth century, and much mountaineering literature reflected this assumption, but there was also a reaction against the new approach. Instead, many writers looked back to what they considered the traditions of their hobby, and to a Romantic tradition of writing about mountains, to form a critique of the New Mountaineer and his ways.

In this chapter, I consider how and why this critique was expressed, and examine the writers who called for a return to earlier values. However, to posit two diametrically opposed approaches to climbing in this period is to create a false dichotomy. In reality, the two camps – the old and new schools of climbing – had a great deal more in common than was often acknowledged. The New Mountaineer was both real and fictional. On the one hand, he represented a genuine shift in the ethos and practice of mountaineering. At the same time, he was also a product of the collective imagination of Victorian mountaineers, representing anxiety about the direction their sport was taking and nostalgia for an imagined past.

## The New Mountaineer and His Critics

For the most part, the proponents of the new approach to mountaineering were unapologetic, at times even rather triumphalist. Writing in 1891, Albert Ernest Maylard, a founding member of the Scottish Mountaineering Club, was candid about how any Romantic or aesthetic notions took a back seat to the physical challenge that a tough, potentially dangerous climb afforded:

> It is in the conquering of difficulties that the true climber most frequently finds his greatest pleasure; and however much he may delight in the glories of the scenic effects, he will often love most to look back upon that bit where he had to hang on to a slippery rock by his fingers, stick the tip of his toes on to a narrow ledge, hitch up his other knee and sprawl to safety on his stomach.[1]

The politician, art critic, author, and mountaineer Martin Conway took a similar view four years later, describing the bracing and unsentimental satisfaction to be gained from the experience of danger and hardship on a climb in terms that clearly owe a good deal to the doctrine of manliness discussed earlier:

> Such struggles with nature produce a moral invigoration of enduring value. They wash the mind free of sentimental cobwebs and foolish imagining. They bring a man in contact with cold stony reality and call forth all that is best in his nature. They act as moral tonics.[2]

This seems to be the authentic voice of the New Mountaineer: disciplined, spartan, professional, concerned with the tangible, and somewhat lacking in aesthetic appreciation. The New Mountaineers also tended to arrogate to themselves a quality of experience that was different and in some ways superior to that of their more Romantically influenced predecessors. Looking back in 1908 to his early experiences of mountain climbing, Lehmann J. Oppenheimer made this claim quite explicitly:

> I could not have believed, in these earlier days, that an intense appreciation of the mountains might be compatible with the most undignified gymnastics upon them, or that hilarious levity brimming over from joyful companions might even enhance the wild beauty of gullies and ridges; but experience has taught me that scenery is best enjoyed in pauses between mental and muscular efforts.[3]

It was this tone that non-mountaineers usually heard, and many outside observers took the authors of such comments at their own estimation. Yet it would be an oversimplification to assume that this attitude was universal. It is true that mountaineering in the late nineteenth century was characterized by the rise of professional values, by close attention to the tangible and the consequent development of a new material culture, and by a dogged concentration on the rigours of physical challenge and the importance of manliness. But it was also marked by a strong reaction against that trend. For this was, paradoxically, the period when what we might call the Romantic strain in mountain culture attempted to reassert itself.

Writing about attitudes to polar exploration in the late nineteenth century, Francis Spufford points to the dangers of assuming a homogenous set of attitudes and beliefs in any historical period. 'A time is never unified', he writes. 'The different generations who share it travel side by side without their perceptions necessarily merging, like the different bands of grit that a glacier carries separately downwards.'[4] Spufford's warning could just as pertinently be applied to the culture of mountaineering; even his glacier metaphor seems apt. A new approach to mountain climbing did emerge in the latter part of the century, but it was by no means without its critics. A shared set of assumptions, expressed through the genre of mountaineering literature, certainly seemed to exist, but it would be wrong to assume a straightforward teleological progression from an old to a new paradigm, or to believe that at some point in the second half of the century the old, Romantic-inflected approach or the attitudes that had characterized the Golden Age of the 1850s and 1860s disappeared altogether. Older attitudes and conventions died hard, and the new values were deeply, sometimes bitterly contested. Many mountaineers continued to write in terms that owed a great deal to Romantic conventions – indeed, some displayed a determined resistance to the values of those they derided as 'mountain gymnasts' or 'rock acrobats',[5] or as 'Philistines'.[6]

The very existence of such epithets is evidence for this resistance. The New Mountaineer may not have joined the New Woman or the New Journalism in the lexicon of *fin-de-siècle* Britain, but several other writers coined terms to describe him – evidence that he was considered both new and controversial. So, for example, the public school headmaster Hely H. Almond used ecclesiastical terminology to divide his fellow Scottish Mountaineering Club members into two groups, the 'Salvationists' and 'Ultramontanes'.[7] Almond's 'Ultramontane' was the climber whose ambition it is to scale the side of inaccessible peaks with unpronounceable names, who look upon a quarry face with great enthusiasm, as affording chances quite as great, and nearly as glorious, of getting badly hurt, as a genuine mountain does.[8]

He was, in other words, the archetypal New Mountaineer. The Salvationists were the more cautious and traditionalist mountaineers 'who, like myself, abominate pain and danger and extreme fatigue, who yet would go to the Highlands in winter, whenever they can snatch two or three days' holiday'.[9] Almond's terms for the two tribes of climber were occasionally repeated by subsequent writers, but like Collie's New Mountaineer they never entered common usage.[10] However, the type of climber he describes – content to climb in a quarry if no mountains are available, and determined to push through pain and danger to conquer difficult new routes – is immediately recognizable as one of the new breed. Whether they called them New Mountaineers, Ultramontanes, rock acrobats, mountain gymnasts, or practitioners of what Dent termed 'flashy athleticism', traditionalists were in no doubt about their polemical target.[11]

Criticism of the ethos of mountaineering was nothing new, of course. As discussed in the Introduction, the Matterhorn disaster of 1865 had led to widespread condemnation of the dangers of Alpine climbing, but even before that Ruskin had been criticizing the approach of mountaineers. In 1856, a year before the formation of the Alpine Club, he insisted, in the fourth volume of *Modern Painters*, subtitled *Of Mountain Beauty*: 'Those who want to know the real facts of the world's outside aspect, will find that they cannot trust maps, nor charts, nor any matter of mensuration; the most important facts being always quite immeasurable'.[12] This was written in the context of a defence of 'Turnerian topography', Ruskin's phrase for what he considered the unique vision that J.M.W. Turner had brought to landscape art, but it also seems to anticipate by several decades the criticisms that would later be levelled at the New Mountaineers and their supposed obsession with the minutiae of mapping, navigation, and measurement.

Although he actually became a member of the Alpine Club, Ruskin continued to criticize the ethos of mountaineering, most famously in his lecture entitled 'Of Kings' Treasuries', published in *Sesame and Lilies* (1865), in which he berated the mountaineers who had, in his view, 'made racecourses of the cathedrals of the earth'. Ruskin's diatribe continued: 'The Alps, which your own poets used to love so reverently, you look upon as soaped poles in bear gardens, which you set yourselves to climb and slide down with shrieks of delight'.[13] He tempered his comments in the preface to the second edition of *Sesame and Lilies*, conceding that his attack would 'fall harshly on the reader's ear' in the light of the Matterhorn tragedy that year, and allowing that 'some experience of distinct peril, and the acquirement of habits of quick and calm action in its presence, are necessary elements, at some period of life, in the formation of manly character'.[14] Nonetheless, he continued to develop his critique of mountaineering, and was especially harsh on the claim that mountaineers had access to a privileged understanding or experience of mountain landscapes.

Ruskin's comments tend to depict all mountaineers as both pretentious in their claims to superiority and shallow in their spiritual experience of mountains: their ability to experience mountains as they deserve to be experienced is hopelessly compromised by their desire to perform athletic feats upon them. Ironically, these were roughly the same charges that critics of the New Mountaineers made, while implying that an earlier generation of mountaineers – the men who formed the Alpine Club and who climbed in the Golden Age – had adhered to different standards.

Milder criticism came from Anthony Trollope in 1866, in a piece on the Alpine Club, in which he poked fun at what he regarded as the conceited attitude of Club members. The Alpine Club man 'does not quite carry himself as another man, and has his nose a little in the air, even when he is not climbing', claimed Trollope.[15] The mountaineer's sense of being 'one of a class permitted to face dangers which to us would be simply suicidal, does give him a conscious divinity of which he is, in his modesty, not quite able to divest himself'.[16] Trollope's sense that the Alpine Club men considered their own experience of mountains far superior to those of tourists or other valley-bound observers was both accurate and ironic. As we will see in Chap. 5, mountaineers made this claim to an elevated quality of experience explicitly and consistently. At the same time, the generation of Alpine Club men mocked by Trollope and attacked by Ruskin were the very people who would later be among the harshest critics of the New Mountaineers and their values.

What is different about the criticism that begins later in the century, however, is that much if not most of it originates with mountaineers themselves. Ruskin and Trollope, like the critics of mountaineering who seized upon the Matterhorn disaster as evidence of its foolhardiness, were essentially viewing the sport from the outside. From around the late 1880s, criticisms of mountaineering more typically originated with climbers themselves. Specifically, the criticism came from those who believed that a new breed of climbers was ignoring and undermining the values of mountaineering, and that something intangible but valuable was being lost.

## The Romantic Backlash

In his first address as president of the newly formed Scottish Mountaineering Club in 1889, Ramsay spoke of his concerns about the direction mountaineering was taking and the type of person it was attracting. He deplored 'the class who look upon mountains simply and solely as a field for exercising or gaining muscle, or the glory which muscle-culture brings' and who

> care for no ascent which is not difficult or new, measure mountains solely by their height, never care to repeat an ascent once made, and love to boast that they have crowded so many first class or second class peaks or passes into a single week.[17]

Ramsay used his speech to set out the type of mountaineer he wished the new club to attract – and the type he hoped would not join. Alongside the devotees of 'muscle-culture' and the boastful in the latter category were those who visited mountain resorts because it was considered fashionable, and fair-weather mountaineers who refused to set out on a climb if there was any chance of mist and rain. Other undesirables included

> the record-climber, who climbs his mountain against time: having rushed to the top in three minutes less than the shortest time on record, he duly inserts a paper stating that fact, with time, place, and person, in a bottle, which he conceals in the cairn upon the top; that done, he has no time to waste upon the view, but plunges down again at record pace, in the hope of gaining three more minutes in the descent.[18]

Such criticisms were unsurprising from a man then in his early fifties who saw the sport he loved being changed by younger participants, but Ramsay was not simply expressing entrenched conservative attitudes. This was, after all, the same speech in which he proudly described modern mountaineering as 'a science of a highly complex character' with 'rigorous methods of its own'.¹⁹ His ideal mountaineer was not an ossified relic of the Golden Age, but an amalgam of old and new who could take the best from both cultures. In this respect he set the tone for some of the critiques of the New Mountaineer that were to follow.

The critics of the new breed of mountaineer tended to frame their attacks in terms of what were perceived to be Romantic values, but this was a new understanding of the Romantic filtered through a distinctive late-Victorian sensibility. This period was characterized by a new fascination with the Romantic movement, taking the form of what Andrew Radford and Mark Sandy describe as a preoccupation with 'a revitalised world of romance'.²⁰ This involved a reconfiguration of Romantic values into the 'civilised and rational' Victorian self-image on the one hand, and on the other an awareness of the Romantic as a 'potentially subversive, ungovernable essence'.²¹

Wordsworth, in particular, had enjoyed a renaissance among the late Victorians. Although his reputation grew throughout the Victorian period, Stephen Gill has demonstrated how the last two decades of the century saw a huge surge in criticism and debate about his work, in the wake of John Stuart Mill's 1873 autobiography and the publication of the pseudonymous *Autobiography of Mark Rutherford* by William Hale White in 1881, as well as the foundation of the Wordsworth Society in Grasmere in 1880.²² Victorian mountaineers were acutely aware of the influence of Wordsworth and other Romantic writers on their own view of mountain landscapes. Ramsay, for example, wrote in 1896 of the profound influence of the Lake Poets, Walter Scott, and other Romantic writers on the contemporary appetite for mountain scenery: 'It is but the day before yesterday that our people began to delight in the beauty of wild scenery, or to look upon mountains as anything but barriers or deformities'.²³ This kind of testimony to the enduring influence of Romantic writing about mountains is common in texts of this period, and the resurgence of what can broadly be termed Romantic attitudes and values in new, characteristically Victorian forms was to provide the basis of many of the critiques of the New Mountaineer that would emerge in this period.

In reality, of course, Romantic attitudes to mountains and mountain travel were far from homogenous. My intention is not to suggest the existence of a coherent Romantic movement but rather to examine the perceptions of late-Victorian writers, who clearly did identify a particular set of values and attitudes and who had started to think in terms of a discrete Romantic period in art and literature. Arguably, this approach also led some observers to overstate the differences between the new generation of mountaineers and its predecessors.

The 1898 article in which John Norman Collie coined the term New Mountaineer provides a fairly representative example of how such critiques were expressed in Romantic language. Collie was, on the face of it, a rather unlikely champion of the Romantic tendency: a prominent research scientist, who among other achievements helped to develop the medical use of X-rays, he was also a pioneer of Scottish mountaineering; he climbed hard routes in the Alps with Mummery (himself a stout defender of the New Mountaineer's ethos), and eventually participated in some of the first climbing expeditions to the Himalayas, including the 1895 expedition to Nanga Parbat on which Mummery was killed.[24] As his scientific credentials would suggest, Collie was certainly not averse to new technical innovations. He was reported as giving a paper to the Alpine Club in 1894 about his ascent of a previously unclimbed peak in the Alps, during which he 'illustrated his paper, not only by lantern slides, but by several admirable diagrams and excellent photographic enlargements, showing in a most clear manner the position of the mountain and the details of his route'.[25] Collie's biographer also notes that he 'had not the slightest doubt that the ends justified the means' when it came to climbing new routes, on one occasion even using an ice axe to hack a step into a difficult rock face on Scafell in the Lake District.[26] All of these factors suggest the kind of approach more usually associated with New Mountaineers.

Yet in 'A Reverie', Collie takes his epigraph from Alfred Tennyson's 1842 poem *Morte d'Arthur* ('The old order changeth | Yielding place to the new') to create a sense of elegy for a vanished sensibility:

> One by one the recollections of all our most cherished climbs will be punctured, flat and unprofitable as a collapsed bicycle tyre they will rotate over the rough roads of bygone memories, whilst that progressive democratical finger will guide the new nickel-plated, pneumatic-cushioned, electrically-driven modern mountaineer on his fascinating career.[27]

Collie's passage identifies – and implicitly criticizes – a new type of climber, with a new sensibility and a new set of values. His language associates this new breed with technology, modernity, and mechanisation; with nickel-plated technological innovation and pneumatic-cushioned modes of transport; with a set of developments that seem urban, scientific, and coldly rational. His description of the 'progressive, democratical finger of the "New Mountaineer"', which 'is laid with equal mockery and irreverence on Sgurr nan Gillean and Cir Mhor' suggests he regards the new generation as guilty not only of irreverence but perhaps also of threatening egalitarianism, although he does not expand on this point.[28] The sort of mountaineer he describes would feel perfectly at home with the juxtaposition of post office and telegraph office in the shadow of the Skye Cuillin, identified by the *Manchester City News* a few years earlier. Collie's appeal to Tennyson, on the other hand, evokes a past time when mountains were associated with romance and mysticism, not with 'life as it is lived nowadays'.[29] Like Tennyson's dying king, the epigraph seems to imply, Collie found his world being changed by a coming generation with a new code of behaviour.

This is not, of course, precisely synonymous with a Romantic perspective, and it may be significant that Collie chose a line from Tennyson and not, say, Wordsworth for his epigraph. By the time Collie was writing, the notion of Tennyson as a quintessentially 'Victorian' poet had taken root; at the same time, as Wim Tigges points out, he was deeply influenced by the Romantic poets while not being wholly defined by their legacy.[30] Joseph Bristow points out that the construction of Tennyson as a 'Victorian' poet had begun with his lengthy entry in Edmund Clarence Stedman's *Victorian Poets* (1875), the work that Bristow suggests fixed the term 'Victorian' as a 'widely accepted period designator'.[31] Tennyson had died just six years before Collie's article was published, and Samantha Matthews notes how a wave of elegies, biographies, and scholarship had reinforced his 'posthumous presence' in the intervening years, further confirming his place as the 'representative Victorian poet'.[32] An 1893 article by Theodore Watts had also presented him as essentially distinct from Wordsworth and Coleridge in his approach to nature poetry, lacking what Watts called 'the Sufeyistic passion of the Nature-intoxicated poet'.[33] To quote Tennyson was to lay claim to a certain kind of lyricism, a degree of introspective melancholy, and a vague inclination towards a Romantic sensibility, without necessarily calling for a wholesale return to what had come to be perceived as Romantic values. It suggested a healthy and moderate appreciation of mountain scenery, without the dangerous intoxication and loss of control implied by Watts's reference to Sufism.[34]

This use of Romantic tropes and conventions repackaged in a form calculated to be more acceptable to a Victorian sensibility is fairly representative of the kind of textual strategy employed throughout the last decades of the nineteenth century as a significant minority of mountaineering writers fought a rearguard action against what they regarded as the reductive, philistine approach that had taken over. Collie was echoing sentiments expressed by numerous contemporaries, who viewed themselves as defending the 'true' meaning of mountaineering against the new mountain gymnasts.

Joseph Gibson Stott was the first editor of the *Scottish Mountaineering Club Journal*. He would later write to his successor, William Douglas, bemoaning what he regarded as the dry, technical, and mechanistic tone that had crept in to recent articles. 'There is too much of the "mere Mountain timetable" these days', he complained in 1895:

> There is too little description, and too much (no, not too much, but too bald and dry) rock-structure narrative [...] What I want is a paper – in which I can hear the roaring of the torrent, and see the snaws and the brown heather, and the clouds and scud flying athwart the blue above the rocky peaks – something in fact that will set my pulses beating; and conjure up dear old Scotland; and what is of no interest to me are some of these papers: all miles and facts and minutes, and endless dissections of the unhappy points of the Compass. To me these are really little more interesting than an architect's specifications for building a dyke.[35]

Stott's dismissive use of the word 'dissection' brings to mind the scientific, analytical approach to mountaineering identified with Collie's 'New Mountaineer'. The 'unhappy points of the Compass' are a direct reference to what he clearly regarded as a modish obsession with the fine details of mapping and navigation. Katrin Lund and Hayden Lorimer suggest that Stott's line of argument contrasts 'the familiar conventions of the romantic landscape canon' with the 'quantification of outdoor practice'.[36] Like Collie, Stott chose to express his regret at this shift to quantification in something approximating to the language of nature poetry, with a direct appeal to sensory impressions and to a sensibility that can only very broadly be termed Romantic.

The use of phonetic spelling ('snaws') to suggest a Scottish pronunciation of 'snows' also hints at conventions of untamed Celtic wildness and authenticity which were still widespread in this period: the novels of Walter Scott remained influential up to the end of the century and were commonly alluded to. Writing in the *Cairngorm Club Journal* in 1889, for example, William C. Smith noted with regret: 'It is now impossible for us to realise the world of solitude and romance that existed in the pre-tourist and pre-mountaineering days'.[37] Smith alluded to the sentiments of Frank Osbaldistone in Scott's *Rob Roy* (1817) upon approaching the Highland hills:

> While I gazed on this Alpine region, I felt a longing to explore its recesses, though with toil and danger, similar to that which a sailor feels when he wishes for the risks and animation of a battle or a gale, in exchange for the insupportable monotony of a protracted calm.[38]

This appeal to the tradition represented (and in part created) by Scott's novels and poetry is tempting for writers who wish implicitly to criticize the new breed of mountaineer, and while Stott does not name Walter Scott, the somewhat contrived coinage of 'snaws' seems unlikely to be wholly coincidental.[39]

Stott and Collie were far from being isolated voices; indeed, Stott's use of the phrase 'mere mountain timetable' in his letter is actually an echo of an article earlier that year by Ramsay. Writing an obituary of Professor John Veitch, another former president of the Scottish Mountaineering Club, Ramsay recalled:

> Deeply as he loved the hills, our late President was not a mountaineer in the modern technical – may I say slang? – sense of the term. He enjoyed, indeed, putting forth his strength, and could glory in a great day's walk [ ... ] But he was no peak-bagger. He never 'broke a record' or 'made a first ascent'.[40]

Ramsay went on in the same article to bemoan the fact that 'climbing, like other things nowadays, must be conducted on scientific principles',[41] and criticized the number of articles appearing in the club journal of the 'mere Mountain Time-Table kind'.[42] He expressed the wish 'that as members of this Club, we shall always remember that our highest object, above everything that can be expressed in mountaineering jargon, is to promote a love – an admiring, reverent, sympathetic love – love of the hills'.[43] This 'admiring, reverent, sympathetic love' seems to have more in common with the legacy of Romantic writing about nature than with some of the more robust and technically detailed accounts of mountain adventure that were filling the pages of the *Scottish Mountaineering Club Journal* by this stage. Stott and Ramsay were both writing just a few years after the introduction of Naismith's Rule, and it is not hard to imagine that they had this kind of development in mind. His dismissal of peak-bagging and record-breaking suggests he was also alarmed by the growing spirit of competitiveness and the practice of collecting Munros.

We encounter this kind of complaint more and more frequently in climbing texts from the late 1880s onwards. If a wide range of texts attest to the importance of mensuration, training, modernity, and professional competence, and to a keen interest in materiality, others from the same genre often provide evidence of resistance and complaints about this ethos. The complainants typically argue that a new spirit, inimical to the values they hold dear, has taken hold of the mountaineering fraternity; that a new generation of climbers is more interested in ticking peaks off a list than in the views to be seen from the summits or slopes of those peaks; that mountain literature is increasingly preoccupied with the prosaic details of routes, distances, and techniques, rather than descriptions of scenery, weather, and atmosphere. Above all they complain, as Collie did, that the old order is changing, and that something has been lost – something they often find hard to clearly identify or articulate, but which is implicit in the language they use and which is analogous though not precisely identical to a Romantic experience of mountains.

What might be termed a Romantic backlash was not confined to the pages of the *Scottish Mountaineering Club Journal*. Robert Adamson wrote in the *Cairngorm Club Journal* in 1895 in terms that bring to mind the criticisms of Collie, Stott, and Ramsay:

> There is a climbing jargon, and a tiresome climbing talk, and, as in all other forms of physical enjoyment to which the British mind has given itself, a thirst for 'records', 'first ascents' and 'new ways', which bids fair soon to leave no corner of the narrow field unexplored.[44]

The longer-established and arguably more conservative *Alpine Journal* was even more frequently the forum for such complaints. Freshfield, a former editor of the *Alpine Journal* and later to become president of the Alpine Club, wrote in 1890 that he wanted 'to do what I can to hinder the specialisation of mountain-climbing as an inferior branch of gymnastics, to be taught by Swiss professors'.[45] Conway, one of Freshfield's successors as president, echoed his concerns a year later. Belying the enthusiasm for the 'cold stony reality' of mountain climbing that he would express just a few years later, Conway warned:

> There is a danger to my way of thinking, in that the gymnastic and quasi-professional element tends to increase; and that tendency should now be combated. Alpine climbing is no mere gymnastic exercise like rowing, but a large and comprehensive sport, wherein the whole nature of man can find stimulus and play. It is not an exercise for the muscles and nerves only, but for the reason and imagination as well.[46]

As well as appealing to the legacy of Romantic writing about mountains, critics of the New Mountaineer tended to set up an idealized type of climber who existed in earlier times. They presented this ideal mountaineer as successfully combining the Romantic and the athletic, capable both of aesthetic pleasure in mountain scenery and physical joy in a challenging ascent – unlike the New Mountaineers of the present who supposedly placed too much emphasis on the physical side of this equation. They also implied that such climbers still existed, but enjoyed less attention and kudos than the brasher New Mountaineers. So when Ramsay had finished enumerating the type of climber he did not want to see join his club, he set out the attributes of the sort of member he would welcome. Such a mountaineer 'delights in the difficulties and danger of a new route; and he is fully sensible of the pride of finding his legs firm beneath him, his wind sound within'.[47] At the same time, however,

> his main and great joy is in the glory of the scenery through which he climbs; he dwells fondly on every view with a reverent humble sense of the fresh glories of creation which each discloses.[48]

Conway, too, expressed a sense that the mountaineering community now fell into two camps, with some climbers cleaving to the old values and others seduced by the new. Writing in the *Alpine Journal* in 1890, he contrasted the 'gymnast' with the 'mountain-climber'. The gymnast, Conway explained,

> likes 'pretty bits' of rocks, with a cracklet here for a finger and a cracklet there for a toe. He does not mind whether he reaches a summit or not. He is not careful to enlarge his knowledge of the Alpine chain as a whole [ . . . ] He does

not care for wandering. He has small affection for trees and mountain forests. He dislikes snow-fields and slopes. Easy climbs are a bore to him.[49]

The true mountain climber, on the other hand, 'is an altogether different type of person, but at present he is not so easy to find.'[50] Conway set out his attributes in some detail:

> What he loves, first and foremost, is to wander far and wide among mountains. He does not willingly sleep two consecutive nights in the same inn. He detests black-coated *tables d'hote*. He hates centres. He gets tired of a district and likes his holiday to be a tour. He loves a good and companionable guide. He always wants to see what is on the other side of any range of hills. He prefers passes to peaks, and hates not getting to the top of anything he starts for. He chooses the easiest and most normal route. He likes to know the names of all the peaks in a view. He cannot bear to see a group of peaks none of which he has climbed. He covers maps with red lines, marking his routes. He willingly explores side valleys.[51]

Conway would return to the contrast between gymnasts and mountain climbers the following year, applying the term 'Alpine gymnast' to 'a man for whom the overcoming of physical obstacles by means of muscular exertion and skill is the chief pleasure of mountaineering'.[52] He contrasted this type of climber with the 'man who plans new expeditions after gathering a full knowledge of a locality, who has the generalship to strike out a new line of route, and the intelligence to understand a mountain'.[53] Dismissing the gymnast, Conway pleaded,

> For heaven's sake let him go to Zermatt by train and stay there! If the Alps are the playground of Europe, let Zermatt be set aside as its gymnasium. There are several unaccomplished gymnast routes up the Matterhorn (straight up the north face, for instance); there remains more to be done in that neighbourhood by our excellent and muscular friends [ ... ] We shall soon no doubt hear of a man holding the 'record of the world' for the Matterhorn, and half a dozen betting agents will set up their summer abodes on the sites of the old wooden houses once so picturesque.[54]

He repeated his concerns about the 'gymnastic' approach yet again in 1895 with the publication of *The Alps from End to End*, his account of a journey across the range, undertaken in order to understand the Alps as a region, 'and not merely as a casual assemblage of crags affording gymnastic problems'.[55] In it he eulogized the earlier generation of climbers 'who gave to mountaineering its peculiar *éclat*' in these terms: 'They were attracted by the peak's position, not its difficulty; they sought the beauty of its view, not any problem to be solved by physical ingenuity or endurance'.[56] The implied contrast with the Munro-baggers and 'acrobats' of the present is very clear.

## Re-Writing Mountaineering History

This idealizing of previous generations of climbers seems odd when we consider the attitudes of the men who formed the Alpine Club back in the 1850s, and of other early pioneers like Albert Smith or Wills. Any reading of the early Alpine Club publications, whether *Peaks, Passes, and Glaciers* or its successor the *Alpine Journal*, must give the impression that, in fact, many of the first generation of recreational climbers spent considerably more time thinking about physical ingenuity and endurance than about the beauty of the view. This generation of mountaineers generally seemed quite unembarrassed by the 'exhilarating consciousness of difficulty overcome'.[57]

In fact the ethos associated with the New Mountaineer can be detected in narratives dating back even further than the formation of the Alpine Club. An account of a successful attempt on Mont Blanc in 1827, written by the elder brother of one of the two climbers, expresses sentiments that seem to have a good deal in common with those of the late nineteenth century. On reaching the summit, 'the first feeling among them was that of satisfaction at having at length completed their bold and arduous undertaking, in which so many before them had failed'.[58] Albert Smith's boisterous account of his 1851 Mont Blanc adventure, in which he described the 'capital fun' to be had on the mountain is perhaps the most famous example.[59] 'Every step we took was gained from the chance of a horrible death', claimed Smith, who emphasized the danger and gymnastic demands of the climb.[60] Another example is the narrative by the Reverend Charles Hudson and future Alpine Club president Edward Shirley Kennedy of their 1856 ascent of Mont Blanc without guides, *Where There's a Will There's a Way*. 'In attempting the ascent', its authors assert,

> we were simply actuated by love of adventure, by the hope of breaking through the exclusive Chamonix guide system, and by the desire of making

ourselves familiar with the beauty and topography of the Alpine regions. We went abroad for recreation: it was pleasure that we sought.⁶¹

This defiance of Romantic convention and deliberate sidelining of notions of sublimity or aesthetic considerations seems more in keeping with the atmosphere of the eighties and nineties than with Conway's notion of a 'large and comprehensive sport, wherein the whole nature of man can find stimulus and play',⁶² or Ramsay's 'admiring, reverent, sympathetic love'.⁶³ Hudson and Kennedy continue in language that again seems to anticipate the professionalised world of advanced mapping, navigation techniques, and strenuous athleticism that would follow a generation later:

> By examining maps and models, we had made ourselves as nearly masters of the route as possible; continued training had put us into capital condition, so that we could have sustained very prolonged exertion; and we *knew* the nature of the difficulties to be overcome, and were constantly enabled to guard against danger.⁶⁴

G.N. Vansittart, who climbed Mont Blanc on the same day as Albert Smith but in a different party, expressed a similar attitude in a letter to the *Daily News*:

> Having walked under the sea in a diving apparatus more than 100 feet deep, and having descended the bowels of the earth, both in the iron mines of Dannemora in Sweden, and the salt mines in Poland, and having ascended both by a balloon and many high mountains, I can safely assert that there is a certain pleasure in all these enterprises unknown to those who have not experienced them.⁶⁵

Again, this is an unapologetic presentation of mountaineering as a form of thrill seeking; an attitude the late Victorian generation seemed to assume had taken hold much later in the history of mountaineering. By the early days of the Golden Age, we can find plenty of examples of attitudes that would not seem out of place in accounts from the 1890s. Tuckett, for example, was viewed by later generations of climbers as not only an adventurous pioneer but also a profoundly Romantic figure. 'In the heroic cycle of Alpine adventure' claimed Stephen, 'the irrepressible Tuckett will occupy a place similar to that of the wandering Ulysses in Greek fable, or the invulnerable Sivrid in the lay of the Niebelungs'.⁶⁶ Stephen may have written this with tongue partly in cheek but there is no doubt that many climbers regarded Tuckett as an archetypal figure of the Golden Age. Yet his own accounts of his various adventures in the late 1850s and early 1860s suggest plenty of interest in the physical, material reality of climbing, and at times he exhibits the kind of robust approach more usually associated with the New Mountaineers. In 1859, for example, he described a bivouac shelter his guide constructed during their ascent of the Aletschhorn that year, taking great care to describe the materials used, the clothes he was wearing, and the precise dimensions of the shelter.[67] Writing the same year, he described an ascent of Monte Rosa in the sort of robust, sporting language more commonly associated with the New Mountaineers:

> Under the best of circumstances, this ridge is a pinch, but when the jagged rocks, which usually afford a holdfast, are masked in soft treacherous snow, which at any moment may give way and descend in avalanches, whilst affording no sure footing, and no support for the *baton*, it requires some 'vim' to go ahead: we did not flinch, however.[68]

Two years later Tuckett was making light of the very real dangers of crevasses on his descent of the Signalkuppe, a peak on the border of Italy and Switzerland. 'The snow was by this time very soft, and the Glacier is here much dislocated', he wrote. 'One or other of the party was constantly falling in, but of course with the rope the only danger was the chance of getting an ugly blow on the shin'.[69] A year later, Whymper – another figure closely associated with the Golden Age, and seemingly far removed from the ethos of the New Mountaineer – would echo this tone when expressing his opinion that in addition to the view from a mountain summit, there is 'a hearty satisfaction to be felt in making the ascent, which is payment enough in itself'.[70]

By the second volume of the *Alpine Journal* in 1865, it is possible to detect an element of wishful thinking in William Mathews' claim:

> There seems to be a growing desire among members of the Alpine Club to turn their mountain expeditions to some scientific account, and so add the charm of intellectual exercise to the comparatively animal pleasure of climbing.[71]

Mathews, a regular correspondent on scientific matters, may have been responding to the erosion of scientific justifications for mountaineering discussed in the Introduction, but his reference to animal pleasure suggests that the unapologetic physicality, hearty celebration of manliness, and ethos of adventure and self-testing that came to be associated with the New Mountaineers was in fact a powerful factor much earlier in the history of British mountaineering.

It is thus hard to avoid the conclusion that many mountaineering writers in the late nineteenth century were essentially reinventing the history of their own sport, whether knowingly or not. The mid-Victorian generation who had begun the sport of mountaineering, with their robust talk of sparring with 'a worthy adversary' and their aspirations to 'make a fair bag of new peaks and passes',[72] were gradually reimagined by their late-Victorian successors as a group of Romantic and spiritual aesthetes, and endowed with values wholly inimical to those of the New Mountaineer.

In part, this may be attributable to the wider *fin-de-siècle* invention of 'Romanticism', a collective desire to reinvent the past with a view to an alternative present in light of what were imagined to be Romantic values. Radford and Sandy write of the late-Victorian 'deep fascination for what is lost, forsaken, compromised or vanquished', a category which for mountaineers could encompass the early days of their own sport: a lost Golden Age, now compromised by the tarnished values of the New Mountaineers.[73] In this reading, the criticisms levelled at the current generation of climbers and the lionising of a fictive version of the sport's history could be seen as indicating a psychological need to ascribe value to the activity of mountaineering over and above the simple 'animal pleasure' that its adherents had in fact ascribed to it from the beginning.[74] For many climbers of what Richard Le Gallienne later dubbed the 'Romantic Nineties', the presence of a telegraph and post office in the vicinity of one of the most remote and mountainous regions in Britain – not to mention the increasingly crowded and commercialized status of the Alps – did not correspond to their self-image as mountaineers.[75] It is easy to imagine how this disjunction between reality and self-image might translate into a wholesale reinvention of the early history of mountaineering and a widely expressed desire to return to values that in truth had rarely been in evidence in the first place. The retrospective invention of a history for their own sport by climbers in the late nineteenth century also brings to mind Eric Hobsbawm and Terence Ranger's suggestion that the 'invention of tradition' involves a set of practices 'which seek to inculcate certain values and norms of behaviour' and to 'establish continuity with a suitable historical past'.[76] Mountaineering, with its very short history, seems a prime candidate for this type of strategy, which Hobsbawm and Ranger suggest was common across a range of activities in the period 1870 to the First World War.

By the same token, some of the more severe criticisms of the New Mountaineer as an oafish philistine owe more to the insistent emphasis on modernity, materiality, and technical detail in the writing of the period than to the reality of what took place in the mountains, suggesting that the New Mountaineer is a literary as much as a historical phenomenon. Sally Ledger, writing about the New Woman who was so widely discussed and criticized around the same period, describes her as both a 'discursive construct' and an actual representative of the *fin-de-siècle* women's movement, and notes the complex and sometimes contradictory relationship between these two versions.[77] A similar point could be made about the New Mountaineer. The period from around 1870 certainly did witness a shift in attitudes and values, and in this respect the New Mountaineer is real. But he can also be seen as a kind of chimera, representing not only modernity but also a collective anxiety about the changes wrought by that modernity.

Some of those who wrote about the New Mountaineer seemed to recognize this paradox, and strove to capture the complexity and ambiguity of the contemporary mountaineer's situation. One of the more interesting commentaries on the new ethos came quite early in the period, from the novelist and literary critic Henry Schütz Wilson. In *Alpine Ascents and Adventures* (1878) he takes a rather more nuanced approach to the question of the correct ethos for the mountaineer: 'I *have* felt the beauty and poetry of these glorious mountains', he insists in his introduction, but that italicised '*have*' serves to warn the reader that this sentiment will be qualified in some way.[78] He then continues:

> That excitement which is needed by the high-hearted English character and temperament is supplied, in part at least, in quiet days when there are no noble wars, and but few chances of stirring adventure, by Alpine climbing. Hence the irresistible attraction of the fascinating pursuit of mountaineering to men of fine physique; to men of ardent, highly-organized, even of ideal, natures. The risk involved in first-class Alpine work is sufficient to lend to climbing the dignity of danger; and the poet may rejoice in the results of the feats which the athlete achieves.[79]

Having first laid out a claim to a conventionally poetic sensibility, then switched tone by setting out a manifesto more characteristic of the New

Mountaineer, Wilson abruptly returns to the traditional language of Romantic mountain worship:

> If a mountaineer be a poet, he feels besides, in his spiritual nature – and feels almost beyond the power of expression – that profound thrill of imaginative rapture which is born of rare and hardly-won contact with some of the noblest and most sublime scenes which exist in God's wonderful creation; and the memory of such high delight remains a joy which lasts throughout, and which ennobles life.[80]

This seems rather confusing. I have suggested that styles of writing about mountaineering can broadly be divided into two camps – one expressing a concern with aesthetic experience that can loosely be termed Romantic in its preoccupations, the other sporting, robust, and concerned with testing one's own physical limits in a challenging outdoor setting. Yet Wilson appears to have a foot in both, straddling a seemingly gaping divide. Wilson imagines two characters, 'Hawley Scrowger' and 'Norman Franklin'. Scrowger is

> a muscular phenomenon, and a mental dwarf. His main object is, to quote his own slang (slang applied to God's Alps!) to 'bag a peak'; and his scarcely secondary aim is to complete the ascent and descent in the fewest possible number of hours [ ... ] The mountains are not connected in his mind with wonder, awe, delight [ ... ] His climbing is a mere match against time.[81]

Franklin, by contrast,

> enjoys worthily the manly exercise of climbing, and the divine scenery in which he works [ ... ] He climbs, not as a machine, but as a man. He probably works well and pluckily; but, as he works for noble enjoyment, he does not care exclusively for making an ascent in a notably short time.[82]

Franklin would appear to represent the old school of climber, who clings to traditional values and eschews the new ethos of measurement, classification, and 'peak-bagging'. The reference to his refusal to climb as a machine emphatically rejects the increasingly common notion of the climbing body as a kind of engine or motor. Even his surname seems to carry echoes of the romantically doomed expedition to seek the Northwest Passage that left Britain in 1845 under Sir John Franklin and was never seen again. Although in many respects Franklin was very much the conventional Victorian hero, there were aspects of his story that had more in common with the values attributed to the early mountaineers than with the world of the New Mountaineers. Writing about the memorializing of Franklin by, among others, Wilkie Collins and Charles Dickens in *The Frozen Deep* (1856), Spufford suggests they

> insisted that the Franklin expedition told a second, spiritual story which took priority over the material one; it recounted to those with ears to hear a victory in the explorers' hearts and minds, which registered where it mattered most, in the hearts and minds of their compatriots, or even in an ideal Arctic truer than the gross Arctic shown on maps.[83]

Spufford also argues that the public memorializing and eulogizing of Franklin and his men 'involved a little more than just the famous English reverence for disaster; it combined bodily loss with spiritual gain, conquest with abnegation'.[84] This is not precisely the same as saying that Franklin was a figure in the Romantic tradition, but it does suggest that his public persona was associated as much with certain spiritual and transcendent values as with the more conventional attributes of the square-jawed Victorian explorer. In particular, the downplaying of the importance of success or failure, and the greater emphasis on the spirit and style with which Franklin had set about his mission, seem to give him an image which is at odds with the late-Victorian emphasis on competence, modernity, and scientific omnipotence. Whether conscious or not, Wilson's decision to give this name to his fictitious climber lays claim to the values and attributes that had been attached to the Northwest Passage expedition.

Yet this fictional Franklin does not fit neatly into the template of Romantic searcher after meaning in nature. He appreciates 'the divine scenery in which he works', but he also enjoys 'the manly exercise of climbing'. Achieving the summit is not his sole aim, but nor is he wandering randomly in the manner of Coleridge. The use of phrases like 'works well and pluckily' and 'manly exercise' suggest he is operating within a set of conventions – the recently established norms of mountaineering, with techniques for the use of rope and ice axes, navigation by map and compass, and set routes and itineraries – rather than indulging in discursive walking. Even the word 'work' suggests something quite different from the kind of ascent associated with Romantic writing about mountains. As we shall see, the use of the term 'work' to characterize this type of activity is a relatively new development, which tends to be associated closely with the typical approach of the late-Victorian mountaineers.

From this perspective, Franklin comes to seem less like the binary opposite of Hawley Scrowger than another facet of the same personality. In fact, many mountaineers of the late nineteenth century felt no obligation to choose between Scrowger or Franklin – instead, they created personas for themselves which encompassed both approaches to mountain climbing, seeing no inherent contradiction between 'bagging peaks' and the 'thrill of imaginative rapture'.[85]

## Defending the New Ethos

Some climbers continued the attempt to square the circle by claiming for the new breed of mountaineers all the attributes of their predecessors. Mummery, one of the most talented and pioneering 'rock athletes' of the late-Victorian period, was unapologetic about the activities of the New Mountaineers, asking rhetorically 'whether the love of rock-climbing is so heinous and debasing a sin that its votaries are no longer worthy to be ranked as mountaineers, but are to be relegated to a despised and special cast of "mere gymnasts"'.[86] One reviewer of Mummery's 1895 memoir described his view of mountaineering succinctly as 'pure play', suggesting an approach that was very much in tune with the New Mountaineering ethos.[87]

However, rather than simply defending gymnastics for its own sake, Mummery framed his defence of the new approach by arguing that criticisms of it were based on what he called the 'recrudescence of Mr. Ruskin's original charge, that we treat the mountains as greased poles. This I venture, on behalf of rock-climbers generally, to most emphatically deny'.[88] He went on to claim that pleasure in exertion was not incompatible with the appreciation of beauty, and to insist that the more skilled the mountaineer, the more likely they were to appreciate the true beauty of their surroundings.[89] The New Mountaineer, in Mummery's view, was no less sensitive to natural beauty and aesthetic pleasure than his predecessor – he simply appreciated it in a different way, through the 'exertion of acquired skill'.

William Brown, in an 1896 article on climbing Ben Nevis in the *Cairngorm Club Journal*, tried to reconcile the differences between old and new approaches to mountaineering by simply dismissing them as untrue and irrelevant. Outlining the merits of climbing versus mountain walking, he includes the commonly levelled charges that 'climbing is mere gymnastics' and that 'the nameless rapture that comes of communion with the "eternal hills" refuses to associate itself with the mechanical details of ropes and ice-axes'.[90] This, Brown retorts, 'is all nonsense', and like Mummery he insists that the true climber is just as sensitive as ever before to 'the wondrous phenomena into the heart of which his sport carries him'.[91]

Jones, encountered in the previous chapter extolling the virtues of the scientifically minded climber, was in many respects the archetypal New Mountaineer – a tenacious, driven, almost fanatical rock climber who forged new routes on Lake District gullies and cliffs previously considered unclimbable and was killed in an Alpine accident at the age of thirty-two. Yet in his guide to *Rock Climbing in the English Lake District* (1897) Jones set out his justification for mountaineering in terms that seem to straddle both old and new motivations and attitudes:

> It satisfies many needs; the love of the beautiful in nature; the desire to exert oneself physically, which with strong men is a passionate craving that must find satisfaction somehow or other; the joy of conquest without any woe to the conquered; the prospect of continual increase in one's skill, and the hope that this skill may partially neutralise the failing in strength that comes with advancing age or ill health.[92]

His list might be balanced in favour of the attractions that mountaineering holds for the 'New Mountaineer', but Jones is careful to put 'the love of the beautiful in nature' at the top. Other writers would deal with the contradictions simply by learning to live with inconsistency. Maylard's 1894 description of having to 'hang on to a slippery rock by his fingers', with which this chapter opened, is a fairly typical of what was perceived to be the attitude of the New Mountaineer.[93] Yet just five years later, Maylard suggested: 'Doubtless, poetry still lingers, and ever will linger, in mountains, however much it may disappear from the necessary grotesque distortions of the mountaineer'.[94] At the same time he conceded,

> a great deal of modern mountaineering literature and modern mountaineering is destitute of much that once savoured of the poetical sentiment. Nor is it to be wondered at when the sole object of a particular expedition is to reach a special spot by some peculiarly inaccessible route.[95]

Maylard went on to issue this warning:

> The danger of deleting from mountaineering literature too much, shall we say, of its picturesque side, is possibly to incur the too greater infusion of the purely physical element; in other words, to make the ascent of a mountain simply an athletic performance, the feat of a gymnast.[96]

This ability to hold two apparently contradictory points of view was surprisingly common among mountaineers in this period. Time and again, climbers who write about their sport do so in terms that undermine the notion of a simple, binary opposition between the Romantic, aesthetic approach on the one hand, and the modern, empirical ethos on the other. In the writings of these mountaineers, Hawley Scrowger and Norman Franklin seem to coexist, even to be two aspects of the same person. Even the most pragmatic of the New Mountaineers displayed the influence of their Romantic antecedents – or perhaps of the reinvention of these antecedents for a renewed Romantic present.

Even the writing of Collie, the man who coined the phrase New Mountaineer, displays evidence of the complexities and downright contradictions that attend mountaineering in this period. Collie could, when he wished, write the kind of prose Stott wanted to see more of (Stott indeed singled out Collie as a writer of whom he approved, and hoped to see more from in the *Scotttish Mountaineering Club Journal*). Consider Collie's 1894 description of the view from Scafell as night approaches:

> Delicate pearl-grey shadows were creeping in amongst the wealth of interlacing mountain forms in the clear air, deepening towards the far east in the darkness of approaching night. No sound breaks the stillness, all around are piled the tumbled fragments of the hills, hoary with memories of forgotten years. The present fades away, and is lost in a vast ocean of time; a life-time seems a mere shadow in the presence of these changeless hills. Slowly this inscrutable pageant passes, but blacker grow the evening shadows; naught remains but the mists of the coming night, and darkness soon will fall on this lonely mountain-land.[97]

This kind of writing seems almost a calculated affront to the new 'rock gymnasts' who had made this Lake District valley their base. But it is worth examining this passage more closely. While the references to the 'vast ocean of time' and 'piled and tumbled fragments' seem commonplace enough to the modern reader, these could be read as allusions to matters which were still fresh in the 1890s, and which had been deeply controversial just a few decades earlier. Charles Lyell's *Principles of Geology* (1830–33) had exploded conventional wisdom about the age of the earth, establishing that the planet was much older than previously believed and subverting Christian conceptions of Biblical time as thoroughly as Darwin's work would later undermine humanity's claim to a special place in the universe.[98] As Gillian Beer points out, Lyell's central argument was that 'earlier geologists had unwarrantably assumed a discrepancy between previous and present agents of change and had supposed the earth to be now in a "period of repose" after periods of catastrophe'.[99] Lyell's work, which synthesized and built upon the work of James Hutton and other uniformitarian geologists, undermined confidence not only in Biblical timescales, but also in the fixed and essentially finished nature of the earth, suggesting that further large-scale and disastrous changes could still be underway.[100]

Collie's allusions to what now seem straightforward and uncontroversial facts – that the large boulders and rock debris seen in Wasdale and other Lake District valleys are the remnants of much older mountains and the result of glacial action in a far distant history; that the history of human life is fleeting in relation to the unimaginable extent of deep geological time – have to be read in the context of the angst and controversy these facts had caused within living memory. It was just over forty years since Ruskin had written to Henry Acland about how the evidence of geology was undermining the foundations of his own religious faith: 'If only the geologists would let me alone, I could do very well, but those dreadful Hammers.'[101] Seen from this perspective, Collie's conventionally lyrical and evocative prose carries with it an awareness of the very modern scientific attitudes discussed earlier.

Even if we discount this reading, Collie was by no means a wholehearted propagandist for the old school of mountaineering writing. Some passages of 'A Reverie' suggest that he also wrote with a keen sense of irony and irreverence towards what had by now become clichés of mountain writing. The essay recounts the various avenues down which his mind wanders over the course of an evening, leading to this reflection: 'Those wonderful mountains! What magnificent outlines, what grandeur, what mystery, what!...stop! Can I be growing sentimental? It must have been the Stilton or the sardines that have produced this particular physiological sensation.'[102] Recalling a visit to a 'beautiful, many-headed mountain, hidden away from democratical enemies of mountaineering', Collie ends his article by describing his party's retreat to the valley as dusk approaches:

> It is now evening, and I ought, if orthodox, here to insert a description of the sunset, to become suddenly poetical, talk about 'The sun-god once more plunges into the baths of ocean'. The sea, too, is always useful at such moments. 'Banks of sullen mist brooding like a purple curtain', etc, sounds well [*sic*].[103]

Collie goes on to list some sharply observed caricatures of purple mountaineering prose, which turn out to be quotations from his own earlier article on Wasdale: 'the shadows of approaching night', 'tumbled fragments of the hills, hoary with the memories of forgotten years', and so on. He particularly commends the phrase, 'the shadows of the approaching night' as forming 'a fitting background for the gloomy and introspective spirit which ought to seize upon one at this particular psychological moment'.[104] Having effectively mocked the tradition of overblown mountain prose (and implied that the approved aesthetic response to mountain beauty is as much a matter of convention and received wisdom as of spontaneous appreciation), he finishes on a bathetic note: 'What the party really did was to hurry down into Allt a Choire Dhuibh Mhor, and haste with more or less empty insides to the "machine" and dinner.'[105]

If his repeated jibes at the 'democratical' nature of the 'new mountaineers' suggest that Collie's aesthetic traditionalism is matched by a degree of political reaction and social conservatism, this parody of the conventions of mountaineering prose conversely suggests a disregard for tradition and an irreverence towards the kind of prose style for which Stott, for example, was agitating. It certainly complicates the picture of Collie as a wholehearted proponent of the traditionalist school of mountaineering and mountain literature. Collie's prose subverts its own ostensible nostalgia, claiming instead a kind of commonsensical celebration of the quotidian – the hungry climbers rushing down to their supper – which seems at odds with his Tennysonian epigraph.

These examples indicate the degree of paradox, complexity, and contradiction that continued at least until the end of the nineteenth century. They suggest that to delineate a straightforward opposition between New Mountaineer and Romantic traditionalist is to indulge in oversimplification. But while Collie, Brown, Jones, and Maylard may have exemplified the degree to which these different attitudes could exist – the extent to which Hawley Scrowger and Norman Franklin could reside in the same personality – they did not necessarily see themselves as deliberately or consciously promulgating such a position. Perhaps the only writer who can be said to have set out a coherent argument for the incorporation of some of the spiritual and aesthetic values of Romantic poets and artists into the seemingly unsentimental and robust ethos of the New Mountaineer was Leslie Stephen. Surprisingly, he did so not at the end of the century when debates about the new ethos seemed to be raging loudest, but almost at the very beginning of the period under discussion.

## Leslie Stephen's 'Sense of Superlative Sublimity'

In a chapter of *The Playground of Europe* (1871) entitled 'The Regrets of a Mountaineer', Stephen looks back over his career and mounts a defence of mountain climbing that eloquently and forcefully combines different strands of mountaineering literature. His strategy in this chapter is to deny that the desire for vigorous exercise and hearty outdoor challenges is in any way incompatible with a poetic and aesthetic appreciation of mountain landscapes. For all Stephen's tone of patrician insouciance and ironic detachment, there is an urgency to his prose in this chapter, a powerful desire to defend the activity of mountaineering both from those who attacked it as unjustifiably dangerous (a charge which was still being levelled at the time of publication, just six years after the Matterhorn tragedy) and from the Ruskinian charge that it reduced the worship of mountains to the undignified equivalent of climbing 'soaped poles in bear gardens'. Above all, he attempts to refute the charge that mountaineering 'is a puerile pleasure – that it leads to an irreverent view of mountain beauty, and to oversight of that which should really impress a refined and noble mind'.[106]

Stephen lists two objections to mountaineering: one from those 'who assume that every pleasure with which they cannot sympathise is necessarily affectation',[107] which he dismisses summarily, and the second, which comes from those who are

> kind enough to admit that there is something genuine in the passion, but put it on a level with the passion for climbing greased poles. They think it derogatory to the due dignity of Mont Blanc that he should be used as a greased pole, and assure us that the true pleasures of the Alps are those

which are within reach of the old and the invalid, who can only creep about villages and along high roads.[108]

The reference to 'the old and the invalid' is clearly aimed at Ruskin, who had insisted in *Sesame and Lilies*: 'The real beauty of the Alps is to be seen, and seen only, where all may see it, the child, the cripple, and the man of grey hairs'.[109] But Stephen also goes to some length to define and analyze the various ways mountain exploits can be described in print. One way is to

> indulge in fine writing about them, to burst out in sentences which swell to paragraphs, and in paragraphs which spread over pages; to plunge into ecstasies about infinite abysses and overpowering splendours, to compare mountains to archangels lying down in eternal winding-sheets of snow, and to convert them into allegories about man's highest destinies and aspirations.[110]

The other school of thought, Stephen suggests, goes to the opposite extreme:

> Tall talk is luckily an object of suspicion to Englishmen, and consequently most writers, and especially those who frankly adopt the sporting view of mountains, adopt the opposite scheme: they affect something like cynicism; they mix descriptions of scenery with allusions to fleas or to bitter beer; they shrink with the prevailing dread of Englishmen from the danger of overstepping the limits of the sublime into its proverbial opposite; and they humbly try to amuse us because they can't strike us with awe.[111]

Those who adopt this latter approach – the breed of climbers who would later come to be termed New Mountaineers – do so not from latent philistinism or an inability to appreciate the finer points of mountain beauty, but because of an inherent English reticence, an unwillingness to indulge in excessively florid language, and a reluctance to risk seeming ridiculous. They tend to be judged dull and unresponsive to aesthetics, Stephen argues, because they fastidiously recoil from what might be considered the excesses of the Ruskinian or Romantic approaches. In fact, however, 'a sense of humour is not incompatible with imaginative sensitivity', and 'it seems rather hard to [*sic*] these luckless writers when people assume that, because they make jokes on a mountain, they are necessarily insensible to its awful sublimities'.[112]

He proceeds to recount a series of his own recollections of mountain experiences that 'harmonise with the sense of superlative sublimity'.[113] He is at pains to argue that the mountaineer is 'not a mere scrambler, but that he looks for poetical impressions, as well as for such small glory as his achievements may gain in a very small circle'.[114]

Stephen suggests that the typical mountaineer may appear on the surface to be of the Hawley Scrowger persuasion, hearty and insensitive, but that this is merely a pose intended to avoid the risk of appearing excessively passionate or of indulging in 'tall talk'. In fact, he proposes, the ideal mountaineer is capable of enjoying vigorous physical challenges and a degree of danger and discomfort while remaining fully alive to the aesthetic and spiritual qualities of the mountains on which he has these experiences. The ideal mountaineer can retain a sense of sublimity without losing his sense of humour, and always retain his sense of perspective.

In a sense, then, the 'strange concatenation of interests' identified on Skye was not simply the ability of the professional men who gathered there to pursue their hobby of mountaineering while staying abreast of the latest news on the Stock Exchange or developments in their businesses; not simply the incongruous modernity of telegraph and post offices under the shadow of the Cuillin. The concatenation there and in other climbing centres was the conjoining of a variety of seemingly irreconcilable attitudes and approaches: the 'noble enjoyment' of Norman Franklin; the 'peak-bagging' of Hawley Scrowger; Collie's 'cherished recollections' of companionable days on the hills; Jones's 'love of the beautiful in nature' and 'desire to exert oneself physically'; and Stephen's 'sense of superlative sublimity' coexisting with 'allusions to fleas or bitter beer'.

Seen in this light, much writing about mountaineering in the latter decades of the nineteenth century seems to have as its unspoken purpose an attempt to reconcile 'the conquering of difficulties' with the 'poetical sentiment' that Maylard wrote of — to amalgamate these different motives and priorities into a unified whole. The concatenation of apparently incompatible interests suggests that paradox, contradiction, and resistance are just as important to the story of how attitudes to mountains and mountaineering developed as any sense of a shift from 'Romantic' to 'post-Romantic' attitudes. In some cases the New Mountaineer was just as capable of aesthetic appreciation and finer feelings as his idealised predecessors. In the next two chapters, I will explore how this aesthetic sense changed and developed in the period under discussion, and how Victorian mountaineers made the physical experience of climbing central to their understanding of mountain experience.

## Notes

1. Alfred Ernest Maylard, 'Winter Ascents: Ben Vorlich and Stuc-a-Chroin on the 1st January 1891', *Scottish Mountaineering Club Journal*, 1 (1890–91), 222–34 (p. 225).
2. Conway, *Alps from End to End*, p. 174.
3. Lehmann J. Oppenheimer, *The Heart of Lakeland* (London: Sherratt and Hughes, 1908), p. 9.
4. Francis Spufford, *I May Be Some Time: Ice and the English Imagination* (London: Faber and Faber, 1996), p. 278.
5. For examples of these usages, see Ramsay, 'The President's Address', p. 6; Martin Conway, 'The Dom from Domjoch', *Alpine Journal*, 15 (1890–91), 104–11 (p. 109); 'Mountain Climbers and Mountain Gymnasts', *Alpine Journal*, 15 (1890–91), 224–25 (p. 224); and Martin Conway, 'Exhausted Districts', *Alpine Journal*, 15 (1890–91), 255–67 (p. 257).
6. See, for example, Claude Wilson, 'The Corno Bianco', *Alpine Journal*, 17 (1894–95), 475–92 (p. 477).
7. Hely H. Almond, 'Ben-y-Gloe on Christmas Day', *Scottish Mountaineering Club Journal*, 2 (1892–93), 235–39 (p. 235). Ultramontanism was a medieval doctrine that insisted papal authority was superior to that of temporal authorities or local bishops, while by 'Salvationist' Almond was simply referring to the Salvation Army.
8. Almond, 'Ben-y-Gloe', p. 235.
9. Almond, 'Ben-y-Gloe', p. 236.
10. See, for example, J.G. Stott, 'Mountain Memories', *Scottish Mountaineering Club Journal*, 4 (1896–97), 224–37 (p. 237), in which the writer refers to 'our worthy friends the Ultramontanes', and describes himself as having 'posed as a Salvationist'.
11. Dent spoke in an address to the Alpine Club in 1889 of 'discouraging mountaineering which is but flashy athleticism': Clinton Dent, 'Address to the Alpine Club', *Alpine Journal*, 15 (1890–91), 3–16 (p. 15).
12. Ruskin, *Modern Painters*, IV, 29.
13. John Ruskin, *Sesame and Lilies* (London and New Haven, CT: Yale University Press, 2002), p. 53.
14. Ruskin, *Sesame and Lilies*, p. 3.

15. Anthony Trollope, *Travelling Sketches* (London: Chapman and Hall, 1866), p. 94.
16. Trollope, *Travelling Sketches*, p. 94.
17. Ramsay, 'President's Address', p. 6.
18. Ramsay, 'President's Address', p. 6.
19. Ramsay, 'President's Address', p. 3.
20. Andrew Radford and Mark Sandy, 'Introduction', in *Romantic Echoes in the Victorian Era*, ed. by Andrew Radford and Mark Sandy (Aldershot: Ashgate, 2008), pp. 1–14 (p. 3).
21. Radford and Sandy, 'Introduction', p. 3.
22. Stephen Gill, *Wordsworth and the Victorians* (Oxford: Clarendon Press, 1998), p. 211.
23. George Gilbert Ramsay, 'Rise and Progress of Mountaineering in Scotland', *Scottish Mountaineering Club Journal*, 4 (January 1896–97), 1–15 (p. 2).
24. F.G. Donnan, 'Collie, John Norman (1859–1942)', *Oxford Dictionary of National Biography* (Oxford: Oxford University Press, 2004). doi:10.1093/ref:odnb/32498.
25. 'Proceedings of the Alpine Club', *Alpine Journal*, 17 (1894–95), 85–98 (p. 87).
26. William C. Taylor, *The Snows of Yesteryear: J. Norman Collie, Mountaineer* (Toronto: Holt, Rinehart and Winston, 1973), p. 29.
27. Collie, 'A Reverie', p. 99; Alfred Tennyson, 'Morte d'Arthur', 420, in *The Poems of Tennyson*, ed. by Christopher Ricks, Longmans Annotated English Poets (London: Longmans, 1969), pp. 585–98.
28. Collie, 'A Reverie' p. 98. Sgurr nan Gillean and Cir Mhor are mountains on the islands of Skye and Arran respectively.
29. NLS, Acc. 11538, *Manchester City News*, p. 14.
30. Wim Tigges, '"Heir of All the Ages": Tennyson between Romanticism, Victorianism and Modernism', in *Victorian Keats and Romantic Carlyle: The Fusions and Confusions of Literary Periods*, ed. by C.C. Barfoot (Amsterdam and Atlanta, GA: Rodopi, 1999), pp. 307–22 (p. 307).
31. Joseph Bristow, 'Whether "Victorian" Poetry: A Genre and Its Period', *Victorian Poetry*, 42 (2004), 81–109 (p. 90).
32. Samantha Matthews, 'After Tennyson: The Presence of the Poet, 1892–1918', in *Tennyson Among the Poets: Bicentenary Essays*, ed. by Robert Douglas-Fairhurst and Seamus Perry (Oxford: Oxford University Press, 2009), pp. 315–35 (p. 328).
33. Theodore Watts, 'Aspects of Tennyson: Tennyson as Nature-Poet', *The Nineteenth Century*, 33 (1893), 836–56 (p. 841).
34. Tennyson's choice of Arthurian legend in this particular poem is also significant. The idea of Romanticism in the late nineteenth century was closely

connected to Medievalism – itelf a 'Victorian coinage', as Clare A. Simmons points out – and the medieval period was frequently used, as Marian Sherwood notes, to represent 'mourning for loss' in the present: See Clare A. Simmons, *Popular Medievalism in Romantic-Era Britain* (Basingstoke: Palgrave Macmillan, 2011), p. 2; Marian Sherwood, *Tennyson and the Fabrication of Englishness* (Basingstoke: Palgrave Macmillan, 2013), p. 104.

35. Joseph Gibson Stott, cited in Robin N. Campbell, 'My Dear Douglas', *Scottish Mountaineering Club Journal*, 34 (1990), 388–99 (p. 392).
36. Hayden Lorimer and Katrin Lund, 'Performing Facts: Finding a Way Over Scotland's Mountains', in *Nature Performed: Environment, Culture and Performance*, ed. by Bronislaw Szerszynski, Wallace Heim and Claire Waterton (London: Blackwell, 2003), pp. 130–44 (p. 130).
37. William C. Smith, 'The Cairngorms', *Cairngorm Club Journal*, 3 (1899–1902), 8–14 (p. 9).
38. Walter Scott, *Rob Roy* (Edinburgh: Edinburgh University Press, 2008), p. 223.
39. Ironically, Naismith also quoted from *Rob Roy* in his 1893 article on Scottish snow and ice climbing, in which he took a typically New Mountaineer approach to the question of guideless climbing and the technicalities of using ice axes. Naismith took Bailie Nicol Jarvie's description of the Highlands as 'a wild kind of warld by themsells' as the epigraph to this article: Naismith, 'Snowcraft', p. 157.
40. George Gilbert Ramsay, 'In Memoriam: Professor John Veitch', *Scottish Mountaineering Club Journal*, 3 (1894–95), 175–82 (p. 181).
41. Ramsay, 'Prof. John Veitch', p. 181.
42. Ramsay, 'Prof. John Veitch', p. 182.
43. Ramsay, 'Prof. John Veitch', p. 182.
44. Robert Adamson, 'Hill Climbing in Skye', *Cairngorm Club Journal*, 1 (January 1893–96), 181–91 (p. 181).
45. Douglas Freshfield, 'The Solitude of Abkhazia', *Alpine Journal*, 15 (1890–91), 237–55 (p. 238).
46. William Martin Conway, 'Centrists and Excentrists', *Alpine Journal*, 15 (1890–91), 397–403 (p. 401).
47. Ramsay, 'President's Address', p. 7.
48. Ramsay, 'President's Address', p. 7.
49. Conway, 'Dom from Domjoch', p. 108.
50. Conway, 'Dom from Domjoch', p. 109.
51. Conway, 'Dom from Domjoch', p. 109.
52. Conway, 'Centrists and Excentrists', p. 400.
53. Conway, 'Centrists and Excentrists', p. 400.

54. Conway, 'Centrists and Excentrists', p. 403.
55. Conway, *Alps from End to End*, p. 9.
56. Conway, *Alps from End to End*, p. 255.
57. Kennedy, 'Ascent of Monte della Disgrazia', p. 3.
58. Benjamin Hawes, *A Narrative of an Ascent to the Summit of Mont Blanc Made During the Summer of 1827 by Mr. William Hawes and Mr. Charles Fellowes* (privately printed, 1828), p. 19.
59. Smith, *Story of Mont Blanc*, p. 209.
60. Smith, *Story of Mont Blanc*, p. 192.
61. Charles Hudson and Edward Shirley Kennedy, *Where There's a Will There's a Way: An Ascent of Mont Blanc by a New Route and Without guides* (London: Longman, Brown, Green and Longmans, 1856), p. xi.
62. Conway, 'Centrists and Excentrists', p. 401.
63. Ramsay, 'Prof. John Veitch', p. 182.
64. Hudson and Kennedy, *Where There's a Will*, p. xi, emphasis in original.
65. G.N. Vansittart, Letter, 'Mr. Vansittart's Ascent of Mont Blanc', *The Daily News*, 26 August 1851.
66. Leslie Stephen, 'The Peaks of Primiero', *Alpine Journal*, 4 (1868–70), 385–402 (p. 385).
67. Coolidge and Howard, eds., *Pioneer in the High Alps*, p. 65.
68. Coolidge and Howard, eds., *Pioneer in the High Alps*, p. 71.
69. Coolidge and Howard, eds., *Pioneer in the High Alps*, p. 99.
70. Edward Whymper, 'The Ascent of Mont Pelvoux', *Peaks, Passes, and Glaciers*, 2 (1862), 233–56 (p. 256).
71. William Mathews, 'On the Determination of Heights by Means of the Barometer', *Alpine Journal*, 2 (1865–66), Part 1, 33–41 (p. 34).
72. R.C. Nichols, 'Excursions in the Graian Alps: The Ascent of the Ste. Helene', *Alpine Journal*, 2 (1865–66), 387–97 (p. 387).
73. Radford and Sandy, *Romantic Echoes*, p. 7.
74. Mathews, 'Determination of Heights', Part 1, p. 34.
75. Richard Le Gallienne, *The Romantic Nineties* (London: Putnam, 1951).
76. Eric Hobsbawm and Terence Ranger, eds., *The Invention of Tradition* (Cambridge: Cambridge University Press, 1983), p. 1.
77. Sally Ledger, 'The New Woman and the Crisis of Victorianism', in *Cultural Politics at the* Fin de Siècle, ed. by Sally Ledger and Scott McCracken (Cambridge: Cambridge University Press, 1995), pp. 22–44 (p. 23).
78. Henry Schütz Wilson, *Alpine Ascents and Adventures* (London: Sampson Low, Marston, Searle and Rivington, 1878), p. xi.
79. Wilson, *Alpine Ascents*, p. xi.
80. Wilson, *Alpine Ascents*, p. xi.

81. Wilson, *Alpine Ascents*, p. 69.
82. Wilson, *Alpine Ascents*, p. 72.
83. Spufford, *I May Be Some Time*, p. 270.
84. Spufford, *I May Be Some Time*, p. 128.
85. Wilson, *Alpine Ascents*, p. xi.
86. A.F. Mummery, 'The Aiguilles des Charmoz and de Grepon', *Alpine Journal*, 16 (1892–93), 159–73 (p. 171).
87. 'Reviews and Notices', *Alpine Journal*, 17 (1894–95), 527–34 (p. 528).
88. Mummery, 'Charmoz and de Grepon', p. 172.
89. Mummery, 'Charmoz and de Grepon', p. 172.
90. William Brown, 'Climbing in Scotland: Ben Nevis', *Cairngorm Club Journal*, 2 (1896–99), 1–8 (p. 2).
91. Brown, 'Climbing in Scotland', p. 2.
92. Jones, *Rock Climbing*, p. xlix.
93. Maylard, 'Winter Ascents, p. 141.
94. Alfred Ernest Maylard, 'Scottish Mountaineering: Retrospective and Prospective', *Scottish Mountaineering Club Journal*, 5 (1898–99), 308–14 (p. 311).
95. Maylard, 'Scottish Mountaineering', p. 311.
96. Maylard, 'Scottish Mountaineering', p. 312.
97. John Norman Collie, 'Climbing Near Wastdale Head', *Scottish Mountaineering Club Journal*, 3 (1894–95), 1–9 (p. 9). The Wasdale valley was commonly known as Wastdale at this time.
98. Robert Macfarlane, *Mountains of the Mind* (London: Granta, 2008), p. 37.
99. Gillian Beer, *Darwin's Plots: Evolutionary Narrative in Darwin, George Eliot and Nineteenth-Century Fiction*, 3rd edn. (Cambridge: Cambridge University Press, 2009) p. 38.
100. Macfarlane, *Mountains of the Mind*, p. 33.
101. John Ruskin, *Complete Works*, ed. by E.T. Cook and Alexander Wedderburn, 39 vols (London: George Allen, 1903–12), XXXVI (1909), 115.
102. Collie, 'A Reverie', p. 95.
103. Collie, 'A Reverie', p. 102.
104. Collie, 'A Reverie', p. 102.
105. Collie, 'A Reverie', p. 102.
106. Leslie Stephen, *The Playground of Europe* (London: Longmans, Green, 1871), p. 267.
107. Stephen, *Playground*, p. 266.
108. Stephen, *Playground*, p. 266.
109. Ruskin, *Sesame and Lilies*, p. 6.

110. Stephen, *Playground*, p. 268.
111. Stephen, *Playground,* p. 268.
112. Stephen, *Playground*, p. 269.
113. Stephen, *Playground*, p. 273.
114. Stephen, *Playground*, p. 296.

CHAPTER 4

# The Climbing Body

## INTRODUCTION

The New Mountaineer's characteristic emphasis on materiality extended to the climber's body itself. Increasingly the responses of the human body to its experience of mountain ascents were recorded and discussed. In this respect, the late-Victorian mountaineers reflected a wider cultural and scientific environment in which the relationship of the physical to the visual and a heightened concern with materiality were important. Experimental work taking place during this period in physiology and psycho-physiology, particularly in the fields of muscular exertion and response to external stimuli, had configured the human body as a kind of engine or motor, capable of harnessing energy for productive work but prone to fatigue. In the same period as these medico-scientific developments, there was widespread discussion in artistic circles about the role of physiology in the response of human beings to aesthetic experiences, notably manifested in the concept of physiological aesthetics.

The notion of the climbing body as a kind of machine, maintained by exercise and training and fuelled by correct nutrition; the interest in the physical responses of the climber to fatigue and the other hardships inherent in high-level mountaineering; the implication that the act of climbing is a kind of 'work'; and the redefining of 'pleasure' as something that can be gained from sensations traditionally considered unpleasant; these were all concerns specific to climbing literature of the period, but they were also influenced by broader cultural, medical, and scientific developments in the late nineteenth century.

## THE HUMAN ENGINE

Owen Glynne Jones died in a mountaineering accident in 1899.[1] Reviewing the second, posthumous edition of his *Rock Climbing in the English Lake District* in the *Climbers' Club Journal* the following year, the pseudonymous reviewer 'E. R. G.' recalled Jones' character and approach to climbing in revealing terms. Jones' life brought to mind the Greek historian Thucydides' description of the Athenians: 'They treat their bodies as if they were the bodies of other men'. E. R. G. went on to say of Jones: 'Surely no one ever treated his body more completely "as if it were another's" than poor Jones. He kept it always in the severest training, and forced it do to the utmost of which it was capable'.[2] The reviewer continued:

> His attitude towards himself was precisely that of a marine engineer towards his engines. He quite admits that the machinery is high-class, but his modest pride centres in [*sic*] the fact that he knows how to make the most of it, and can get more work out of it than another man would.[3]

The choice of an engine as metaphor for Jones's attitude to his own climbing body is apt.[4] It points to a wider cultural interest in the potential and limitations of the human body for work, and to the way that interest was consistently reflected in mountaineering texts. The second half of the nineteenth century had seen a surge in research on the effect of fatigue. More generally, it had also witnessed dramatic progress in the understanding of how the muscular and nervous systems responded to external stimuli – to cold, pain, and the effects of altitude, to give just three examples with obvious relevance to the pursuit of mountaineering – and how the physical responses of the body were relevant to mental and physiological processes.

This was a time of increased concern with what Rabinbach terms the notion of 'the human motor' – the idea of the human body as an engine for productive activity, and as an example of both the principle of conservation of energy and of the inevitable dissipation and exhaustion of energy.[5] Rabinbach attributes this concern to a widespread sense that 'the endemic disorder of fatigue'[6] presented a threat to industrial and economic productivity, even to European hegemony in general, as well as to the concept of the body as a 'thermodynamic machine capable of conserving and deploying energy'.[7] This became the subject of a great deal of scientific and medical research in this period. At the same time, the description of climbing mountains as type of work to be carried out by the mountaineer's body was a common trope of climbing literature.

Seen in this context, the suggestion that Jones treated his own body like an engine – a machine from which the skilled engineer can extract the maximum of work by accurately calibrating the amount of fuel and maintenance required – and that he forced his body to do 'the utmost of which it was capable', reads less like a description of Jones's personal idiosyncrasies than a wider statement of how the climbing body had come to be regarded by the end of the century. The late-Victorian emphasis on the physical manifested itself not only in the material culture of mountaineering, but also in a growing interest in the experience of the body while climbing, and the way in which it would respond under the stress of exhaustion, freezing conditions, and other challenges. In some instances it also led to a new emphasis on the *pleasure* of extreme physical exertion – which, I will suggest, represents an almost entirely new approach, just as the New Mountaineers represented a break with other aspects of the past.

The experience of the mountaineer was first and foremost physical. A typical day in the Alps would involve the climber rising in the early hours of the morning to avoid being on dangerous slopes when the heat and sunshine of the day had started to melt the snow. A hasty breakfast would be followed by several hours of walking in darkness. 'We carefully husband our resources', pointed out Charles Edward Mathews in 1892, 'for who can tell whether we shall be out for twelve hours, or fifteen, or even twenty?'[8] The challenges of the day ahead were varied, but would almost inevitably include climbing on rocks and on steep snow, sections of glacier to be negotiated, and a range of physical obstacles to be overcome. 'We evade crevasses, we thread our way through séracs, we wrestle with the rocks, we pull each other up or let each other down, we clamber up great staircases hewn in the blue ice, we wade through the snows', wrote Mathews.[9] The precise nature of such manoeuvres would vary according to the weather and to the climber's own fitness and experience. Many accounts of the period stressed the huge difference that bad weather, for example, could make to the physical experience of climbing. Charles Pilkington pointed out the contrast that the same mountain could present under differing conditions:

> That steep and narrow ridge of rocks, its handholds and ledges small, but firm and not too far apart, so interesting and pleasant to climb when the rocks are dry and warm, can be very different when the wind is howling over it, seeking to tear you from its glazed and slippery crest; your half-frozen fingers scratching the falling snow out of the hidden cracks and crevices; your feet numb and cold, scraping and kicking to find the narrow steps; your eyes half-blinded by the biting sleet, and your body covered in frozen clothing.[10]

The Alpine climber faced the risk of frostbite, snow-blindness, sunburn, and possibly altitude sickness. Although mountaineers embraced technology, the act of climbing itself was largely accomplished without technological assistance: a rope would be used, ice axes would be deployed on snow and ice, and some more technically minded climbers would also use crampons by this stage, but even by the end of the century there were few other technical aids to climbing.[11] The rope was typically looped around spikes of rock and other projections for security, but there was none of the safety equipment that later generations of climbers developed to protect themselves from falls; even the technique of abseiling to descend cliffs safely was not developed until 1911.[12] The climber was thus reliant on strength, balance, agility, and on the proprioceptive powers of his or her own body to move itself through mountainous terrain.

Protective clothing was also rudimentary. The climber might have to spend a night out on the mountains, either as a planned bivouac on a long route or through becoming accidentally benighted. In either case, it was invariably a cold and uncomfortable experience, sheltering under stones with little more than a spare sweater and sometimes a light blanket for warmth.[13] Even on the much smaller mountains of Britain, the physical challenges of climbing were considerable. In an environment where heavy rain was common, and in the absence of lightweight waterproof clothing or fast-drying fabrics, climbers had to tolerate great physical discomfort (see Fig. 4.1). Ascending the mountain of Suilven in north-west Scotland in 1895, Scottish Mountaineering Club president George Gilbert Ramsay and his son were forcibly reminded of the contrast between the harshness of the mountain environment and the

4 THE CLIMBING BODY 113

**Fig. 4.1** 'British Hill Weather', from the *Badminton* guide

vulnerability of their own bodies. Having rather unwisely chosen to climb in kilts, they found themselves

> drenched to the skin; the wind made merry with our kilts, blowing them anywhere but where they ought to be; and we often had to clasp the dripping rock with bodies as bare as – but less hard than – its own.[14]

Above all, the climber had to deal with the constant problem of fatigue. 'Fatigue is a condition that the mountaineer cannot wholly escape', wrote Dent, and a good deal of mountaineering literature of the period reflects the climbers' awareness of the potential and limitations of their own human engines.[15] This interest grew directly from their experience of the physical demands and rewards of climbing, but it was also informed and influenced by the work that was being done in experimental science. Interest in the performance of the 'human motor' found its evidential basis in the series of discoveries made by researchers in this period, and in the decades leading up to it, particularly in the field of physiology.

Physiology had developed in the early part of the nineteenth century from a rather marginal offshoot of anatomy to a recognised scientific discipline in its own right, with the rise of experimental methods and laboratory techniques.[16] This new discipline had its roots in the work on tactile stimuli carried out in Leipzig in the 1820s by Ernst Heinrich Weber, laying the foundation for a new interest in and exploration of the importance of touch.[17] By the 1850s physiologists throughout Europe were concentrating their efforts on taking 'a human sense that was imprecise, variable, and fleeting and translat[ing] it into the movement of an instrument', with inventions as varied as the mercury column of the thermometer, the polygraph, and the electrocardiograph.[18] In the same decade, Hermann von Helmholtz carried out the first work on the measurement of the speed with which stimuli such as pain are translated into muscular response, using an instrument known as the myograph to record the contractions.[19]

The 1860s saw further attempts to measure and register physiological actions, such as the invention of the sphygmograph, to measure the pulse without the need for any surgical attachment.[20] Much of the early pioneering work was done in France and in the German-speaking countries of Europe, but the first specialist physiological laboratories in Britain were established towards the end of the 1860s and the Physiological Society was formed in 1876, with the *Journal of Physiology* beginning publication two years later.²¹ Between roughly 1870 and 1885, physiology in Britain took on its modern characteristics, with the introduction of practical classes by the Royal College of Surgeons from 1870, the growth of animal experimentation (which in turn had become more acceptable with the use of anaesthesia), and great leaps forward in both teaching and research methods.²²

As with the other institutions increasingly dominated in this period by middle-class male professionals, the Physiological Society had its share of mountaineering members. One of its founders was Francis Maitland Balfour, whose work on animal morphology was cut short in 1882 when he was killed in a fall while climbing in the Alps.²³ Dent, editor of the *Badminton* guide, president of the Alpine Club in the late 1880s, and author of many other mountaineering books and articles, was appointed to the Society in 1893, after a career as Demonstrator in Physiology at St Georges Hospital in London from the late 1870s.²⁴

It was not only in Britain, however, that mountaineers were involved in physiological research. Back in Leipzig, Hugo Kronecher had been carrying out studies on muscle fatigue in frogs during the 1870s, assisted by an Italian physiologist, Angelo Mosso.²⁵ Mosso continued to work on muscle fatigue upon returning to his native Turin, transferring his attention to human subjects and eventually publishing his groundbreaking work *La Fatica* in 1891; the book was translated into English and published in Britain as *Fatigue* in 1904. His research on fatigue is central to the mountaineering physiology of the late nineteenth century, combining as it does an experimental interest in the effect of fatigue on both physical and mental processes, a scientific methodology for measuring and calibrating the changes thus brought about, and an interest in the wider concern about fatigue in society.

Mosso's work was the most important and influential in this field, but he was building on research that had been carried out by, for example, psychologist Adolf Fick and chemist Johannes Wislicenus in Switzerland as far back as the 1860s. Fick and Wislicenus had climbed the Faulhorn in 1865 as part of their work on the chemical changes that took place in muscles as a result of fatigue, using the ascent to measure the amount of muscle protein used up in their own bodies.²⁶ Mosso, a keen Alpinist who would later publish on the *Physiology of Man in the High Alps* (1898), wrote in *Fatigue* of the relation between mental and muscular exhaustion, using the example of his own experiences on the summits of Monte Visto and Monte Rosa. He reported: 'The physical conditions of thought and memory become less favourable as the blood is poisoned by the products of fatigue, and the energy of the nervous system consumed'.[27]

This was clearly of interest to anyone concerned with how the human body operated, not just at high altitude but in any stressful or physically tiring situation, and the research Mosso carried out between the 1870s and the 1890s was revolutionary. His 1884 invention of the ergograph, to measure muscle fatigue accurately, led directly to the discovery that different human subjects respond to fatigue at differing rates despite having similar ages, physiques, and other factors. He was among the first scientists to suggest that fatigue was a chemical process involving the production of such toxins as carbonic acid, and he identified the effects of variation in 'atmospheric pressure, environmental temperature, time of day, nutritional status of the subject' and other variables on the onset of fatigue.[28] As his allusion to his own Alpine climbing experiences suggests, he also made the connection between mental and muscular fatigue – a connection which reflects the wider project among researchers in this period to link the physical with the mental.

Mosso's research reflects wider social concerns about physical work, fatigue, and the impact of modern life on the individual human subject. These concerns found an outlet in numerous studies of fatigue and a perception that the unique strains and stimuli of modern life were leading to an increase in the problem of 'neurasthenia'.[29] Physiology in the 1880s and 1890s was increasingly concerned with problems of fatigue, with the precise measurement and management of human responses to tiredness, pain, and external stimuli, and with what Crary calls the 'relation between sensation and motor behaviour'.[30] In the 1880s scientists began to distinguish between the localized sensations of heat and pressure; to work on the electrophysiology of muscle; and to measure changes in muscular electric currents during fatigue, leading to the discovery of the 'causal primacy of electrical action' in muscle function.[31] In the 1890s this work on the muscular system was complemented by a wave of new research on the impact of external stimuli on the human body; for example, the development of William D. Krohn's 'Apparatus for Simultaneous Touches' in Illinois in 1892, which allowed up to ten points on the body to be stimulated at the same time,[32] and Max von Frey's work in Germany which finally proved the existence of pain points in the body.[33]

The focus in the discipline of physiology on precise measurement, and on the transformation of the seemingly intangible and ephemeral into something that could be measured, enumerated, and replicated had its counterpart in the new spirit of codification and classification that had taken hold of mountaineering in the same period. Munro's Tables and Naismith's Rule might seem a world away from the laboratory work of experimental physiologists, but the transformation of mountaineering from an ad hoc and sometimes rather haphazard activity into a disciplined sport, carried out 'systematically and of set purpose', clearly reflects this same desire to measure and record that can be identified in physiology and in so many other disciplines in this period.[34]

The new drive to understand the precise nature of physiological processes also had a more direct relationship to mountaineering than this metaphorical one. Some of the experiments carried out had a direct bearing on the world of mountaineering – in particular, those undertaken by Mosso, Flick, and Wislicenus on fatigue in the climbing body – while other work was done by Dent and Balfour, who also happened to be mountaineers, and who in Dent's case played an important role in articulating the philosophy of mountaineering in this period. More generally, mountaineers took a keen interest in any physiological or medical developments that had a bearing on their pastime, and in the causes and effects of fatigue in particular. From the beginning of our period, the question of how fast the climber could acclimatize to altitude, and how far the climbing body could be pushed, is a frequent concern of mountaineers. Recalling an ascent of a pass below the Jungfrau in 1871, Tyndall vividly described his feelings of exhaustion:

> At every brow I pause; legs and breast are laid against the rough rock, so as to lessen by their friction the strain upon the arms, which are stretched to grasp some protruberance above. Thus I rest, and thus I learn that three days training is not sufficient to dislodge London from one's lungs.[35]

In a paper given to the Royal Society in the same year, and reprinted in the *Alpine Journal*, the physician (and inventor of the clinical thermometer) Thomas Clifford Allbutt described how the effective climber must have 'not good legs alone, but also a good heart, capacious lungs [...] and plenty of those foods known as the carbohydrates, which foods burn in the body, giving off as products water and carbonic acid.'[36] This interest in the optimum fuel for the human motor would continue with Craufurd Grove's 1885 article on the 'Alpine Training Diet'. Writing that same year, Dent noted how the experienced mountaineer conserves his energy: 'He never puts forth more strength at each step than is necessary, thus saving his powers, being always ready in an emergency and never degenerating into that most dangerous of encumbrances, a tired member of a united party'.[37]

This interest in mountaineering physiology was not confined to fatigue. The *Alpine Journal* and other mountaineering publications discussed in some detail the causes and prevention of sunburn and snow blindness.[38] Allbutt addressed frostbite and its treatment in an 1876 paper that debunked some of the more eccentric and dangerous cures for this condition.[39] Contributors discussed the effects of altitude on human physiology, still very imperfectly understood at this stage; Dent was one of the first people to speculate that a climber might one day be able to reach the summit of Everest, almost twice the altitude of the highest Alpine peak.[40] The *Alpine Journal*, in particular, kept its readers informed of the latest research on the cause and prevention of altitude sickness.[41] There was even some rather eccentric speculation about evolutionary adaptations that might account for the superior performance of mountain guides born and brought up in an Alpine environment, attributing to the guide 'some structural difference, both hereditary and acquired, actually permitting more freedom of movement at the ankle-joint, which neither muscular action nor power of balance could ever give to the amateur'.[42] But these obvious connections of physiology to mountaineering are perhaps less significant than the way in which the ethos of mountain climbing in this period reliably reflects the preoccupations of physiology with fatigue, muscular response, and the measurement and classification of physical activity.

It is, for example, unlikely to be coincidental that around the same period, writers on mountaineering begin to use the word 'work' to describe their pastime, something which is virtually unheard of in earlier accounts of climbing mountains but which becomes routine as the century progresses. As late as 1885, Dent would note that the use of the phrase was newly fashionable in climbing literature: a previous generation of mountaineers, he wrote, 'did what it is now the fashion to call their "work" thoroughly'.[43] By the 1890s, however, Ramsay would use the word without any need for explanation, proclaiming on behalf of his fellow Scottish Mountaineering Club members in 1895: 'We climb mountains because we love them; and we welcome all who love them, and have done good work on them, whether they be accomplished pole-climbers or not'.[44] Two years later William Brown, writing disparagingly about an influx of tourists to Sligachan on Skye, complained: 'The climber, however, bent on difficult work must get nearer to his mountains'.[45] There are numerous other examples of the word being used to describe an activity that is clearly not work, in the traditional sense of the word, but rather a leisure activity involving physical toil and potential fatigue. Rabinbach suggests it is only in the late nineteenth century that the word 'work' becomes 'universalized to include the expenditure of energies in all motors, animate as well as inanimate'.[46] The fact that mountaineering literature pushed this semantic expansion still further, using the word to describe an activity that might more obviously be called a type of play or pastime, suggests that the preoccupations of experimental physiology and the anxieties of *fin-de-siècle* society about the role and nature of physical labour were having an impact on climbing as on so many other areas of life.

### 'Giving Tactile Values to Retinal Impressions'

The relevance of the seemingly disparate experiments described above lies in their common interest in the various types of human physical response, whether the simple response of nerves to pain stimuli or the more complex response of the whole body, including the brain, to fatigue. By the 1890s, there was an accumulating body of work, starting with Weber in the 1820s, in which the human body was measured, tested, and experimented upon, and theories were expounded about the way in which physical stimuli and experiences had a corresponding impact on mental impressions. As William James put it in one of the culminating works of psycho-physiology of the nineteenth century, his *Principles of Psychology* (1890): 'No mental modification ever occurs which is not accompanied or followed by a bodily change'.[47]

The belief in the inextricable linkage of the physical to the mental inevitably had important implications for the discipline of psycho-physiology. By the end of the century, as David Parisi puts it, 'tactile experience and its mental correlate became part of a mechanistic and quantifiable universe'.[48] Just as late nineteenth-century physiologists looked to the work of Weber in the 1820s for the basis of their work, so psycho-physiology had its roots in the period from the 1790s to about 1830. During this period a series of new discoveries about the brain and nervous system established the physical brain as 'the organ of thought'[49] – something that had been fiercely disputed up to this point – and led to the rise of what Alan Richardson calls 'anti-dualistic psychological models founded on the mind's embodiment, placing novel emphases on automatic and unconscious mental processes and mind-body interaction'.[50] It was not until the early 1870s, however, that localization of brain function was finally established, and the rest of the decade saw a further series of discoveries that allowed the various regions of brain function to be identified.[51] As with physiology, many of the major steps forward would be made in German speaking countries, and the founding of Wilhelm Wundt's laboratory in 1889 once again saw the centre of gravity in experimentation shift towards Leipzig.[52] The last thirty years or so of the century mark what Crary calls a shift 'from the *structural* psychology of associationism to various kinds of *functional* psychological accounts', a change he attributes at least in part to 'the increasing importance and richness of a physiological understanding of the human subject'.[53]

The insights of physiology and psycho-physiology were by no means confined to the world of science and medicine. In the arts, too, a new significance was attributed to the role of touch, both in the understanding of what had previously been considered the purely visual field, and in the broader concept of how human consciousness is constituted. What Hilary Fraser describes as the 'conceptualisation of touch in the visual field' had by the late nineteenth century become a key issue for writers, artists, and theorists as diverse as Bernard Berenson, Aloïs Riegl, and Grant Allen, as well as for poets 'Michael Field' (Edith Cooper and Katharine Bradley), Vernon Lee, and Kit Anstruther-Thomson.[54]

One of the first texts to address this issue directly was Grant Allen's *Physiological Aesthetics* (1877). Allen declared his purpose to be to demonstrate the 'purely physical origin of the sense of beauty, and its relativity to our nervous organisation',[55] and he attempted to establish a correspondence between the pleasure of 'Play', experienced when 'we exercise our limbs and muscles, not for any ulterior life-serving object, but merely for the sake of the pleasure which the exercise affords us',[56] and the aesthetic feelings similarly stimulated when we 'exercise our eyes or ears'.[57] Allen's theories were mechanistic and in many ways crude, but they do demonstrate that certain topics were being thought about and discussed by the 1870s: the relationship of physical movement to perception, the physiological basis of pleasure, and the centrality of embodiment in human experience.

These same preoccupations were starting to emerge in mountaineering narratives at roughly the same time as Grant was writing. Assumptions were made in these texts that are analogous to Allen's, even if they were not necessarily spelt out explicitly. Mountaineering literature from this period begins to stress the interconnectedness of sight, touch, and movement; of visual evidence being supplemented and corroborated by close physical contact and by physical action. Tyndall's *Hours of Exercise in the Alps* (1871) was described by its author as being 'for the most part a record of bodily action', and while Tyndall's prose is actually considerably more complex and sensitive to mountain aesthetics than this suggests, he does tend to present visual images of mountain scenes swiftly followed by a description of the climber's own physical movement through those same scenes, as in this account of climbing the Weisshorn:

> We find the rocks hewn into fantastic turrets and obelisks, while the loose chips of this sculpture are strewn confusedly on the ridge. Amid these we cautiously pick our way, winding round the towers or scaling them amain. The work was heavy from the first, the bending, twisting, reaching, and drawing up calling upon all the muscles of the frame.[58]

Tyndall moves seamlessly from the impressions gleaned by sight to the sensations gained by moving through the landscape; this is an experience characterized and defined by movement as much as by sight. Writing in the same year, Freshfield recalled his group's first reaction upon coming across an unclimbed peak in the Dolomites:

> The mountaineers amongst us pulled out opera-glasses, and began at once to dissect the peak; decide this couloir was snow and available, that rib of rock broken and useless – in short, to converse in that Alpine jargon which marks the race considered by Mr. Ruskin capable of treating the Alps only as greased poles.[59]

This was, of course, a riposte to Ruskin's accusation that mountaineers treated the Alps 'as soaped poles in bear gardens'.[60] But it also indicates how the first instinct of Freshfield and his companions was to examine the mountain closely for places where it was feasible for the climbing body to ascend. While this is ostensibly a description of mountaineers using vision to make a judgement, the judgement they are making is about the physical practicability of the mountain for the human frame. The rock is 'useless' because it does not look as if it will bear the climber's weight; the snow is 'available' because the particular angle at which it is lying makes it unlikely to avalanche when the mountaineer steps on to it. This is an instrumental approach to mountain scenery, in which the aesthetic response of the viewer takes second place to the anticipation of the physical sensation of climbing it.

These are early examples of how the climbing body started to be placed in the foreground of the mountain scene. Later in the century, the focus in mountaineering literature on the climber's corporeal interaction with the landscape became far more pronounced and frequent. By 1890, when Conway was writing his account of an ascent of the Dom, the third-highest summit in the Alps, it was implicit that perception – and in this case, memory – was closely linked to physical experience. Conway noted how certain moments of this particularly gruelling climb were imprinted in his memory, not only because of their visual impact but also from the physical sensations he had undergone:

> Two or three very nasty places remain photographed in my memory – one where there was a kind of elbow in the ridge, and we had to jump from an oval-topped ice-covered block across a gap of no particular width, landing on a knife-edge of rock, from which we had instantly to step again on to firm footing. The thing would have been easy enough without the glazing and the gale, but the memory of the moment before that flying step comes back to me sometimes like a cold horror.[61]

It is worth recalling that this is the same article in which Conway made clear his disapproval of the antics of mountain 'gymnasts'.[62] Given this context, it is clear that Conway is not simply boasting about his athletic feats. Instead, he is writing with the implicit assumption that the physical sensation of mountain climbing is central to the experience, and that this will be recalled afterwards just as clearly as any visual impressions.

This belief that physical sensation can provide sense impressions as reliable and accurate as those afforded by sight became a consistent theme in mountaineering writing. Writing in 1892 about a winter trip to north Wales undertaken some fourteen years earlier, Henry George Willink recalled how the evidence of the eyes could be misleading, and had to be verified by direct physical experience:

> We could see that the windward flank of Crib-y-ddysgl ahead of us was of a dull grey, and we floundered slowly towards the nearest part of this, cheering ourselves with the thought of the good progress we should make when we reached it.[63]

The dull grey tone had led his party to expect that this side of the mountain – part of the Snowdon range – comprised exposed rock rather than ice and was therefore possible to climb. Physical engagement with the mountain would soon prove otherwise:

> To our surprise, however, when we did set foot on this promised land, we found that it was neither more nor less than a coating of granulated snow-ice some inches thick, not rough enough to give foot-hold even at the moderate angle of thirty degrees, or thereabouts, at which it was set, and too hard to stamp the feet into. There was nothing for it but cold steel, so the axe went to the front, and for twenty minutes it was necessary to enjoy the pleasure of making the back ache with cutting steps.[64]

Eyesight has here proven inadequate to assess the mountain landscape; only the act of setting foot on the mountain can provide an accurate measure of its suitability for the mountaineer. I am suggesting not that such accounts were directly or knowingly influenced by physiological or psycho-physiological research, but rather that they were symptomatic of a milieu in which physical sensation was allotted an increasingly important role. This was partly to do with the practicalities of climbing, but it was also related to the wider concern about the relation of movement to perception.

Mountaineers from the 1870s onwards were also more likely to describe these sensations in sensuous, almost voluptuous language than that used by their predecessors. Again, this reflects what was taking place in literary and artistic discourse of the time. Walter Pater's Conclusion to *The Renaissance* (1873), for example, seems to echo both the newly sensuous preoccupations of the mountaineers, with its references to the 'physical life' of 'delicious recoil from the flood of water in summer heat', and the wider cultural and scientific concern with physical response to stimuli.[65] Pater's book, and in particular the Conclusion, is often presented as one of the texts which laid the groundwork for aestheticism and even for *fin-de-siècle* decadence, but it can equally be regarded as sharing the concern for the immediate, sensory experience of the human being in nature – which may include visual experience, but does not necessarily have to be mediated by sight. Lene Østermark-Johansen describes one of Pater's key themes as 'the relation between pain and beauty, touch and sight', a concern that does not seem so far removed from that of the Victorian mountaineers.[66] Like Allen's work, Pater's Conclusion represents an increased awareness of and interest in the way that all the senses feed in to what is perceived visually, and a belief that the 'physical life' is not distinct from but wholly integrated with the visual.

A comparable sensibility can be identified in mountaineering accounts from this period onwards. Leslie Stephen, writing three years before Pater, gave an account of his sensations during a solitary climb in the Dolomites in terms that bring to mind Pater's concern with 'physical life':

> A languor stole over me, and though I resisted the tempter, I raised my feet slowly and sleepily; I groaned at the round, smooth, slippery pebbles, and lamented the absence of water. At length I reached a little patch of snow, and managed to slake my parched lips and once more to toil upwards.[67]

This sort of language, richly detailed in its examination of physical sensations, becomes increasingly common in mountaineering literature. An 1883 article by J. Stafford Anderson on his ascent of the Dent Blanche provides a good example of the loving detail with which both the pleasures and pains of mountain experience were recounted – and the degree to which the two were increasingly conflated. On a day of enforced idleness before their ascent, Anderson writes:

> We had the cabine [sic] to ourselves, and slept the sleep of the just, not turning out till seven o'clock the next morning, as we had only an idle day before us, which was spent in lying about on the rocks, revelling in the sunshine, drinking in the magnificent panorama spread before us, and now and then trying to catch its beauties in the camera.[68]

Later, having completed the climb, the mountaineers' physical sensations are very different but no less satisfying:

> We turned our attention to the injuries we had sustained; constant contact with the snow and ice in the latter part of the ascent, had turned our hands into a half-frozen and pulpy condition, and the steel of our axes being frozen, every time a finger rested on it a piece of skin peeled off. I had suffered the most, and for an hour or two the blood had oozed from my fingertips, sullying the purity of the snow, and leaving quite sufficient traces to show our route up. Not having tasted food for seven hours, our thoughts naturally turned to the provision bag, and a very scanty one we found it – about two cubic inches of very dry tongue, one leg of a fowl, some bread-and-butter, and a little wine and brandy. We did not smoke, for the simple reason that we had not the wherewithal, but we were too much elated to grumble at anything.

In the first extract, the 'magnificent panorama' and the sensation of resting in the sunshine meld into a languorous experience; in the second, frozen and peeling flesh and hunger mix with elation. Both move beyond simple accounts of majestic mountain views or traditional travellers' accounts of perilous journeys, gesturing instead towards an embodied form of experience in which it is almost impossible to separate 'pain and beauty, touch and sight'.[69]

Theodore Cornish's 1890 account of winter climbing in the Alps, for instance, includes a description of a New Year's Eve spent shivering in a hut high up on the Schreckhorn, after which the narrator and his companions

> were rewarded for our toil by the most magnificent sunrise I ever beheld. We could not see the sun, which was on the other side of the mountain, but gradually our numbed limbs and weary frames were inspirited, as peak after peak, clearly-cut and snow-clad, was bathed in the rich pink hues of the unfolding morn. With renewed energies we pressed on.[70]

This seamless melding of the visual and the physical into an indivisible sensual experience – physical toil rewarded by scenic beauty, the visual impression of the sunrise inspiriting the cold and tired bodies of the climbers – suggests Pater's seemingly esoteric aesthetic musings were not so far removed from the concerns of the late Victorian mountaineers. Willink, too, on the same Welsh excursion recounted above, experienced the impact of the mountain environment on his body and described it in language that seems to call upon the full sensorium rather than one individual sense:

> Five minutes after taking our gloves off they were frozen hard; my beard and moustache were stiff with congealed breath and frozen snow which had got there from some tumble in a drift; our woolly clothes were tagged with little bobbins of ice which tinkled as we walked, and later on towards evening we found our axe and alpenstock covered with jackets of ice formed by the freezing of snow melted by the friction and warmth of our hands.[71]

Later in the century, Fraser suggests that Berenson's art criticism, based as it was on the concept of physiological aesthetics, was an important contribution to the 'emergent theory of the tangibility of the visual in the nineteenth century'.[72] Berenson, in texts including his 1896 *The Florentine Painters of the Renaissance*, argued: 'Sight alone gives us no accurate sense of the third dimension', the third dimension in this context being depth.[73] In childhood, Berenson believed, the sense of touch, aided by muscular sensations of movement, 'teaches us to appreciate depth', while in adulthood, 'every time our eyes recognise reality we are, as a matter of fact, giving tactile values to retinal impressions'.[74] Berenson believed it was the task of the painter to

> rouse the tactile sense, for I must have the illusion of being able to touch a figure, I must have the illusion of varying muscular sensations inside my palm and fingers corresponding to the various projections of this figure, before I shall take it for granted as real.[75]

This 'illusion' was, of course, precisely the sense that many writers on mountaineering were aspiring to – although they would have been more likely to designate the connection between muscular sensations in palm and fingers and the projections of rock face as a manifestation of their own heightened awareness of the corporeal reality of mountains. As early as 1871, Tyndall had noted how the process of climbing sharpened his awareness of his own muscular system and the contact of his hands with the mountain: 'The fingers, wrist, and forearm were my main reliance, and as a mechanical construction the human hand appeared to me this day to be a miracle of constructive art'.[76] Dent, too, noted that 'examination of rocks by what surgeons term palpation is *sine qua non* in rock climbing'.[77]

The Austrian art historian Aloïs Riegl similarly argued that the tactile sense was necessary to supplement and support the visual. As he noted in *Historical Grammar of the Visual Arts* (1897), 'the optical sense alone does not suffice to present us with a true sense of form [ . . . ] To convince ourselves of the actuality of depth, we must call on another sense, the sense of touch, or tactile sense'.[78] Riegl believed that only by calling upon previous tactile experiences could the human viewer 'mentally flesh out into three-dimensional form the two-dimensional surface that our eyes actually perceive',[79] and he argued strongly that the sense of touch had been downplayed in favour of the sense of sight in much previous art theory.[80]

Riegl regarded perception as embodied and dependent on the physical situation of the perceiving subject. His perceptual psychology aimed to delineate the various stages of perception and the role of both touch and vision in these stages. As Linda M. Shires points out, many Victorian artists and writers understood that 'vision is intimately bound up with the physiological space of the viewer and all his or her senses'.[81] Shires identifies a shift in perception in the nineteenth century, 'from a single, seemingly objective, universal perspective to an increasing preoccupation with the processes of perception'.[82] This focus on the physical and material underpinning of perception was by no means limited to art theory in this period, but was characteristic of what Fraser calls a 'general exploration of the embodied nature of vision in the nineteenth century'.[83] That exploration clearly extended to the subculture of mountaineering, even if its expression was largely implicit. But mountaineering narratives moved beyond the objective examination of physicality. For the other striking feature of accounts written by late nineteenth-century climbers is their insistence on the *pleasure* of physical sensation.

## Bodily Pleasures

If social and medical concern in this period centred on fatigue as a problem, there was a concurrent strand in mountaineering literature that took a quite different approach. Much writing about climbing in this period actually seems to welcome fatigue as part of the multifaceted experience of climbing, rather than regarding it as an inevitable but regrettable side-effect of physical exertion. Just as the New Mountaineers who gathered at the Sligachan Hotel seemed rather more relaxed about the impact of technology and other manifestations of fast-paced modernity than might be expected from people who had chosen to spend their time in the remote wilderness of the Cuillin hills, so many mountaineers left accounts of their activities in which they seemed quite comfortable with the notion of fatigue and other discomforts as integral to their enjoyment.

These accounts moved well beyond the simple 'pleasure in the exertion of acquired skill' that Mummery would defend as the prerogative of the climber. They were written by what was arguably the first generation of travellers claiming to actively enjoy sensations of exhaustion, cold, and fear, and to delight in their own physicality, in the responsiveness of their bodies to the demands placed upon them by climbing, and in the development of skills and knowledge that allowed them to travel safely in mountainous terrain. Of course, some acceptance of fear was an essential part of the sublime as traditionally understood, and the notion of a kind of 'delightful Horrour' had been common in accounts of mountain landscapes since John Dennis coined the phrase after crossing the Alps in 1688.[84] But the degree of direct physical involvement in the writing of late-Victorian climbers goes well beyond this rather more distant and theoretical experience. This new emphasis on pleasure operated on both an individual and a social level, and it required a degree of comfort, safety, and health in everyday life to be taken for granted before it could become widespread. Climbing in this period remained the preserve of a relatively wealthy middle class, and mostly male elite, whose lives in the city were safe, healthy, and physically easy in a way that was virtually unprecedented in history. As the literary critic I. A. Richards would put it, looking back in 1927 at his climbing career in the late nineteenth and early twentieth centuries: 'To enjoy unnecessary discomfort or insecurity, we must first be bored with comfort.'[85] It was perhaps a search for something outside the comfort, safety, and convenience of their own lives that led many climbers to pursue this new activity. Whatever the motivation, in their emphasis on pleasure the late Victorian mountaineers seem to move beyond the scientific and medical preoccupations and social anxieties of their time. Instead they present a positive, confident account of the pleasures of the climbing body which annexes even sensations like fatigue and cold that a generation or so previously would have been considered negative, incorporating them into a new ethos of embodied perception.

Like the shifts identified in Chap. 2, this new approach begins to take shape from around the early 1870s. In his 1870 paper to the Alpine Club, Craufurd Grove enumerated the qualities of a 'first class mountaineer' in terms that would become familiar in the decades to follow:

> He must have some power of determining from below the best way up a mountain, or to the top of a col, a thing requiring a long-practised eye and considerable judgement. He must be able to see his way through the complicated entanglement of an ice-fall; to tell from a distance whether rocks are likely to be practicable or not; to follow his line of ascent down again with certainty over a wilderness of rock, where footsteps have left no trace; few know how difficult this is until they try to do it for themselves. He must be able to judge rapidly and surely whether séracs are likely to fall; must be strong and enduring, able to undergo the severe labour of making steps in the snow, or cutting steps in the ice, and, most important of all, must have that singular combination of strength with activity matured by long practice, which makes a man a good iceman and a good cragsman.[86]

Craufurd Grove's list is, of course, entirely consistent with a growing emphasis on technical skill and an increasingly professionalised approach to climbing.[87] However it is notable not just for the combination of physical and visual skills demanded of the mountaineer, but also for its sense of relish and satisfaction at hard-won knowledge and physical superiority. This emphasis on the pleasures to be gained from the experience of climbing mountains became a regular feature of mountaineering texts, as what Hansen calls the 'tactile, visceral, physical' aesthetic of mountaineering came to be explicitly promulgated and defined.[88] The notion of physical pleasure was to play an increasingly central role in the way climbers wrote about and discussed their pastime, but the definition of just what constituted 'pleasure' would be extended to cover a much wider range of physical sensations than perhaps ever before.

We can illustrate the novelty of this sense of relish for the full range of experiences offered by climbing by comparing the articles published in the early volumes of *Peaks, Passes, and Glaciers*, from 1859, with its successor volume, the *Alpine Journal*, which began publication in 1863. Writing in the first volume of *Peaks, Passes, and Glaciers*, Wills admitted: 'You cannot – at least I never could – appreciate the picturesque while the teeth are chattering with cold and the inner man loudly proclaims its detestation of that which nature also abhors'.[89] In the same volume William Mathews noted that the summit of Mont Vélan, on the border between Italy and Switzerland,

> consists of a rather extensive flattened dome of snow; a circumstance greatly in its favour, as standing on a knife edge, holding on to an alpenstock thrust into the snow, is not, except with persons of very peculiar temperament, conducive to the enjoyment of fine scenery.[90]

Finally, the Reverend J. Llewelyn Davies, writing about the view from the Dom, noted:

> There is a particular charm in such a view, which secures every one who ascends a high mountain in fine weather from being disappointed; although, it must be admitted, he may have to set against his pleasure considerable fatigue, and what is more disagreeable, extreme cold.[91]

The contrast with the tone of later accounts is striking. Far from relishing the sensations of cold, danger, fatigue, and exposure to vertiginous positions, these writers present them as unpleasant but inevitable accompaniments to the pursuit of mountaineering, with no sense that they actually form part of the pleasure of the whole experience. Fatigue, for example, is described in terms analogous to those that Mosso might use – simply as an unavoidable effect of physical exertion. This attitude was not confined to contributors to *Peaks, Passes, and Glaciers*. Two years later, in 1861, the philosopher Francis Galton edited *Vacation Tourists and*

*Notes on Travel in 1860*, a compendium of travel writing. In the chapter on 'The Graian Alps and Mount Iseran', J.J. Cowell described the sensation of being benighted on a mountain path as 'very unpleasant, as one constantly knocks one's feet against the great stone that are sure to be sticking up, and one takes long steps where one ought to take short ones, and *vice versa*'. The path had been flooded at various points, with the consequence that

> for nearly an hour we went dabbling on over land and water, leaping the pools by help of our alpenstocks, and trusting to luck for a firm footing beyond; fortunately, I never fell down on any of these occasions, though my knapsack made me feel very top-heavy.[92]

Once again, we note the lack of any sense of physical pleasure or satisfaction: the tone is one of frustration, irritation, discomfort, of a traveller far from at ease in his situation and lacking confidence in his own physical skills. There is none of the exhilaration and delight that climbers begin to express a decade or so later.

From around 1870 onwards we can identify a change in the way writers on mountaineering present the incidental hazards and discomforts of their sport. Increasingly, they describe the chattering of teeth, fatigue, extreme cold, and precarious perches on knife-edge ridges with relish, satisfaction, and a kind of grim pleasure or black humour (see Fig. 4.2). Consider A.W. Moore, writing in the *Alpine Journal* in 1870 about a pioneering winter expedition to the Alps. His group had hoped to make a winter ascent of Mont Blanc but in the event had to be satisfied with reaching only one relatively small summit. 'This is therefore a narrative of failure,' Moore concedes, 'but of failure from which we derived more enjoyment than from many of our summer successes in past years'.[93] Later in the same article, he describes climbing about a thousand feet from a pass, during which ascent his group was frequently brought to a standstill

> by the smoothness of the slabs of rock beneath the snow, which was itself too powdery and incoherent to give footing. We lay basking in the sun until the wind, which seemed temporarily to have gone to sleep, woke up to the fact of our presence, and by a spiteful gust, which seemed to freeze the very blood in our veins, drove us down helter-skelter to a more sheltered position. Both in ascending and returning from the pass we had the satisfaction of going straight across the Dauben See, which was, of course, hard frozen with about five feet of snow on the ice.[94]

**Fig. 4.2** Grim pleasure and black humour: 'Serves Him Right', from the *Badminton* guide

This is something quite new. The description of struggling to stay upright on smooth, snow-covered rock; the primal, almost reptilian responsiveness of the blood to the stimuli of warm sunlight and cold wind; the satisfaction in traversing a frozen lake – these are sensations which it is hard to imagine a writer of any previous generation describing with such obvious relish. Yet this kind of writing quickly becomes the norm, and the relish is expanded to cover, for example, such incidental details as the unpleasant effects of high-altitude ultraviolet exposure on the climber's skin. Here is Edward Whymper in 1871 describing a group of British mountaineers in Zermatt:

> Their peeled, blistered, and swollen faces are worth studying. Some, by the exercise of watchfulness and unremitting care, have been fortunate enough to acquire a fine raw siena complexion. But most of them have not been so happy. They have been scorched on rocks, and roasted on glaciers. Their cheeks – first puffed, then cracked – have exuded a turpentine-like matter, which has coursed down their faces, and has dried in patches like the resin on the trunks of pines. They have removed it, and at the same time have pulled off large flakes of their skin [ ... ] Their lips are cracked; their cheeks are swollen; their eyes are blood-shot; their noses are peeled and indescribable. Such are the pleasures of the mountaineer![95]

Whymper was not being entirely ironic when he talked about 'pleasures' in this context. Many climbers regarded sunburn as a badge of honour, visible proof that the sufferer had indeed spent time above the snow line; it was this attitude that Ruskin alluded to when he depicted mountaineers as 'red with cutaneous eruption of conceit'.[96] Although subsequent writers would provide advice on preventing and treating severe sunburn, they also tended to present it not just as an occupational hazard of climbing, but a part of the complex of sensations that make up the full gamut of mountaineering experience.[97]

The suggestion that a degree of discomfort, whether from sunburn, cold, or physical exertion, was a tonic for the climber, allowing him to slough off the enervating effects of city life and attain a higher state of physical self-awareness and prowess, became common from around this time. Describing a climb on Mont Blanc, Stephen reported: 'the heavy, sodden framework of flesh and blood I languidly dragged along London streets has undergone a strange transformation, and it is with scarcely a conscious effort that I breast the monstrous hill which towers above me'.[98] The feelings being described here are not precisely those of physical pleasure in the normal sense of the word, yet the language has a degree of palpability and a relish in the details of the physical. Stephen's 'sodden framework of flesh and blood' sometimes remained weak and unsuited to the task of climbing, but even when the physical business of climbing was painful and exhausting it was described with an almost masochistic sense of relish. Girdlestone, writing around the same time, was similarly explicit about the weaknesses of the flesh that mountain excursions could expose, and described them with a similar degree of relish. On a short trip to get in training for a longer expedition he recalls:

> We soon raced up the mule-path to the summit of the Gemmi, and then, concealing our knapsacks among the rocks, made an excursion to the left up the Lämmeren Glacier, which descends from the Wildstrubel, so as to gain some notion of ice-work before attempting the Tschingel the next day. As we were none of us in training, some snow slopes which we ascended expanded our lungs and reduced our weight considerably; we had a few crevasses to jump and a few steps to cut; but our excursion was limited by speedily-increasing appetites, which compelled us at length to turn, and after regaining our sacs to hasten somewhat exhausted down to the little inn.[99]

Compare the quotations from Wills, Mathews, and Cowell just a few years earlier, and the contrast is striking. Writers increasingly recalled fear, exhaustion, and discomfort with a degree of satisfaction and pride. This tendency grew more marked as the century progressed – so much so that even Ruskin seemed to participate in the new delight in physical activity.[100] He describes in his autobiography, *Praeterita* (published between 1881 and 1886) descending the Montenvers by glissading – a kind of controlled but rapid slide down a snow or ice slope, checked by braking with an ice axe or alpenstock. 'We took Richard back to the first couloir', he recalls, referring to his friend from childhood, Richard Fall, 'showed him how to use foot and pole, to check himself if he went too fast, or got head-foremost; and we slid down the two thousand feet to the source of the Arveron, in some seven or eight minutes'.[101] Ruskin adds in a footnote that this estimate of the time taken to descend is 'including ecstatic or contemplative rests; of course one goes much faster than 200 feet a minute, on good snow, at an angle of 30 degrees'.[102] Even Ruskin, it seemed, could sometimes enjoy the sheer physical exhilaration of finding oneself moving at speed down a mountain slope.

Before long, even non-climbers were starting to remark on this new phenomenon of the physical pleasure that climbers took in their 'work'. In his memoir of living and working at the meteorological station on Ben Nevis, which had been established on the summit in 1883, William Kilgour recalled his impressions of one of the Easter meetings of the Scottish Mountaineering Club on the mountain in the mid-1890s. 'The misty cold weather which prevailed on the occasion, far from deterring, only added to the zest with which these mountaineers tackled their work', he noted. 'They did not seem to revel in the view from the summit so much as in the enjoyment of surmounting the difficulties of the tasks which they imposed on themselves'.[103] By this time, the approach that Kilgour identified was widespread, and much mountaineering literature seems to take particular satisfaction in physical discomfort. Here is Maylard, writing in 1891 about the delights of winter mountaineering in Scotland:

> What so bracing to the mountaineer as a keen, fresh, frosty breeze! What so inspiring as a rock face coated with snow and ice, that must be conquered somehow! Where such fun as when you see your companion struggling to extricate himself from a snowdrift into which he has sunk up to his waist![104]

This was the same article in which Maylard argued that the mountaineer was happiest when forced to 'hang on to a slippery rock by his fingers'.[105] Maylard continued:

> Instead of snow and ice to lightly and rapidly tread upon, we may find ourselves sinking into, and heavily toiling over, miry bogs, and a deluge of rain may replace the more seasonable snowstorm. But to the real climber, whose love centres primarily on the pleasures connected with physical exercise, these inclemencies will not detain him, and he will not miss reward.[106]

The assumption that the true climber was motivated primarily by the gratification to be gained from physical exertion would not have been widespread until this period. Nor would earlier generations of mountain travellers have been likely to share Naismith's enthusiasm for extreme mountain weather, expressed in his 1893 article on Scottish winter climbing:

> You find yourself in the midst of a howling tempest [ ... ] You can hardly see your companions, much less make them hear. With hair and clothes hard frozen, you stagger on with a 'list' to windward; crouching down at times

and holding on with your axe, when a more furious gust strikes you. 'Where does the pleasure come in?' somebody asks. *It is all pleasure!* If the nature of the ground allow the whole party to move together, the fight with the wind quickens the circulation, and puts you in a glow of exuberant health and high spirits. When at last, after doing your climb, you get out of the clouds and down to the road, you are as jolly as possible.[107]

Instead of the menacing, potentially deadly hazards that they had been considered in the past, the sensations of sinking into a snowdrift or being caught out in inclement weather were now being presented as invigorating and pleasurable. Writing in the *Cairngorm Club Journal* the following year, John Gordon was keen to refute those sceptics who failed to understand the pleasure to be gained from bad weather, exertion, and discomfort:

'This you call enjoyment', sneer some. Well, yes; to the healthy human mind there is a wild delight in meeting and fighting the unchained forces of nature – a pleasure in seeing the wind sculpture on the snow fields, and the growth of ice flowers.[108]

As Naismith's italicised exclamation suggests, these were component parts of the wider experience of mountain climbing. Many accounts from this period seem to have as their underlying project an attempt first to delineate the components of the pleasure of mountaineering, and then to consider them in the context of the whole mountain experience – textually breaking down the pleasures of climbing and then putting them back together again. So writing in the *Alpine Journal* in 1873, Clinton Dent was already sufficiently attuned to the physical pleasures of climbing to be able to differentiate between those gained from rock and snow climbing:

It is the diversity of obstacles that meet one in rock-climbing, the uncertainty as to what may turn up next, the doubt as to the possibility of finding the friendly crack and the apposite ledge on some huge tower of rock one has to storm, that constitute some of its main charms. Every step is different; every muscle is called into play as one is now flattened against the rough slabs, now abnormally stretched from one hold to another, or gathered into a heap like the conventional pictures of the ibex – and every step can be recalled afterwards with pleasure and amusement as the mountain is climbed over again in imagination.[109]

Dent concludes that rock climbing allows the amateur a greater degree of satisfaction than climbing on snow, in part because he 'can and must exercise his own powers, and not be wholly dependent on his guides. On snow the amateur is but an impediment, an extra burden, as has often been said, to the guides', whereas on the rock he can climb almost as an equal.[110] He writes of the 'huge satisfaction' to be gained from looking back at a rock ridge or cliff and feeling

> that it has been climbed with no other assistance than that which Nature provided herself; to feel, as it were, that one has successfully translated oneself over a stiff rock passage set by the female examiner (such things may yet be) Nature, without surreptitious aid from one's neighbour, in the shape of steps.[111]

However, returning to the topic of snow climbing in 1885, Dent now appears to believe that the superior level of skill and experience required on snow slopes enhances their satisfaction to the mountaineer:

> The accurate sense of touch in probing doubtful snow with the axe requires and deserves very much more practice than most people would imagine. The unpractised mountaineer may climb with more or less ease a difficult rock the first time he is brought face to face with it, but long and carefully acquired experience is necessary before a man can estimate with certainty the bearing power of a snow bridge with a single thrust of the axe.[112]

This attempt to break down the components of climbing pleasure would become increasingly common in mountaineering prose. James Bryce, radical politician and president of the Cairngorm Club, attempted an analysis of the varied elements that make up the pleasure of climbing in the first volume of the Club's journal in 1894. Bryce first suggests a pre-reflective form of satisfaction, in which, 'those who love the mountains, and have from childhood been wont to range over them, find their delight so natural and obvious that they hardly know how to discriminate the elements that make it up', but he then goes on to attempt just such a project.[113] Bryce lists love of exertion; the satisfaction of successfully surmounting difficulties; pleasure in exerting and testing one's skill; danger ('it may be wrong to enjoy danger, but one must confess that the enjoyment is intense while it lasts'); the love of scenery; and the ability to find solitude.[114] He suggests that the attraction of mountain scenery is fairly low down this list of priorities: 'Those who really enjoy scenery are still a minority even amongst mountaineers.'[115] Instead, the corporeal pleasures of exertion, exposure, and mastery of an array of skills predominate.

Maylard went still further in attempting to delineate the different elements that make up the pleasure and satisfaction of climbing. As a medical man, he used his specialist knowledge to write two articles for the *Scottish Mountaineering Club Journal*, published in 1897 and 1898, on 'Climbing considered in its physiological aspects'. His concerns were in some respects similar to those of Mosso and his fellow researchers – the physiology of the climbing body, and its performance at altitude or under severe physical exertion. But he also linked these matters directly to the question of how and why the mountaineer gains pleasure from the act of climbing.

In the first of the two articles, he outlines his view that 'it is in the structure of the human frame and its innumerable functions that we must seek for the reasons why, in the first place, we enjoy ourselves; and why, in the second, each of us individually does so more by indulging in one pastime than in another'.[116] He goes on to ask the basic question, 'Why does a man climb?' and concludes that a variety of motives might predispose someone to the hobby of mountain climbing:

> To some it is a horrible grind, as the expression usually goes, but then they say the more than reward rests in the after enjoyments connected immediately with the varied and changed conditions met with in high regions, and remotely with the improvement in general bodily health which results.[117]

For others, however,

> the pleasure itself is directly associated with the energy put forth. The mere physiological exercise involved in raising or lifting the body puts into action certain parts of our body that, had they the power to express an opinion, would say they liked it.[118]

A third group of climbers is motivated more by 'the overcoming of physical obstacles, the conquering of difficulties which call forth not only the pleasures connected with muscular exertion, but the faculties of discrimination, observation, and judgement associated with purely mental efforts'.[119]

In his second article, Maylard moves on to an investigation of the influence of climbing on the various organs of the body, suggesting both a local influence upon specific organs, as well as more intangible benefits from the environment in which climbing is carried out and from the act itself. Thus, in the case of eyesight, the climber is supposed to benefit from viewing varied effects of light, colour, and perspective. While this might be claimed of any outdoor activity, he argues that it is particularly pronounced in mountaineering. In addition to this supposedly scientific analysis of the visual pleasure to be gained from climbing, he also suggests a more abstract benefit. 'Is there any other pursuit', he asks, 'where the eye conveys to the brain impressions so keenly pleasurable, so completely enthralling, so abstracting that the mind can dwell on nothing in the past, nothing in the future, but all in the present'.[120] A similar combination of immediate physical and more abstract moral benefits are outlined for the ear, nose, and brain.

Maylard's article is eccentric in places and it is interesting less for any genuine medical or physiological insights than for the way it illustrates the preoccupation of mountaineers in this period with analyzing their own hobby. Like Bryce, he attempts to break the pleasure of mountaineering down into its constituent parts, but he starts from the assumption that climbing is an activity enjoyed in the round, with every organ of the body involved and with physical, psychological, and philosophical pleasures intermingled. This approach – of separating out the component elements of physical pleasure, enumerating them, and even allotting them a different importance in the overall mix of sensation – is consistent with the wider tendency towards classification, enumeration, and codification, but it also suggests an understanding of pleasure in which multiple physical experiences and sense impressions feed into each other to create the holistic experience of mountaineering. Such an approach might be said to have reached its apotheosis in Frederic Harrison's *My Alpine Jubilee*, the 1908 memoir in which Harrison, one of the founders of the Alpine Club, looks back at his mountaineering career. In an extended passage of descriptive prose, Harrison recalls in chronological order the varied delights of a day's Alpine mountaineering, from the moment when the party leaves their hut before sunrise to the point of reaching the summit. These snapshots of pleasurable moments include the following:

> The tramp in silence under the morning stars; the hush which precedes the dawn, and the glowing circles of sunlight round the distant peaks; the ring of the crisp ice in the early morn; the study of the path, and the halt merry with shouts and jests; the snatched meal, preposterous but delicious; the grappling with some mad ice-torrent, and the cunning path wound upwards through a chaos of séracs; the wild and fairy loveliness of cavern and chasm; then the upward strain across some blinding wall of snow; the crash of the

ice-axe and the whirr of the riven blocks; the clutch at the hewn step; the balanced tread along the jagged ridge; the spring at the last crag, and then the keen cheer from the summit.[121]

In his melding of the scenic and the sensual, Harrison typifies the way in which mountaineering writing attempted to create a unified picture of the sensory experience of climbing, while retaining a sense of the components that make up that experience. But many writers were also keen to emphasize that the pleasures of mountaineering were not limited to the time actually spent on the mountain.

## THE INADEQUACY OF LANGUAGE

Pleasure could potentially be gleaned from the whole range of mountain experience, from pre-planning before leaving home to the recollection of the trip once safely returned. Girdlestone, for instance, expanded on the pleasures of anticipation and of resting and luxuriating in the lowlands before a mountaineering expedition:

> There is a delicious luxury in such occupations, greatly enhanced by a not too obtrusive consciousness that a day or two will bring the hardest of work, the poorest of food and shelter, and the wildest and most savage solitude in nature. Mountaineers, indeed, often lose half their pleasures by plunging at once into desolation, without 'wasting', as they say, a day; measuring out their holiday in the most business-like manner, 'doing' rather than *enjoying* nature's noblest scenery.[122]

Tuckett, writing in the *Alpine Journal* in 1873, was equally eager to stress the satisfaction to be gained from recalling one's climbing experiences after the event. He wrote of carrying away

> no fleeting image of the scene, but a carefully composed picture, around which those numerous little incidents cling which suggest the 'I say, old fellow, do you remember how?' &c. in the long winter evenings, calling up a host of pleasant memories and details which – empty nothings to the uninitiated – are, to a quondam comrade, stamped with a Mint-mark that will always give them currency.[123]

These were the social rather than the strictly physical pleasures of mountaineering, but the two types of pleasure were not entirely separable.

Climbing offered both a social experience, in which mountaineers came together to recall and compare their experiences, and an intensely personal physical experience. The social pleasure was closely linked to the class element of climbing, but this second, personal experience presents an interesting paradox, in that it was widely written about yet often presented as something that could not be communicated to the non-climber. However, this is a more mediated version of pleasure than the immediate sensory gratification to be gained from the act of climbing itself. Mountaineers certainly did not dismiss these mediated pleasures, but they did tend to allocate them a less privileged status than direct physical experiences.

As we have seen, much of the writing about mountains in this period involved not so much a downgrading of the visual as a determined linking of the visual to the physical. So Moore's haptic sense of the smoothness of icy rocks and the chilling wind are supplemented by the sight of the ice and snow of the frozen Daubensee; Dent's stretching muscles and contact with rough slabs, and the feel of snow under the thrust of his ice-axe are complemented by the view back over the ridge that has just been climbed and the appearance of the peak still towering above; and Harrison's list of varied sensory impressions – the silence of dawn, the sound of ice, the crash of the axe, and the spring of the climber's step on to the summit – also includes the visual impressions of stars and sunlight and the 'blinding wall of snow' facing his party. This combination of the auditory, the haptic, and the visual is presented as allowing the mountaineer to create (or recreate) a 'carefully composed picture' in a way that visual impressions alone would be unable to.[124]

Yet this attempt to incorporate the visual and the physical in order to give a fuller impression of reality often seems doomed by the writer's implicit or explicit admission that the task is ultimately futile. For the other powerful impression given by much of the writing about mountain climbing in this period is that it involves the task of trying to convey by words something which cannot really be fully communicated to the non-climber. As we have seen, climbing prose frequently emphasized the essential incommunicability of the climbing experience, while the genre of climbing literature in the latter part of the nineteenth century increasingly tended to speak to the community of climbers rather than to the wider reading public. This sense of the inadequacy of words to convey mountain experiences accurately has partly to do with a sense that the nature of these experiences was either beyond language or perhaps pre-linguistic. Stephen was in the vanguard of this scepticism about the ability of language – or, for that matter, art – to convey the facts of mountain scenery. Writing in 1873, he suggested:

> My readers must kindly set their imaginations to work in aid of feeble language; for even the most eloquent language is but a poor substitute for a painter's brush, and a painter's brush lags far behind these grandest aspects of nature. *The easiest way of obtaining the impression is to follow in my steps.*[125]

The emphasis is mine. Stephen is asserting the indivisibility of experience, and the inadequacy of either language or visual images to recreate that experience. A couple of years later, Freshfield wrote about the 'limitations' of art or language in this context:

> To represent to others the glory of the mountain-tops requires, it is true, either a poet or one of the greatest and rarest landscape painters. But even if these fail, if the scenery of the high Alps proves altogether unpaintable and indescribable, it may yet be in the highest sense beautiful. The skill of the interpreter cannot be accepted as the measure of that which is to be interpreted, nor can the noble and delightful in nature be made subject to the limitations of art.[126]

Ashley Abraham made a similar point when writing about his experience of climbing on Skye. Writing in 1908, but looking back to the 80s and 90s, Abraham remarked that 'pen and ink' were relatively useful for describing 'hairbreadth escapes, critical situations, and physical discomfort', but were largely powerless

> to convey the thrill of exhilaration that comes to those who scramble along a serrated rock-ridge on which the hand- and foot-holds are abundant, and into the ascent of which excitement and peril only enter in a small degree. Similarly, powerless are they to convey the feeling of delight experienced in clinging to a steep rock-face in perfect safety, or to bring home to one the joys of being out amongst the bare gabbro rocks above the moor.[127]

Significantly, Abraham did not deny the power of language to reproduce the feeling of danger or discomfort, but rather pointed out its inadequacy to communicate the kinetic pleasures of movement and coordination, and the delight of one's own situation in the mountain landscape. His downgrading of the capacity of writing to reproduce this sort of experience is implicitly extended to all language, written or spoken, when he goes on to claim: 'To appreciate these things, it is necessary to penetrate into these sanctuaries – to be a rock-climber, in short'.[128]

As we have seen, scientific and other disciplines played an increasingly important role in the construction of the late nineteenth-century mountaineer's identity, but there is also a sense in which this idea of an almost pre-linguistic experience which can never be adequately conveyed by words, and thus is never subject to accurate analysis and classification, is being reflected in the writing we have examined here. Craufurd Grove, with his detailed list of the complex and interrelated skills required of the climber, or Dent, writing of the 'diversity of obstacles' which cause every muscle to be called into play, seem to be groping towards a conception of the climber's bodily unity that suggests it can only be experienced by the climber himself, and cannot really be written about – an ironic position, given the vast number of words written about mountaineering in this period.

Writing in 1908, Oppenheimer imagined a visitor to Wasdale being invited to come on a climb, and replying that he would like to, since, 'Merely as a lover of Wordsworth I should like to see the Pillar.' The reply is emphatic and unsentimental: 'Yes, but don't come in a Wordsworthian frame of mind: if your brain is preoccupied with that "something far more deeply interfused" you won't do your share of looking after the rope'.[129] The 'Wordsworthian frame of mind' was no longer a valid approach to experiencing mountains; instead the practical details of engaging with the mountains engaged the climber in a richer, more direct, and more holistic experience of mountains than that to which previous generations of writers had laid claim.

## Notes

1. Alan Hankinson, *The First Tigers: The Early History of Rock Climbing in the Lake District* (London: J. M. Dent, 1972), p. 157.
2. E.R.G., 'Reviews', *Climbers' Club Journal*, 3 (1900–01), 42–46 (p. 43).
3. E.R.G., 'Reviews', p. 43.
4. E.R.G. was not the only commentator who regarded Jones in this light. Walter Parry Haskett Smith was reported as saying that Jones 'studied his own physical powers as a chauffeur studies his car'. Cited in Hankinson, *The First Tigers*, p. 99.
5. Rabinbach, *Human Motor*, p. 3.

6. Rabinbach, *Human Motor*, p. 4.
7. Rabinbach, *Human Motor*, p. 48.
8. Charles Edward Mathews, 'The Recollections of a Mountaineer', in *Badminton Library of Sports and Pastimes: Mountaineering*, ed. by Clinton T. Dent (London: Longmans, Green, 1892), pp. 348–79 (p. 377).
9. Mathews, 'Recollections', p. 378.
10. Charles Pilkington, 'Climbing Without Guides', in *Badminton Library of Sports and Pastimes: Mountaineering* ed. by Clinton T. Dent (London: Longmans, Green, 1892), pp. 307–24 (p. 308).
11. Crampons had been used in the Austrian Tyrol by local climbers since around the 1880s, but it was not until the twentieth century that their use became widespread among British climbers. Eckenstein was a key figure in popularizing them, developing his own model and organising public crampon races in 1912: Ed Douglas, *Mountaineers: Great Tales of Bravery and Conquest* (London: Royal Geographical Society, 2011), p. 99.
12. Douglas, *Mountaineers*, p. 42.
13. See, for example, J. Oakley Maund, 'Mountain Misadventures', *Alpine Journal*, 7 (1874–76), 409–21.
14. G.G. Ramsay, 'Ascent of Suilven by the Grey Castle', *Scottish Mountaineering Club Journal*, 4 (1896–97), 23–34 (p. 32).
15. Clinton T. Dent, ed., 'Mountaineering and Health', in *Badminton Library of Sports and Pastimes: Mountaineering* (London: Longmans, Green, 1892), p. 85.
16. Sven Dierig, 'Engines for Experiment: Laboratory Revolution and Industrial Labour in the Nineteenth-Century City', *Osiris*, 2nd ser., 18, 'Science and the City' (2003), 116–34 (p. 117).
17. Parisi, 'Tactile Modernity', p. 191.
18. Robert G. Frank, 'The Telltale Heart: Physiological Instruments, Graphic Methods, and Clinical Hopes', in *The Investigative Enterprise: Experimental Physiology in the Nineteenth Century*, ed. by William Coleman and Frederic L. Holmes (Berkeley, Los Angeles, and London: University of California Press, 1988), pp. 211–90 (p. 213).
19. Angelo Mosso, *Fatigue*, trans. by Margaret and W.B. Drummond (London: Swan Sonnenschein, 1904), p. 76.
20. Rabinbach, *Human Motor*, p. 97.
21. Rick Rylance, *Victorian Psychology and British Culture, 1850–1880* (Oxford: Oxford University Press, 2000), p. 71.
22. W.J. O'Connor, *Founders of British Physiology: A Biographical Dictionary, 1820–1885* (Manchester and New York: Manchester University Press, 1988), p. 132.
23. O'Connor, *Founders*, p. 248; 'In Memoriam, Francis Maitland Balfour', *Alpine Journal*, 11 (1882–84), 101–03.

24. O'Connor, *Founders*, p. 227.
25. Mosso, *Fatigue*, p. 82.
26. Rabinbach, *Human Motor*, p. 125.
27. Mosso, *Fatigue*, p. 200.
28. France Daniele, Camillo di Giulio, and Charles M. Tipton, 'Angelo Mosso and Muscular Fatigue: 116 years After the First Congress of Physiologists', *Advances in Physical Education*, 30 (2006), 51–57 (p. 55).
29. Rabinbach, *Human Motor*, p. 146.
30. Crary, *Suspensions of Perception*, p. 169.
31. Frank, 'Telltale Heart', p. 247.
32. Parisi, 'Tactile Modernity', p. 208.
33. Martin Grunwald, *Human Haptic Perception: Basics and Applications* (Basel: Birkhäuser, 2008), p. 11.
34. Smith, *Climbing in the British Isles*, I, vii.
35. Tyndall, *Hours of Exercise*, p. 10.
36. T. Clifford Allbutt, 'On the Effect of Exercise Upon the Bodily Temperature', *Alpine Journal*, 5 (1870–72), 212–18 (p. 214).
37. Clinton T. Dent, *Above the Snow Line* (London: Longmans, Green, 1885), p. 326.
38. See, for example, R.L. Bowles, 'Sunburn', *Alpine Journal*, 14 (1888–89), 122–27; Dent, 'Mountaineering and Health', p. 82.
39. T. Clifford Allbutt, 'On the Health and Training of Mountaineers', *Alpine Journal*, 8 (1876–78), 30–40 (p. 39).
40. Dent, *Above the Snow Line*, p. 315.
41. See, for example, C.G. Monro, 'Mountain Sickness', *Alpine Journal*, 16 (1892–93), 446–55; Percy W. Thomas, 'Rocky Mountain Sickness', *Alpine Journal*, 17 (1894–95), 140–41.
42. George Wherry, *Alpine Notes and the Climbing Foot* (Cambridge: Macmillan & Bowes, 1896), p. 120. Wherry was an Alpine Club member and a surgeon at Addenbrooke's Hospital, Cambridge. The book was dismissed in a review in the *Cairngorm Club Journal*, the reviewer pointing out that any structural difference in feet was most likely due to a lifetime spent walking up steep slopes: 'Reviews', *Cairngorm Club Journal*, 2 (1896–99), p. 69.
43. Dent, *Above the Snow Line*, p. 264.
44. Ramsay, 'Prof. John Veitch', p. 181.
45. William Brown, 'The Coolins in '96', *Scottish Mountaineering Club Journal*, 4 (1896–97), 193–208 (p. 208).
46. Rabinbach, *Human Motor*, p. 4.
47. William James, *Principles of Psychology*, 2 vols (London: Macmillan, 1890), I, 5.
48. Parisi, 'Tactile Modernity', p. 199.

49. Alan Richardson, *British Romanticism and the Science of the Mind* (Cambridge: Cambridge University Press, 2001), p. 1.
50. Richardson, *British Romanticism*, p. 2.
51. Edwin Clarke and L.S. Jacyna, *Nineteenth-century Origins of Neuroscientific Concepts* (Berkeley, Los Angeles, and London: University of California Press, 1987), p. 306.
52. John Harrison, *Synaesthesia: The Strangest Thing* (Oxford: Oxford University Press, 2001), p. 26.
53. Crary, *Suspensions of Perception*, p. 43, emphasis in original.
54. Hilary Fraser, 'Foreword', in *Illustrations, Optics and Objects in Nineteenth-Century Literary and Visual Cultures*, ed. by Luisa Calè and Patrizia Di Bello (Basingstoke: Palgrave Macmillan, 2010), pp. ix–xv (p. ix).
55. Grant Allen, *Physiological Aesthetics* (London: Henry S. King, 1877), p. 2.
56. Allen, *Physiological Aesthetics*, p. 34.
57. Allen, *Physiological Aesthetics*, p. 34.
58. Tyndall, *Hours of Exercise*, p. 98.
59. Douglas Freshfield, 'The Dolomites of Val Rendena', *Alpine Journal*, 5 (1870–72), 249–59 (p. 249).
60. Ruskin, *Sesame and Lilies*, p. 53.
61. Conway, 'Dom from Domjoch', p. 106.
62. Conway, 'Dom from Domjoch', p. 108.
63. H.G. Willink, 'Snowdon at Christmas, 1878', *Alpine Journal*, 16 (1892–93), 33–42 (p. 37).
64. Willink, 'Snowdon at Christmas', p. 37.
65. Walter Pater, *The Renaissance: Studies in Art and Poetry*, ed. by Kenneth Clark (London: Collins/Fontana, 1961), p. 220.
66. Lene Østermark-Johansen, *Walter Pater and the Language of Sculpture* (London: Ashgate, 2011), p. 73.
67. Stephen, 'Peaks of Primiero', p. 389.
68. J. Stafford Anderson, 'The Dent Blanche from Zinal', *Alpine Journal*, 11 (1882–84), 158–72 (p. 159).
69. Østermark-Johansen, *Walter Pater*, p. 73.
70. Theodore Cornish, 'An Ascent of the Weisshorn from Zinal; and Some Notes on Winter Climbing', *Alpine Journal*, 15 (1890–91), 192–205 (p. 202).
71. Willink, 'Snowdon at Christmas', p. 38.
72. Fraser, 'Foreword', p. x.
73. Bernard Berenson, *The Florentine Painters of the Renaissance*, 3rd edn. (New York and London: G. P. Putnam and Sons, 1908), p. 3.
74. Berenson, *Florentine Painters*, p. 4.
75. Berenson, *Florentine Painters*, p. 5.

76. Tyndall, *Hours of Exercise*, p. 102.
77. Dent, *Above the Snow Line*, p. 114.
78. Aloïs Riegl, *Historical Grammar of the Visual Arts*, trans. by Jacqueline E. Jung (New York: Zone Books, 2004), p. 395.
79. Riegl, *Historical Grammar*, p. 187.
80. Riegl, *Historical Grammar*, p. 341.
81. Linda M. Shires, *Perspectives: Modes of Viewing and Knowing in Nineteenth-Century England* (Columbus, OH: Ohio State University Press, 2009), p. 4.
82. Shires, *Perspectives*, p. 5.
83. Fraser, 'Foreword', p. xiv.
84. Macfarlane, *Mountains of the Mind*, p. 73.
85. I.A. Richards, 'The Lure of High Mountaineering', in *Complementarities: Uncollected Essays*, ed. by John Paul Russo (Manchester: Carcanet New Press, 1977), pp. 235–45 (p. 236) (First publ. in *Atlantic Monthly*, January 1927, pp. 51–57).
86. Craufurd Grove, 'Comparative Skill', p. 89.
87. It should be recalled, though, that Craufurd Grove's purpose was to point out how difficult it was for the amateur mountaineer to emulate the skills of the professional guide, and his paper was partly intended as a rebuke to Girdlestone's claims that guides were often unnecessary. Guideless climbing was still controversial in 1870 – later in the century, mountaineers tended to be less modest about their own abilities.
88. Hansen, 'British Mountaineering', p. 219.
89. Alfred Wills, 'The Passage of the Fenêtre de Salena', *Peaks, Passes, and Glaciers*, 1 (1859), 1–38 (p. 31).
90. W. Mathews, 'The Mountains of Bagnes', *Peaks, Passes, and Glaciers*, 1 (1859), 76–125 (p. 82).
91. Rev. J. Llewelyn Davies, 'Ascent of One of the Mischabel-Hörner, Called the Dom', *Peaks, Passes, and Glaciers*, 1 (1859), 194–206 (p. 202).
92. J.J. Cowell, 'The Graian Alps and Mount Iseran', in *Vacation Tourists and Notes on Travel in 1860*, ed. by Francis Galton (London: Macmillan, 1861), pp. 239–63 (p. 241).
93. A.W. Moore, 'On Some Winter Expeditions to the Alps', *Alpine Journal*, 5 (1870–72), 62–76 (p. 63).
94. Moore, 'Winter Expeditions', p. 66.
95. Whymper, *Scrambles*, p. 262.
96. Ruskin, *Sesame and Lilies*, p. 53.
97. See, for example, Bowles, 'Sunburn'.
98. Leslie Stephen, 'Sunset on Mont Blanc', *Cornhill Magazine*, October 1873, pp. 457–67 (p. 460). Tyndall, writing two years earlier, had found the

mountain atmosphere took longer to have its effect: of a solo ascent undertaken 'for the sake of training', in which he struggled physically and mentally, Tyndall wrote, 'London was still in my brain, and the vice of Primrose Hill in my muscles': Tyndall, *Hours of Exercise*, p. 3.
99. Girdlestone, *High Alps*, p. 73.
100. See Colley's discussion of Ruskin's 'physical and kinetic relationship to the mountains': Colley, 'Ruskin', *Victorian Literature and Culture*, p. 43.
101. John Ruskin, *Praeterita*, ed. by Tim Hilton (London: Alfred A. Knopf, 2005), p. 390.
102. Ruskin, *Praeterita*, p. 390.
103. William T. Kilgour, *Observers at the Highest Meteorological Station in the British Isles* (Paisley: Alexander Gardner, 1905), p. 141.
104. Maylard, 'Winter Ascents', p. 223.
105. Maylard, 'Winter Ascents', p. 225.
106. Maylard, 'Winter Ascents', p. 226.
107. Naismith, 'Snowcraft in Scotland', p. 162, emphasis in original.
108. John Gordon, 'An Arctic Summer Day on Cairn Toul', *Cairngorm Club Journal*, 1 (1893–96), 157–63 (p. 163).
109. Clinton T. Dent, 'Rothhorn from Zermatt', *Alpine Journal*, 6 (1872–74), 268–74, (p. 269).
110. Dent, 'Rothhorn from Zermatt', p. 269.
111. Dent, 'Rothhorn from Zermatt', p. 269.
112. Dent, *Above the Snow Line*, p. 25.
113. James Bryce, 'Some Stray Thoughts on Mountaineering', *Cairngorm Club Journal*, 1 (1893–96), 1–6 (p. 1).
114. Bryce, 'Stray Thoughts', p. 4.
115. Bryce, 'Stray Thoughts', p. 3.
116. Alfred Ernest Maylard, 'Climbing Considered in Its Physiological Aspects', *Scottish Mountaineering Club Journal*, 4 (1896–97), Part 1, 267–75 (p. 267).
117. Maylard, 'Physiological Aspects', Part 1, p. 268.
118. Maylard, 'Physiological Aspects', Part 1, p. 268.
119. Maylard, 'Physiological Aspects', Part 1, p. 269.
120. Maylard, 'Physiological Aspects', Part 2, p. 18.
121. Frederic Harrison, *My Alpine Jubilee* (London: Smith, Elder, 1908), p. 122.
122. Girdlestone, *High Alps*, p. 59, emphasis in original.
123. F.F. Tuckett, 'The Col Vicentino, Bosco del Consiglio, and Monte Cavallo', *Alpine Journal*, 6 (1872–74), 124–44 (p. 126).
124. Tuckett, 'Col Vicentino', p. 126.
125. Stephen, 'Sunset on Mont Blanc', p. 464.

126. Douglas Freshfield, *Italian Alps: Sketches in the Mountains of Ticino, Lombardy, the Trentino, and Venetia* (1875; Oxford: Basil Blackwell, repr. 1937), p. 151.
127. Ashley Abraham, *Rock Climbing in Skye* (London: Longmans, Green, 1908), p. 6.
128. Abraham, *Rock Climbing*, p. 6.
129. Oppenheimer, *Heart of Lakeland*, p. 40.

CHAPTER 5

# The Haptic Sublime

## INTRODUCTION

The insistent emphasis on the quality of physical experience of mountaineering gave rise to a new mountain aesthetic that I would like to call the 'haptic sublime'. The sublime, so important to eighteenth and early nineteenth-century theories of aesthetics, might seem to have been banished from mountaineering discourse by this stage. Yet it stages a dramatic reappearance in the second half of the nineteenth century, reinvigorated and transformed by an infusion of physical exercise and hazardous contact with mountain landscapes, and by a heightened concern with materiality.

There is a certain irony in the fact that materiality and vigorous physicality were the very qualities most closely associated with the New Mountaineers, the breed of climbers accused by some commentators of being immune to mountain aesthetics. Many of the same writers who took positions on the New Mountaineer question also emphasized that the ability to estimate the true nature and magnitude of mountain features was at least partly contingent on the prior physical immersion of the viewer in that landscape. In many cases they presented that physical connection as directly responsible for creating a powerful, even transcendent emotional experience in the climber. For all that mountaineering writers rarely used the word 'sublime', I contend that a new version of the sublime is precisely what they were claiming to have experienced.

## A New Type of Subjectivity

Writing in 1900, the mountaineer and literary critic Ernest A. Baker described a new route up one of Scotland's most famous mountains. Baker, along with the renowned Lakeland climbers George and Ashley Abraham, had completed the first direct ascent of the Crowberry Ridge of the Buachaille Etive Mor, the great pyramid-shaped peak that dominates the entrances to Glencoe and Glen Etive. His article was for the most part a straightforward account of techniques and precise details of the route, typical of the style of writing about mountaineering that had become prevalent. At one point, however, he allowed himself a moment of reflection on his feelings during this and previous ascents:

> The vividest emotions of the rock-climber arise from the conflict between his rational perception of dangers overcome and eliminated, and the impression that these dangers inevitably make on the sub-consciousness; in climbing a broad and open precipice like the front of this ridge these emotions are at their keenest.[1]

The word 'sublime' does not appear anywhere in Baker's account of this climb, and it would have been uncharacteristic for a late nineteenth-century mountaineer to use the term. Yet what he describes nonetheless has a striking and rather surprising degree of continuity with the definitions of the sublime that had been developed during the eighteenth century, notably by Edmund Burke and Immanuel Kant. The idea of a powerful, even overwhelming emotion resulting from exposure to a spectacular and intimidating natural feature, a perceived threat that is overcome or survived and the resulting sense of mastery, and a lingering psychological tension between this sense of mastery and the overwhelming nature of sublime affect would all have been familiar to a reader of Kant.[2] The sublime – a concept whose antecedents stretch back to Titus Lucretius Carus in first century BC Rome and to the Greek Dionysius Longinus in the first century AD – had enjoyed a period of renewed vigour and interest in Europe after Nicolas Boileau's French translation of Longinus' *On the Sublime* (1674), and was a key element of eighteenth-century aesthetic theory.[3] Although it was far less frequently discussed by this era, the basic tenets of the concept were certainly familiar to late Victorians through the influence of Romantic literature.

As he continues, however, Baker describes his emotional state during the climb in terms that suggest something new:

> Here, with every part of the body, we have direct sensation of the vast space over which we are suspended; the infinite modulations of the sound of rushing water, giving perception of distances apart from sight, the touch of wind currents, glimpses of crags and of voyaging cloud-shadows far below through the depth of air, all enter the soul with an intensity the merely contemplative spectator cannot know.[4]

Baker's insistence on the climber's physical immersion in the environment and consequent heightened ability to perceive his surroundings 'with every part of the body' is perhaps the most explicit statement of an assumption that begins in the period under discussion. This notion that the climber's engagement with the material reality of mountains leads to a heightened, unique, and incommunicable experience was expressed in a variety of ways, and was made more or less explicitly by different mountaineering writers. But certain assumptions were made consistently enough that it can justifiably be described as a new aesthetic of mountain appreciation – one I will call the haptic sublime. This aesthetic developed in the period from around the end of the Alpine Golden Age to the end of the century, and was therefore taking shape at exactly the same time as the debates about the New Mountaineer.

The haptic sublime involves an encounter with mountain landscapes in which the human subject experiences close physical contact – sometimes painful and dangerous, sometimes exhilarating and satisfying, but always involving some kind of transcendent experience brought about through physical proximity to rock faces, ice walls, or snow slopes. Like the eighteenth-century sublime, it is to some degree an aesthetic of mastery, of overcoming a threat or difficulty. To this extent it represents continuity with the sublime of the previous century, and can be seen as continuing a particular type of human subjectivity into the late nineteenth century. Yet at the same time, its emphasis on the physical proximity of the human subject to the object of sublime experience and its insistence on the privileged status of the mountain climber – over and above that of Baker's 'merely contemplative observer' of mountain scenery – involve quite a new type of subjectivity. It also involves the presence of real danger, rather than the potential or imagined threat that had previously been associated with the sublime. This change is connected to the wider preoccupations of the period outlined in the previous chapter; in particular, to the growing interest in and understanding of the physiology of effort and fatigue, and to theories about the physical basis of aesthetic feelings and the physiology of the mind. Above all, perhaps, it is linked to the unprecedented phenomenon of human beings taking pleasure, or at least a kind of satisfaction, in physical effort, exhaustion, and deliberate exposure to discomfort and danger.

The phrase 'haptic sublime' was not used by the mountaineers themselves, and the word 'haptic' was not in widespread use until the late 1890s; it was coined by the philosopher and aesthetician Max Dessoir, and shortly afterwards used in the context of art history by Riegl in his *Late Roman Art Industry* (1901).[5] However, just as Norman Collie's coinage of the phrase 'New Mountaineer' in 1898 would give a name to a phenomenon that had been observed and described considerably earlier, Dessoir and Riegl were formalizing and naming a concept that had been widely discussed and theorized over the preceding decades.[6] Differing from the term 'tactile', which primarily refers to sensations involving skin contact, haptic refers to the wider system of hand-eye-body coordination and the related physical sense of proprioception that allows the individual to move around in the world and to make sense of it both visually and physically.

The Victorian mountaineers privileged this supposed ability to make sense of the mountain world through which they moved, and made ambitious claims for their superior quality of experience. They emphasized their own embodied understanding of the mountains, in contrast to that of the tourist or artist – the 'merely contemplative observer' – who viewed the mountains from a safe distance, eschewing the danger and discomfort of physical proximity and contact. This close proximity to the object of sublime experience is what above all distinguishes this new form of sublimity from its predecessors. From Lucretius, with his description in the second book of *De Rerum Natura* of the satisfactions of watching a storm-tossed sea from the shore or warfare from a safe distance,[7] through to Burke's dictum that terror 'produces delight when it does not press too close',[8] the sublime had always been experienced from a position of relative safety and security, in which the sublime object appeared threatening but did not present immediate physical danger. Mountaineering in its late nineteenth-century form changed that, by putting the human subject into close and potentially deadly contact with the sublime object.

This discourse of the sublime was haptic rather than tactile in that it involved the whole body, and it did not claim to replace visual with physical perception. Instead it assumed that the two types of perception were inextricably linked – that the quality of visual experience was heightened by physical experience. This claim was made explicitly and repeatedly by a number of mountaineering writers, most notably Stephen. It conflicted directly with Ruskin's position that the 'real beauty of the Alps' was available to any observer with the correct tools to perceive it, and with his earlier insistence in *Of Mountain Beauty* (1856) on the essentially visual nature of mountain beauty and at the same time on the important role of 'mystery' in mankind's relationship with mountains. As Ruskin put it: 'We never see anything clearly [ ... ] What we call seeing a thing clearly, is only seeing enough of it to *make out what it is*'.[9] Later in the same book, Ruskin argued: 'Our happiness as thinking beings must depend on our being content to accept only partial knowledge, even in those matters which chiefly concern us'.[10] This insistence on 'partial knowledge' would be challenged by the late-Victorian mountaineers, who claimed with varying degrees of explicitness that their knowledge of mountains was necessarily less partial and more complete than that of other observers.

Ruskin was dismissive of this notion that the mountaineer enjoyed some kind of special access to the essential nature of mountain landscapes. As Schama notes, Ruskin was of the opinion that 'climbing was the *least* likely activity to yield the truth of the matter'.[11] He believed that only through accurate vision can human beings accurately apprehend mountains, and that the only way to understand mountains was to look at them with an educated and discriminating eye. The requisite education was to be acquired not by physical exertion but by deep reading, immersion in the traditions of western art, and an understanding of the providential and moral purposes of landscape and nature. He believed that the person who truly appreciates and understands mountain scenery was not the climber who feels 'with every part of his body' the physical solidity of the mountain he is climbing, but rather the observer who can look long and hard at a mountain and recognize both its literal, objective reality and also its artistic truth and even its mythic qualities. The person who truly appreciated mountain landscapes was not the climber who struggled to the summit of a peak, but the sensitive observer who could examine a fragment of gneiss rock and recognize the way it was, as Ruskin put it, 'all touched and troubled, like waves by a summer breeze; rippled far more delicately than seas or lakes are rippled'.[12]

He was concerned with close observation of mountains and indeed with the precise details of geology, and in particular with mineralogy. But he was not simply calling for close observation or arguing that mountaineers should reinstate science as the motive for climbing. Ruskin was primarily concerned with careful viewing, whether from close up or from a distance, and with the need to banish subjectivity from one's experience of mountain landscapes. 'Mountains are the beginning and end of all natural scenery',[13] he wrote in the same book, and he proceeded to set out an aesthetic that expressly dissociated itself from the personal, physical experience of the mountaineer in favour of a more formal, impersonal – and to Ruskin's mind, deeper – understanding:

> The best image which the world can give of Paradise is in the slope of the meadows, orchards, and corn-fields on the side of a great Alp, with its purple rocks and eternal snows above; this excellence not being in any wise a matter referable to feeling, or individual preferences, but demonstrable by calm enumeration of the number of lovely colours on the rocks, the varied grouping of the trees, and quantity of noble incidents in stream, crag, or cloud, presented to the eye at any given moment.[14]

Ruskin's views on mountain aesthetics were concerned less with the question of distance or proximity than with attempting to delineate an understanding and appreciation of the landscape that moved beyond subjective personal experience. There was, for Ruskin, no question of what Baker would term 'direct sensation' felt 'with every part of the body' being available to the privileged mountaineer, or unavailable to the 'merely contemplative spectator'.[15]

This was his position in the mid-1850s and it remained broadly consistent throughout his career. However, fairly soon after climbing emerges as a leisure activity we begin to find descriptions of mountaineering that ignore or sideline Ruskin's doctrines and fit my definition of the haptic sublime. As early as 1864, for example, John Hill Burton noted in his book *The Cairngorm Mountains* how the scenery of the region 'does not tell what it is at a distance', and how the cliff face of 'Lochin-ye-gair' (presumably the mountain now known as Lochnagar) only assumes its true shape when viewed from up close. The cliff, he wrote,

> when viewed from many miles off, looks like a mere puckering in the folds of the mountain, and has been treated with a disrespect which has abruptly

vanished on sudden close acquaintance – as, for instance, when the bemisted wanderer sitting or standing unconsciously on its edge, the mist at his feet is suddenly blown away, revealing a vista twelve hundred feet down. Such an incident is apt to confirm Burke's theory that the sublime is made emphatic by a little of the terrible.[16]

Burton's remark exemplifies some of the assumptions which were to become widespread among mountaineers during the second half of the century, and which were in direct contrast to Ruskin's position: that direct physical experience and close proximity are the only reliable way to acquire accurate knowledge of, and in this case respect for, a particular geographical feature, with the strong implication that such proximity is to be gained only through a certain degree of personal physical risk. Like Baker writing nearly four decades later, Burton both reflects traditional notions of the sublime and articulates a new and qualitatively different version – the haptic sublime.

The writer's appeal to the authority of Burke's *Philosophical Enquiry into the Origin of Our Ideas of the Sublime and Beautiful* (1757) and his conformity to the definition of the sublime as being inspired by the terrible or the overpowering suggest Burton is writing in a tradition that runs from Burke and Kant through the Romantic writers. In this tradition, the sublime is a powerful subjective experience that comes upon one in a sudden, unexpected, and overwhelming rush of sensation. Although Kant locates the sublime in the perceiving human subject rather than in the perceived object, the invocation of great physical magnitude and the image of a mist-shrouded mountain are fairly typical of the kind of natural features traditionally considered appropriate objects for sublime experience in Romantic art and literature. Indeed, Burton's image of the 'bemisted wanderer' brings to mind such well-known Romantic images as Caspar David Friedrich's painting *The Wanderer Above the Sea of Fog* (1818) or Wordsworth in *The Prelude* looking down over a sea of mist from the summit of Snowdon.[17]

But Burton is also describing a qualitatively different sublime experience to the ones depicted by Wordsworth or Friedrich. Typically, the sublime as described in earlier accounts did not extend to the point of real physical danger; instead it operated where the human subject was sufficiently close to the natural object – be it waterfall, avalanche, or cliff face – to feel awe and a sense of threat, but not close enough to be truly endangered by it. As Burke put it in the *Philosophical Enquiry*:

> Whatever is fitted in any sort to excite the ideas of pain, and danger, that is to say, whatever is in any sort terrible, or is conversant about terrible objects, or operates in a manner analogous to terror, is a source of the *sublime*; that is, it is productive of the strongest emotion which the mind is capable of feeling.[18]

The key phrase here is '*ideas* of pain and danger': the Romantic sublime, like the Lucretian, involved exposure to a scene that brought to mind the possibility or threat of danger or of being overwhelmed, but which was sufficiently distant to pose no actual physical risk. Instead of the distant or imagined danger or threat which the sublime object was traditionally held to pose, the Lochnagar precipice described by Burton presents a real, tangible physical danger to the perceiving subject. Stumbling over it in the mist would almost certainly prove fatal, unlike the avalanche witnessed from a safe distance or the waterfall seen from a secure vantage point. Neither Friedrich's Wanderer nor Wordsworth were discovered on the edge of a real, named cliff that posed the danger of a real fall. By contrast, the Victorian mountaineer faced the possibility of real physical danger in specific, named locations. So Edward Whymper and his companions, shortly after crossing the Moming Glacier in Switzerland, sat down to rest, 'keeping our eyes on the towering pinnacles of ice under which we had passed; but which, now, were almost beneath us'.[19] What followed involved elements of the Romantic sublime, but with an added specificity and genuine physical threat:

> Without a preliminary warning sound, one of the largest – as high as the Monument at London Bridge – fell upon the slope below. The stately mass heeled over as if upon a hinge (holding together until it bent thirty degrees forwards), then it crushed out its base, and, rent into a thousand fragments, plunged vertically down upon the slope that we had crossed! Every atom of our track, that was in its course, was obliterated; all the new snow was swept away, and a broad sheet of smooth, glassy ice showed the resistless force with which it had fallen.[20]

Whymper describes the sublimity of this force in precise degrees of angle and in terms of familiar urban edifices. It is also unleashed in a specific, named location and on terrain that has very recently been crossed by the human subjects who witness it. Had it happened a short time earlier, it would have obliterated not only their tracks, but the climbers themselves.

The Victorian mountaineer's sublime, then, is something qualitatively new. It not only substitutes genuine peril for the slightly contrived sense of threat that the Burkean sublime, for example, had involved. It also places relentless emphasis on what Burton called 'close acquaintance' and Baker termed 'direct sensation' through 'every part of the body' – the physical contact or proximity of the perceiving subject to a sublime mountain object that is specific and tangible. It is this insistence on the physical contact with the mountain that above all distinguishes the haptic sublime from its precursors, and which helps give much of the literature of nineteenth-century mountaineering its tone of distinctive modernity. Between Burton in 1864 and Baker in 1900 we can trace a history of similar writing by mountaineers. While the sublime might seem to have been eroded in the New Mountaineer's approach to mountains, in fact it lingered on well into the late nineteenth century, transformed from its eighteenth-century antecedents into something different.

Here, for example, is Dent writing in 1873 about the satisfaction of having mastered and overcome the fear that is a component of sublime affect:

> It is a grand moment that just when the real difficulty of the expedition opens out; as you grasp the axe firmly, settle into the rope, and brace up the muscles for the effort of the hour. On a fine day, when your peak towers clear and bright above you, when you feel that at last you are on the point of deciding whether you shall achieve, or fail in achieving a long wished-for success, or what I may perhaps be allowed to call a cutting-out expedition: it is that moment which is probably the most pleasurable of the whole expedition; the excitement on getting near the top rather fades away than increases, and you clamber as calmly often on to the actual summit of a peak as on to the knifeboard of an omnibus.[21]

On one level, this is the characteristic tone of the New Mountaineer, concerned with vigorous physical exercise and excitement rather than with finer aesthetic feelings. On the other hand, Dent's description of the feeling of doubt followed by calm is also consistent with Kant's proposition in *The Critique of Judgement* (1790) that the sublime involves first of all a concern about obliteration, or the mind's inability to grasp the enormity before it, then a subsequent feeling of renewed confidence in one's own rational powers.[22] At the same time, Dent is describing a much more direct and present physical threat – not simply a threat to the faculty or reason, but to the integrity of the human body – and the satisfaction that follows is consequently felt physically as much as mentally.

Dent would return to this theme in 1885 when describing an unsuccessful attempt to climb the Aiguille du Dru, in the Mont Blanc massif. On the way down from this climb, the snow and ice had become dangerously soft, and melting ice above them caused stones to shoot down the gully his party was attempting to descend. Alarmed by this threat, the group made their way down the face of the mountain instead – a route that held its own dangers:

> Often, in travelling down, we were buried up to the waist in soft snow overlying rock slabs, of which we knew no more than that they were very smooth and inclined at a highly inconvenient angle. It was imperative for one only to move at a time, and the perpetual roping and unroping was most wearisome. In one place it was necessary to pay out 150 feet of rope between one position of comparative security and the one next below it, till the individual who was thus lowered looked like a bait at the end of a deep sea line. One step and the snow would crunch up in a wholesome manner and yield firm support. The next, and the leg plunged in as far as it could reach, while the submerged climber would, literally, struggle in vain to collect himself [...] Now another step and a layer of snow not more than a foot deep would slide off with a gentle hiss, exposing bare, black ice beneath, or treacherous loose stones.[23]

What was clearly a dangerous and unpleasant experience continued for much of the day as the group descended to the valley. Yet Dent then concludes his description of this episode with these words:

> It was not till late in the evening that we reached Chamouni; but it would have mattered nothing to us even had we been benighted, for we had seen all that we had wanted to see, and I would have staked my existence now on the possibility of ascending the peak.[24]

This is the haptic sublime in action. The human subject's sense of agency and power is reinforced rather than diminished by the experience of danger and physical suffering. He has been exposed not only to the idea or impression of peril, as in earlier versions of the sublime, but to real, specific danger that could have resulted in his death. Having survived it, he emerges with a renewed confidence in his own abilities.

Mummery, writing in 1892, gave a similar account of how a desperate and potentially dangerous physical struggle with a mountain could be followed by a sense of triumph, renewal, and power. His attempt to get to the top of the first of two linked summits of the Chamonix aiguilles, the Charmoz and Grepon, involved a series of uncomfortable and downright painful physical manoeuvres, including a difficult chimney where the climbers had to jam their backs against one wall and knees against the other in order to avoid falling. Mummery then describes how his companions

> were ruefully gazing at their torn and bleeding elbows, for it appears they had only succeeded in attaching themselves to the gully by clasping their hands in front of them, and then drawing them in towards their chests, thus wedging their elbows against the opposing walls.[25]

His account of this physically bruising ascent concludes as follows:

> Long hours of exertion urged to the utmost limit of the muscles, and the wild excitement of half-won but yet doubtful victory, are changed in an instant to a feeling of ease and security, so perfect that only the climber who has stretched himself in some sun-warmed, wind-sheltered nook, can realize the utter oblivion which lulls every suspicion of pain or care, and he learns that, however happiness may shun pursuit, it may, nevertheless, be sometimes surprised basking on the weird granite crags.[26]

Although he chose the word 'happiness', I suggest that what Mummery describes here is another example of the haptic sublime; intense physical struggle and 'wild excitement' followed by the 'ease and security' of the mind that has experienced and survived danger and finds itself 'surprised' by the resulting powerful feelings. Jones, discussing an 1893 attempt on the Dent Blanche in Switzerland, would later express much more succinctly this linkage of physical sensation to enhanced mental *and* physical power. 'The mountain was in a dangerous condition,' Jones recalled, 'and the last five hours on the way home we spent in wading, waist-deep, through soft snow. It was rather painful, of course, but there was a certain pleasure even in our pain, for it helped to make philosophers of us'.[27]

## The Return of the Sublime

On the face of it, it seems surprising that the sublime continued to retain any currency at all among the Victorian mountaineers, who were often presented as more interested in athleticism than aesthetics. As we have seen, the growth of mountaineering as a sport, and the influence of Albert Smith's Mont Blanc show and then the publications of the Alpine Club, had the general effect of moving away from sublime, Romantic, and scientific approaches to mountains towards an adventurous, sporting ethos. By the middle of the nineteenth century, direct references to sublime experience were much less common both in writing about mountains and in literature in general.[28] By the latter part of the century, as Reuben Ellis puts it, the prosaic details of 'frozen toes and compass bearings' were a more common topic of mountaineering prose than the 'sublimity of the eternal'.[29] The frequent references to the material culture of mountaineering and the often irreverent or facetious tone of accounts of mountain adventures seemed to undermine the sublime aesthetic.

Even when the word 'sublime' was used in the second half of the nineteenth century, it increasingly seemed to be in a way that had come adrift from its eighteenth-century definitions, often being used simply as a synonym for awesome or majestic. Thus as early as 1860 we find Tyndall remarking almost in passing about some boulders on Mont Blanc: 'When they fall their descent must be sublime'.[30] By 1893 Maylard was suggesting that the typical mountaineer climbed for a variety of motives:

> He climbs not only because he feels the exercise to be healthful and invigorating, but because he enjoys the exquisite freshness of the air, the varied sounds in nature around him, and, when on a summit, that sublime peace and stillness which gives such feelings of rest and repose.[31]

'Rest and repose' are sufficiently far removed from, for example, Burke or Kant's definition of the sublime to suggest that Maylard was using the word quite casually.[32]

Part of the difficulty in tracing the differences between the haptic sublime and its predecessor lies in the sheer heterogeneity of the concept. The meaning of the sublime continues to be contested to the present day. Andrew Ashfield and Peter de Bolla, writing against the tradition of teleological progress towards post-Kantian subjectivity represented by Samuel Monk,[33] suggest that three distinct shifts take place in the discourse of the sublime through the eighteenth century.[34] First, the sublime object – mountain, volcano, or waterfall – is presented as the source of sublime affect. Next, the sublime becomes identified with the perceiving subject, a position typically associated with, but by no means exclusive to Kant. Finally (although they are careful to avoid proposing a simple linear chronology for this change) Ashfield and de Bolla identify what they describe as increased 'attention to the discursive production of the sublime', which is newly focused on 'an investigation of the mechanism or technology by which one comes to know the sublime at all'.[35] This last approach has the effect of diminishing interest in the sublime object, and even to a certain extent in the perceiving subject, concentrating instead on the processes by which sublime affect is produced.

The Victorian mountaineers, then, were neither reacting against nor conforming to a single, stable tradition of the sublime, but rather were climbing (and, crucially, writing) with this very mixed legacy behind them. Furthermore, the sublime had been filtered through the sensibility of the Romantic poets and writers.[36] It is perhaps not so surprising, given this complex and fractured history, that late-Victorian climbers tended to use the word in a way that would have made little sense to an aesthetician of a century earlier.

Yet even if the term itself was no longer used with any precision or conviction by the Victorian mountaineers, their material practices and their manner of writing about their experiences were in fact responsible for a kind of rejuvenated and reinvented sublime – one more amenable to the values of the New Mountaineer. In this new version – the haptic sublime – the experience of sublimity is linked not simply to witnessing the 'visual objects of great dimensions' among Burke's categories of the sublime;[37] it is also linked to the perceiving subject's physical location on or within the natural object, which in the context of mountaineering typically meant the climbers' presence on rock face, ice slope, or mountain summit. This is not in itself contradictory to the Burkean sublime, since Burke's own definition extended to conceding that 'bodily pain, in all the modes and degrees of labour, pain, anguish, torment, is productive of the sublime'.[38] Nor does it directly conflict with Kant's subjectivist dictum that 'true sublimity must be sought only in the mind of the judging Subject, and not in the Object of nature that occasions this attitude'.[39] However, it does considerably extend the definition of how one experiences the sublime, adding to Burke's theory a new emphasis on physical proximity and the centrality not only of 'bodily pain' but all manner of corporeal experience. It certainly moves well beyond Kant's doctrine of the 'dynamic sublime' that the human subject can, 'provided our own position is secure',[40] gain satisfaction and even an enhanced sense of safety and self-possession in the face of the sublime object, since a considerable degree of physical *insecurity* was an inevitable component of the new approach. This new haptic sublime encompasses not only exhaustion, cold, and vertigo, but a whole range of other physical sensations.

Descriptions that fit the definition of this new form of the sublime appear in climbing narratives throughout the period in question. Freshfield recounted his 1873 ascent of the main face of the Pelmo, a peak in the Belluno Dolomites, in the following terms:

> This portion of the ascent of the Pelmo is, in my limited experience, one of the most impressive, and at the same time enjoyable, positions in which a climber can find himself [ ... ] The stones he dislodges, after two or three long bounds, disappear with a whirr into a sheer depth of seething mist, of which the final far-off crash reveals the immensity. The overhanging rocks above, the absence of any resting-place even for the eye below, do not allow him for a moment to forget that the crags to which he clings form part of one of the wildest precipices in Europe.[41]

Freshfield's vivid language here brings to mind conventional evocations of the Romantic sublime, and in one sense his description of this landscape as both impressive and enjoyable conforms fairly closely to Burke's definition of the sublime. However, what makes it a form of the haptic sublime is the mountaineer's insertion into the sublime object – on the face of a precipice – as well as his confidence in his own physical and mental powers to cope with this formidable natural feature:

> To walk for a mile or so along a ledge no broader than the sill which runs underneath the top story windows of a London square, for twice the height of St Paul's cross above the pavement, no shelf below wide enough to arrest your fall, must sound an alarming feat to anyone, except perhaps a professional burglar. And yet to a head naturally free from giddiness, and to nerves moderately hardened by mountain experiences, the full sense of the majesty of the situation need not be disturbed by physical fear.[42]

Even when forced to retreat back along this same route, Freshfield and his fellow mountaineers do so with 'the confidence of experience'.[43]

Not all expressions of the haptic sublime were as explicit as this, but climbers continued to betray a new sense of satisfaction in a wide range of physical experience, including danger, and an assumption that their fellow mountaineers felt the same way. So an unsigned 1877 account of an ascent of Monte Rosa by a new route concludes by recommending it 'to future climbers, who would enjoy magnificent views [ ... ] and do not mind rotten rocks, plenty of falling stones, and but little good handhold or footing during three and a half hours of steady work'.[44] An 1881 report of glacier exploration in New Zealand noted:

> We were very tired, as we had climbed for nearly seventeen hours, with heavy packs on our shoulders; our knuckles were all barked and the skin quite worn off the tips of our fingers from clutching the sharp rocks, as we had not time to select the smooth ones.[45]

The writer makes this comment virtually in passing, with no indication that this spoilt their enjoyment of the experience. The following decade saw Ellis Carr describe how, after a gruelling two days spent on a steep ice climb, including a cold bivouac forced upon his party,

> The intense feeling of relief on gaining, at 5.55 pm, safe and easy ground, where the lives of the party were not staked on every step, is difficult to describe, and was such as I had never experienced before. I think the others felt something like the same sensation. Fatigue, kept at bay so long as the stern necessity for caution lasted, seemed to come upon us in a rush, though tempered with the sense of freedom from care.[46]

A couple of years after Carr, Geoffrey Hastings published an account of a climb on Mont Blanc in the company of Mummery and Collie, during which the trio suffered considerable discomfort. Over the course of his article, Hastings recounts a bivouac on a narrow ledge:

> We took off our boots and stowed them away carefully under the overhanging rock, and wrung the water out of our stockings, and then put them on again. Our legs were soaked above the knees by the ice chips and snow.[47]

The following morning even the technical equipment carried by the group seemed to reflect the bodily suffering they had undergone, and both human body and inert climbing rope respond in similar fashion to the mountain environment:

> The rope, I have noticed after a night out, is in sympathy with one's bodily feelings: it is stiff, full of kinks, and swollen by the encrusted ice to twice its size, giving it an appearance that is most depressing. While we slowly plodded up the snow, so as to get on to the ice-ridge once more, the sun gradually thawed out our kinks and the kinks in the rope, and we were put into good heart.[48]

After further physical suffering, including an ascent through frozen ice blocks where 'our wet fingers froze to the ice when we touched it',[49] the group finally reached the summit: 'In what condition we reached it twere best not told; reach it we did. That final slope had been a weary task'.[50] Yet after this brutal experience, Hastings concludes by recommending the merits of the route to other climbers: 'It is a route which is very seldom done, and one that is wholly exceptional for the grandeur and beauty of the ice scenery, and the sustained interest which the climbing affords.'[51]

As the spread of dates and the range of writers quoted suggest, this was not simply an attitude confined to New Mountaineers; Freshfield and Dent, for example, were both critics of the 'gymnastics' and 'flashy athleticism' that they believed had tainted mountaineering.[52] The assumptions underlying the haptic sublime pervaded the culture of late-Victorian mountaineering, combining as they did the legacy of the Romantic sublime with the new emphasis on the physical and the material.

## Embodied Experience and 'Cold Stony Reality'

This emphasis on the sublime as something apprehended through direct physical experience was deeply influential among the Victorian mountaineers, but it was sometimes criticized as a kind of solipsism on their part. An unsigned review of an exhibition of sketches of the Caucasian mountains in an 1896 edition of the *Alpine Journal* gives an idea of how this criticism was expressed. The artist was Arthur David McCormick, who had already accompanied Conway on one of his Himalayan expeditions.[53] The review is interesting less for its comments on McCormick's work than for its ruminations on the aesthetic tastes of mountaineers in general and Alpine Club members in particular. Its author suggests that Alpinists can, when viewing mountain paintings and drawings, 'recognise and condemn unrealities [and] put an end to the muddled memories of Alpine scenery which used to pass muster with a public no better instructed than its painters'.[54] So far he seems to concur with the widely expressed view that the mountaineer has access to a more accurate picture of mountains than other observers. But the anonymous reviewer goes on to make this point:

> The artistic perceptions of the average Alpine Clubman are exceedingly limited. He looks on mountains primarily as climbs; he estimates views by quantity, by the miles he can sweep over with his 'circumambient eye', and cares only for the 'blue, unclouded weather' most favourable to his pursuit. His ideal is a photograph which shows the crack up which he wriggled, or the chimney in which he cut steps. He finds relief from the too oppressive grandeur of Nature by asserting his own place in the foreground, and that in attitudes which might make an angel, or any winged creature, weep.[55]

The human subject – in this case, the climber – is deliberately inserted into the foreground of the mountain scene. While the mountaineer may enjoy a privileged view, it is evidently not a view to be appreciated solely for its own merits. Instead, the mountain landscape has become the venue for human beings to perform feats of physical bravery, endurance, and athleticism, and the scene is interesting only insofar as these performances are inserted into it. The writer implies that mountaineers are retreating into solipsism, placing themselves in the foreground of the picture from entirely instrumental motives, rather than seeking the 'relief from the too oppressive grandeur of Nature', which Kant might have suggested could be found in the reassertion of one's own faculty of reason. The references to 'blue unclouded weather' and the 'circumambient eye' are clearly intended ironically, constituting an implicit criticism of this approach. The first is a quotation from Tennyson's *The Lady of Shallot* (1842).[56] The 'circumambient eye' alludes to Romantic writing: Byron's Childe Harold is 'lost in circumambient foam'[57] during a storm at sea, while Wordsworth in *The Prelude* refers to the 'circumambient world'.[58] To late-Victorian ears, these phrases would have had associations with Romantic poets in particular, and a poetic sensibility in general, and it is to this sensibility that the writer appeals in his criticism of the current mountaineering aesthetic.

The anonymous Alpine Club reviewer's comments are significant not simply in their contention that the typical Victorian mountaineer 'asserts his own place in the foreground', but also in the clause that he does so 'in attitudes which might make an angel, or any winged creature, weep'.[59] The human subject, it seems, can best be moved by the sublime when he himself is placed centrally within the sublime landscape, and preferably in a precarious and vertiginous posture. The haptic sublime thus involves an embodied experience of the world. In this sense, it represents both continuity and change: this new sublime does not necessarily demand danger, although danger is certainly present in many such situations, but it does require physical effort, bodily stamina, and a degree of appetite for risk, and it places the perceiving human subject not only intellectually at the centre of the experience but also physically in the foreground. This is something quite different from the 'technological sublime' which Jennifer Daryl Slack and John Macgregor Wise suggest had already emerged in this period, with its characteristic 'fear of being overwhelmed, attraction to the beauty of the perfection of the machine and its products, and most of all, reverence for the awesome power of the machine'.[60] Nor is it the same as what Colley suggests is the return of the sublime in the mid- to late-nineteenth century through photography. Colley argues that mountain photography, as practised by artistic exponents like Donkin and Elizabeth Le Blond, works 'to rescue the sublime from the damage inflicted by commerce, crowds and spectacles' in the newly commercialized and overcrowded Alps.[61] Both these phenomena, however, are quite different from the haptic sublime in that they lack the direct physical contact essential to the new aesthetic. Photography was certainly an increasingly important part of the material culture of mountaineering, and photos regularly appeared beside paintings in the Alpine Club's annual exhibitions. Reviewers in the *Alpine Journal* often noted approvingly that both photos and paintings, in proficient hands, could give non-climbers some idea of what mountaineers experienced. A review of a posthumous 1889 exhibition of Donkin's mountain photos at the Gainsborough Gallery on Bond Street suggested that it 'must have opened the eyes of many people to a new world', and that in the absence of an opportunity to visit the gallery 'most tourists can never form any accurate idea of the great, strange world above their heads'.[62] But viewing the mountain world through painting or photography was necessarily a mediated experience, and thus was considered anaemic and unsatisfying compared to the experience of the mountaineer. Part of what makes the haptic sublime distinct from earlier versions of the sublime is the unmediated nature of the mountaineer's experience and, as we will see later in this chapter, the notion of hard-won experience leading to an elevated or privileged view was very important in climbing literature.

Nor is the haptic sublime the same as the 'material sublime' that had been theorized in a variety of ways by Romantic writers. Like the wider concept of the sublime, the material sublime means different things to different writers, with Blake and Coleridge mostly using it in a pejorative sense to indicate what Steve Vine calls a 'defect of the imaginative faculty'.[63] Keats, who was probably the first to use the phrase, had a more positive interpretation, wishing in his 1818 poem 'To J. H. Reynolds Esq.' that the imagination would take its object 'from something of the material sublime', rather than either the dreamlike state that he describes earlier in the poem or alternatively the artificial creations of art.[64] Onno Oerlemans notes that for Keats, the material sublime 'is a recognition that the physical world has a reality – including a "core" characterized by predation and carnivorism – which lies quite apart from the world of beauty and pleasure toward which his art has been aspiring'.[65] Clearly this Keatsian definition of the material sublime has something in common with the insistence of late-Victorian mountaineering writers that they were uniquely attuned to the harsh reality of the mountain environment, through what Martin Conway described as their 'contact with cold stony reality'.[66]

But the material sublime involves an emphasis on the natural object itself and its effect upon the imagination of the beholder: that effect can be deleterious or enriching, but it ultimately involves a much greater emphasis on the natural object itself and its impact on the human imagination or power of creativity than on the human subject's actual physical contact with it. The haptic sublime, on the other hand, is by definition about the contact of human being with the materiality of nature. Louis Norman-Neruda's 1891 account of his ascent of Piz Bernina in the Swiss Alps illustrates the detailed attention that climbers paid to the relationship between the physical features of the mountain and their own physical responses:

> We stuck to the left side of the couloir but later on had several times to change from one side to the other, in order to avoid pieces of ice or hard snow the sun began to detach from the rocks at the top [...] We were in an altogether uncomfortable position and began to wish we could turn back; but it was too late, and, after considering the matter under the shelter of a friendly projecting rock, we came to the conclusion that we could do nothing but proceed. Proceed we did; but I assure you that, however calmly

we both behaved, and however successfully we dodged – sometimes by a few inches – the often large pieces of ice and the stones whizzing by, I, at least should have given more than a great deal for a pair of wings for each of us. However, by carefully looking out for corners where we should be comparatively sheltered, and sometimes, certainly, trusting to Providence – a practice I cordially disapprove of – we managed to reach the top of our couloir at 7.23, the height of which is scarcely less than one Eiffel Tower and a half. Thus we had been in the couloir for three hours and eight minutes.[67]

The reference to the Eiffel Tower, completed just two years earlier, strikes a note of characteristic modernity, as does the typically New Mountaineer concern with precise timings – Norman-Neruda goes on to list a series of exact times at which he and his companions reached specific points on the route. But what is most striking about his account is its close interest in the way he and his fellow climbers have to respond physically to the demands made on them by falling rocks and ice, and how they use the natural features of the mountain for protection and for a route upwards. Shortly afterwards the climbers were threatened by an electrical storm. 'Our ice-axes began to sing, and the irregular gusts of wind threatening to knock us over, compelled us to seek shelter on the Morteratsch side of the arête', he wrote. 'We found but scant accommodation; in fact, we had to tie ourselves to the rocks, so as not to be swept away by the ever-growing power of the storm'.[68] Once again we find the climbers in direct physical contact with the mountain and the elements – literally tied to the mountain, to prevent being blown away.

A year later, Willink – describing the same winter visit to Snowdonia quoted in Chap. 4 – was similarly specific about the effect of mountain weather on the climber's body. He combined a description of the hanging valley of Cwm Idwal that features many conventional attributes of the Romantic sublime with a succinct example of how knowledge about the 'meaning' of atmospheric conditions was based not just on sight but also on physical sensation:

> It was a wild scene. The great hollow of Cwm Idwal is boiling with ragged clouds, which come tearing up as the fancy seizes them, to sweep overhead, and then whirl down again to the Devil's Kitchen, whence they have come. There is a mysterious lurid light in the mist; and through the gaps you catch glimpses of Snowdon and his supporters – how changed from yesterday – pallid and grim now. You can see the snow whisked up into driving whirlwinds

along his ridges; and you know very well what those columns mean from the stinging of the icy particles against your face up here even under the lee of this big stone.[69]

These writers were clearly concerned not with the primacy of imagination but with the impact of the tangible on their embodied experience of nature. This is fundamentally different from the characteristic mode of responding to nature in Romantic literature.

## DANGER AND ITS REWARDS

Rather surprisingly, given the robust and undemonstrative image of the typical New Mountaineer, the experience of dizziness, terror, and being overwhelmed do seem to return in late nineteenth-century accounts of mountain climbing, in a form different from but comparable to the experience described by Romantic travellers. Some mountaineers were prepared to admit to experiences so overwhelming that they seemed not only to fall squarely into the category of the sublime, but also brought to mind Romantic accounts of transcendent emotional experiences. In these descriptions, vertigo and other distortions of the senses produce kinetic and haptic effects that turn the climbing body into the site for the production of sublime experience.

Girdlestone, for example, reported how, finding themselves in an exposed spot in the Alps, two of his climbing companions complained of giddiness:

> The scene was terribly wild, and it was no wonder that a couple of men out for the first time among the mountains should experience a certain trial of nerve on these gigantic precipices. There was one column towering above us on the left, nearly to the summit of the final peak, which produced a remarkable effect on Winkle, for though we were below and at some distance from it, he could not look up at it without giddiness.[70]

An inability to look at a natural object without feeling giddy seems more characteristic of earlier, Romantic accounts of sublime experience; Wordsworth's account in *The Prelude* of stealing a boat in childhood and being terrified by the wholly imaginary impression of a huge cliff rearing up and striding after him in pursuit is perhaps the most famous example.[71] This is surprising in a mountaineering text from the latter part of the nineteenth century, yet accounts of this kind of experience do continue. When Dent finally made it to the summit of the Dru in 1878, after the failed attempt quoted earlier, he recalled this sensation:

> I had tried so hard and so long to get up this little peak, that some reaction of mind was not improbable; but it took a turn which I had never before and have never since experienced in the slightest degree. For a second or two – it cannot have been longer – all the past seemed blotted out, all consciousness of self, all desire of life was lost, and I was seized with an impulse almost uncontrollable to throw myself down the vertical precipice which lay immediately at my feet. I know not now, though the feeling is still and always will be intensely vivid, how it was resisted, but at the sound of the voices below the faculties seemed to return each to its proper place, and with the restoration of the mental balance the momentary idea of violently overturning the physical balance vanished. What has happened to one may happen to others. It appeared to me quite different from what is known as mountain vertigo. In fact, I never moved at all from where I stood, and awoke, as it were, to find myself looking calmly down the identical place.[72]

He goes on to speculate that some unexplained tragedies might have been caused by similar impulses in other climbers. This seems an extraordinary admission, made all the more surprising because Dent confesses that he has previously omitted all mention of it when discussing his experience of this mountain. He is here describing an experience that is irrational, uncontrolled, and overwhelming, and which does not admit of easy comprehension; in short, an experience with all the hallmarks of the sublime, as well as of Romantic accounts of intense and even transcendent emotional experience. Like Wordsworth on Ullswater, Dent is dealing not with the known and understood dangers of a mountain summit, amenable to training, technical skill, and physical prowess, but with something closer to 'a dim and undetermined sense | Of unknown modes of being'.[73]

Ashley Abraham, one of Ernest Baker's climbing companions on the 1900 Crowberry Ridge ascent, gave the impression that this sensation had by the early twentieth century become a recognized phenomenon among climbers (rather as its cultural corollary, Stendhal Syndrome, would later become a recognized tendency among Florentine visitors). Describing the sheer drop from the Skye summit of Am Basteir, he notes:

> To lie on one's chest and look straight over the edge into Lota Corrie or Basteir Corrie will induce, in people whose 'heads' are not very good, all

those delightful thrills down the spine and sensations of wishing to throw themselves over which they say they feel when on a height.[74]

If his characterization of those who experience this sensation as lacking a good 'head' for heights suggests it may be considered a shortcoming, his next comment – on the physiological explanation for such experiences – equally suggests that the phenomenon is not amenable to simply being explained away by science. Noting that a medical friend had described the cause as 'temporary paralysis of the cerebellum' brought on by having no object near at hand to break the focus of the eye, Abraham comments wryly, 'May a remembrance of the reason prove a comfort when next these unpleasant feelings arise!'[75]

These kinds of anecdote, in which something approximating to the sublime seems to stage a reappearance in all its irrationality and overwhelming power, are reminiscent of Romantic mountain experiences yet are also distinct from them in the sense that the climbers are not simply viewing the mountain landscape but are physically immersed in it, perhaps even joined to it. Dent's vertigo takes place after he has completed a physically gruelling ascent of a peak that had already defeated him on an astonishing seventeen previous attempts.[76] Even the *Alpine Journal* reviewer of his book implied that the mountain had become an obsession for him by the time he finally reached the summit.[77] Girdlestone's companions are inexperienced, a condition that necessitates a process of education through what one writer would later describe as 'disappointment and fatigue'. Abraham's putative vertigo sufferer is lying on his chest on a ledge above a deep precipice. In each case, the terrifying sensation of dizziness and the momentary obliteration of self are aligned not simply with the vision of a sublime landscape but with a physical immersion in it.

In its most extreme form, of course, the obliteration involved in the haptic sublime would not be momentary but permanent. If the mountaineers had moved from a Burkean version of the sublime where danger was apparent but reassuringly distant, to a more physically engaged version in which real danger existed, the inevitable result was that accidents and deaths would occur. For the most part the mountaineers, and the wider public, treated these incidents as straightforward human tragedies. But in a few cases, we can discern an attitude to mountain deaths that invokes the sublime, at least implicitly. The popular public lecturer John Stoddard published his collected lectures in a number of volumes towards the end of the century, and in his 1897 volume he dealt with his travels in Switzerland.[78] While discussing the Matterhorn tragedy, Stoddard quoted without attribution the poem 'On a Grave at Grindelwald' by Frederic W. H. Myers.[79] The full poem reads as follows:

> Here let us leave him; for his shroud the snow,
> For funeral-lamps he has the planets seven,
> For a great sign the icy
> Stair shall go
> Between the heights to heaven.
>
> One moment stood he as the angels stand,
> High in the stainless eminence of air;
> The next, he was not, to his fatherland
> Translated unaware.[80]

The final stanza of the same poem is inscribed on a gravestone in Saint Olaf's churchyard in Wasdale Head, the Cumbrian valley that became the centre of climbing in the Lake District from the 1880s. The memorial is to three climbers, Henry Jupp, Algernon Garrett and Stanley Risdale, who died on Scafell in 1903, and the word 'eminence' has either been misspelled or deliberately altered to 'imminence' on the gravestone, but the wording is otherwise identical. The use of these lines to memorialize two separate climbing accidents, nearly forty years apart, suggests that the danger of death was not simply regarded as an occupational hazard of mountaineering, but also had an element of the sublime in it; the very real danger of physical annihilation seems to echo the more figurative annihilation of self implied in the Burkean sublime, while moving beyond it to a haptic sublime grounded in the physical reality of mountain dangers.[81]

If the dangers were greater, however, so were the corresponding rewards. The reward for Victorian mountaineers was, in one sense, not so far removed from that of the Kantian subject, who finds that the experience of the sublime first threatens and then diminishes him, but then bolsters his sense of autonomy and power as a rational human being with the ability to make sense of the world. For the climber, an encounter with the possibility of actual physical destruction was at first terrifying and sobering, but successfully negotiating such an experience and coming through it unscathed allowed him to take pleasure in a renewed sense of personal agency and confidence in his own powers.[82] One of the ways this manifested itself was in the confident assertion that the climber, uniquely among mountain observers, had the ability to accurately judge scale, magnitude, and detail.

## The Authority of Physical Contact

Throughout our period, climbers repeatedly claimed, with varying degrees of specificity and clarity, that perception in the mountains was contingent on physical experience. This new approach was connected to what Hevly terms 'the Authority of Adventurous Observation'.[83] From around the 1860s, writers on mountaineering began to extend the scientist-mountaineer's claim to authority to the non-scientific, sporting mountaineer, insisting with increased confidence that only the person who has engaged in a physical struggle to climb a mountain can look at its natural features and judge their scale with anything like total accuracy.

These writers commonly made three other related assertions: first, that mountain views were by their nature misleading to the uninitiated observer; second, that those individuals who did choose physical engagement with mountains, by scaling them, came back with a changed perspective, both in the visual and intellectual senses of the word; and third, it was impossible for the mountaineer thus changed to convey accurately the nature of this transformative experience to those who had not shared it. They also shared a less explicit but nonetheless common assumption: these experiences would be limited to male climbers. Just as science-based authority was implicitly assumed to be a male characteristic, so this new claim to the authority of physical experience was almost invariably assumed to be the preserve of men. The language of many of these accounts reflects this assumption, as does the marginalizing of women climbers discussed earlier.

These claims were repeated over roughly the same period that the discourse of the haptic sublime takes shape in Britain. Burton's comment on Lochnagar, quoted at the start of this chapter, that respect for the mountain's true physical nature only comes from 'close acquaintance', is an early example of this new approach. For Burton, as for many mountaineering writers after him, actual physical proximity was the only reliable way to acquire accurate knowledge of, and in this case respect for, a particular geographical feature.

A few years after Burton, Girdlestone published his account of travelling without guides, in which he set out his philosophy of mountaineering:

> Far beyond the mere pleasure in climbing is the ennobling and purifying effect of wandering amid the grandest scenery, far from man's abodes, practically alone, with thirty or forty feet of rope separating one from one's comrade, able, 'To hold / Converse with Nature's charms, and view her store's unrolled'. The feelings so gained it is impossible to communicate

to one who has never experienced them, and they are produced in many to a
far higher degree by the eternal snows and the weird forms of the Alps than
by any other kind of scenery.[84]

The quotation is from *Childe Harold's Pilgrimage*.[85] This allusion to a
Romantic poet, and the references to conversing with and viewing nature
(as opposed to engaging physically with it), suggest that the new preoccupation with the mountaineers' elevated quality of physical experience
had by no means fully displaced the subtly different emphasis of Romantic
writing about mountains by this stage. However, the emphasis on the
impossibility of explaining or demonstrating to non-climbers the privileged perspective that the mountaineer enjoys is clearly on display, as it is
again when Girdlestone claims that, 'it is impossible to describe, to one
who has not experienced it, the effect which the solemn boom of an
avalanche at night produces on a traveller in difficulties'.[86]

In 1871, a year after Girdlestone's book was published, John Tyndall
brought out his own climbing memoir, *Hours of Exercise in the Alps*,
which included an account by his companion F. Vaughan Hawkins of
their first attempt on the Matterhorn in 1860. Hawkins' description of the
view of Matterhorn at dusk contrasts sharply with his understanding of it
after close physical contact. 'The dark outline of the Matterhorn is just
visible against the sky', he records, 'and measuring with the eye the
distance subtended by the height we have to climb, it seems as if success
*must* be possible: so hard is it to imagine all the ups and downs which lie in
that short skyline'.[87] This turns out to be a naive and unrealistic view on
the part of the observer, in sharp contrast with the more experienced eye
of the same observer once the ascent has begun. 'Above us', he continues,
'rise the towers and pinnacles of the Matterhorn, certainly a tremendous
array. Actual contact immensely increases one's impression of this, the
hardest and strongest of all the mountain masses of the Alps'.[88]

'Actual contact' is the key phrase here; from around this date on, virtually
all mountaineering writers – whether New Mountaineers or otherwise –
emphasize the importance of actual physical contact with the material reality
of mountains. Note how, for example, Hawkins's account downgrades the
faculty of imagination in favour of experience, and of an understanding of
empirical fact that would have been impossible without that experience. In
some respects, this seems to echo the more negative definitions of the material
sublime, where a preoccupation with the material sidelines imagination. But
for Hawkins there is no suggestion that this is a shortcoming or a failure of the

individual imagination. On the contrary, it is the faculty of imagination that he depicts as unequal to the challenge of rigorously assessing the mountain landscape; instead, the climber's body, in 'actual contact' with the mountain, has become the more finely attuned instrument for making sense of that landscape. It was only through this physical contact, the mountaineers believed, that they could make palpable the quiddity of mountain scenery. The non-climber, who had not experienced 'actual contact', could only hope for an anaemic and partial experience of the mountains.

Perhaps the most explicit proponent of this attitude was Stephen, who devoted considerable space in his mountaineering prose to what Schama calls his 'confident belief that physical experience yielded the *truth* about the relative scale of mountains and men'.[89] He had begun to formulate this position as early as 1861, when he wrote: 'A man can no more feel the true mountain spirit without having been into the very heart and up to the tops of the mountains, than he can know what the sea is like by standing on the shore'.[90] He continued:

> It is just as easy to evolve the idea of a mountain-top out of the depths of your moral consciousness as that of a camel. The small patch of glistening white, which you are told is a snow-slope, looks very pretty out of the valley to any one, but it will look very different to a man who has only studied it through an opera glass, and to one who has had to cut his way up it step by step for hours together.[91]

This emphasis on the qualitative difference of experience between the mountaineer and the casual observer was to become a repeated theme of Stephen's, but it was in *The Playground of Europe* (1871) that he developed it at greatest length. In *The Playground*, he sets out in detail his thoughts on the shortcomings of standard quantification when it comes to assessing the true scale of mountain scenery and features, proposing instead what one would call today a phenomenological approach to mountain scenery – one where the notion of embodiment is central, and where the lived bodily contact of the mountaineer with the rock face or snow slope allowed the human subject to 'assign something like its true magnitude' to this physical feature.[92] He begins this section of the book by acknowledging that size and steepness are important features of mountain beauty as conventionally accepted. 'That a mountain is very big, and is faced by perpendicular walls of rock', he notes, 'is the first thing which strikes everybody, and is the whole essence and outcome of a vast quantity of poetical description'.[93]

For Stephen, however, these qualities of size and steepness are not self-evident, but need to be 'impressed upon the imagination' in order for their true magnitude to be appreciated:

> The mere dry statement that a mountain is so many feet in vertical height above the sea, and contains so many tons of granite, is nothing. Mont Blanc is about three miles high. What of that? Three miles is an hour's walk for a lady – an eighteen-penny cab-fare – the distance from Hyde Park Corner to the Bank – an express train could do it in three minutes, or a racehorse in five. It is a measure which we have learnt to despise, looking at it from a horizontal point of view; and accordingly most persons, on seeing the Alps for the first time, guess them to be higher, as measured in feet, than they really are.[94]

The only way to understand the magnitude of Mont Blanc, and to compare Mont Blanc accurately with, say, Snowdon, is to have climbed every step to the summit. Only this direct physical experience – as distinct from the visual experience gained by looking at the mountain from the valley of Chamonix – will allow the observer to gauge and implicitly understand Mont Blanc's size:

> Now the first merit of mountaineering is that it enables one to have what theologians would call an experimental faith in the size of mountains – to substitute a real living belief for a dead intellectual assent. It enables one, first, to assign something like its true magnitude to a rock or snow-slope; and secondly, to measure that magnitude in terms of muscular exertion instead of bare mathematical units.[95]

Stephen has borrowed the phrase 'experimental faith' from the eighteenth-century Methodist preacher John Wesley, who used it to describe the way in which religious faith could be reinforced and assured by direct personal experience: in other words, it represents a tangible and experiential rather than a theoretical experience of faith, in Wesley's case, or physical magnitude, in Stephen's.[96] He contends that the mountaineer,

> measures the size, not by the vague abstract term of so many thousand feet, but by the hours of labour, divided into minutes – each separately felt – of strenuous muscular exertion. The steepness is not expressed by degrees, but by the memory of the sensation produced when a snow-slope seems to be rising up and smiting you in the face; when, far away from all human help, you are clinging like a fly to the slippery side of a mighty pinnacle in mid-air.[97]

To illustrate this profound difference between the mountaineer's experience of mountains and that of the tourist or other casual observer, he takes the example of a 'round white bank' visible between two mountains, the Eiger and the Mönch. The ordinary tourists who spot it from their hotel, Stephen suggests, see an inaccurate and attenuated representation of this feature:

> They may see its graceful curve, the long straight lines that are ruled in delicate shading down its sides, and the contrast of the blinding white snow with the dark blue sky above; but they will probably guess it to be a mere bank – a snowdrift, perhaps, which has been piled by the last storm.[98]

The mountaineer knows that it is in fact a huge snow-covered rib of rock at a steep angle, somewhere between 500 and 1,000 feet in height, but this knowledge might easily be shared by, for example, an engineer surveying the range or an artist observing the mountains from the valley. The mountaineer, however, has further sources of knowledge unavailable to these two imagined observers, and can thus understand the true significance of this natural feature. The mountaineer

> can translate the 500 or 1,000 feet of snow-slope into a more tangible unit of measurement. To him, perhaps, they recall the memory of a toilsome ascent, the sun beating on his head for five or six hours, the snow returning the glare with still more parching effect.[99]

Only with the memory of such haptic sensations can the observer fully understand or 'decipher' the landscape, and he is adamant that those who have not been through this experience will necessarily remain relatively ignorant: 'I am certain that no-one can decipher the natural writing on the face of a snow-slope or a precipice who has not wandered amongst their recesses, and learnt by slow experience what is indicated by marks which an ignorant observer would scarcely notice'.[100]

Stephen is proposing here that the body can be regarded as an instrument of measurement and a source of knowledge more precise and more attuned to its environment than the human eye alone. Like Girdlestone and Burton, he is claiming that the mountaineer has access to a more intense and rarefied quality of experience: 'These glories, in which the mountain spirit reveals himself to his true worshippers, are only to be gained by the appropriate service of climbing [ … ] And without seeing them, I maintain that no man has really seen the Alps'.[101]

It is worth noting that Stephen is not downgrading or dismissing the sense of sight in favour of touch, but is instead insisting on its *embodiment* in the perceiving human subject. His stress on the climbing body as a unified, holistic instrument of measurement rejects any notion of a split between the visual and the corporeal. In some respects, this insistence on embodied vision seems to correspond to the shift Crary identifies as taking place a few decades earlier, in the period roughly 1810–1840, in which a variety of scientific and cultural developments 'grounded the truth of vision in the density and materiality of the body'.[102] However, where Crary argues that one consequence of this shift was to make the functioning of vision 'dependent on the complex and contingent physiological makeup of the observer, rendering vision faulty, unreliable, and, it was sometimes argued, arbitrary',[103] Stephen is proposing almost the precise opposite – that grounding the faculty of vision in the wider physical experience of the climbing body rendered it more precise, less prone to error and confusion, more able to translate an abstract measurement of distance into 'a tangible unit of measurement'.[104]

He is not contending that the quality of physical experience is superior to that of the purely visual. He is suggesting that the appreciation of the view – the ability to comprehend the scale and significance of mountain landscapes – is actually dependent not just on the power of sight but also on the experience of movement and touch. In other words, he is not just proposing a shift from a visual aesthetic to a valorizing of the physical. Instead, he is suggesting that the proper appreciation of the visual can only be achieved through the physical; through the experience of muscular effort, pain, fatigue, cold, and possibly danger. Just as Hawkins's 'actual contact' was necessary to understand the physical reality of the Matterhorn, and as the sensation of ice particles stinging his face would later allow Willink to interpret the columns of snow on the Snowdon ridges, so the 'appropriate service' of climbing is required for Stephen's observer accurately to interpret visual signals. This has clear parallels with Crary's proposition that the rise of physiological optics and the emergence of an embodied observer in the nineteenth century had by this stage made it clear that 'perception was not a matter of a relatively passive *reception* of an image' but rather that the 'makeup and capacities of an observer' had a role to play in what was perceived.[105] As we saw in the previous chapter, this also sprang from the wider intellectual, medical, and scientific culture of mid- to late-Victorian Britain.

## Learning from 'Disappointment and Fatigue'

*The Playground of Europe* sets out clearly and in detail the propositions that accurate perception depends on physical experience; that mountain landscape is prone to fool the inexperienced eye; and in Stephen's concluding remarks to this section, that the mountaineer is changed by his physical encounter with the landscape in ways that will remain incommunicable to the non-climber:

> I say that the qualities which strike every sensitive observer are impressed upon the mountaineer with tenfold force and intensity. If he is as accessible to poetical influences as his neighbours – and I don't know why he should be less so – he has opened new avenues of access between the scenery and his mind. He has learnt a language which is only partially revealed to ordinary men.[106]

He thus presents the mountaineer's experience as more intense, more personal, and more subjective than that of the mere spectator, and the difference between the two experiences results from differing levels of physical engagement. Yet at the same time as he proposes this intense subjectivity, his emphasis on accurate measurement – on the 'true magnitude' of a mountain feature, the 'force and intensity' of the climber's understanding of it – seems, paradoxically, to claim a degree of *objective* knowledge denied to less physically active mountain observers. There is a constant tension in his writing between the dismissal of 'bare mathematical units' inherent in his privileging of the mountaineer's subjective experience and his insistence that the mountaineer can translate or decipher measurements made in feet and inches into 'a more tangible unit of measurement'. Stephen's mountaineer responds to nature not just subjectively but also by registering accurate, measurable sense impressions.

This kind of claim did not go unchallenged. Ruskin, who had set out his own position on mountain aesthetics back in the 1850s and had explicitly challenged the ethos of mountaineering in the mid-1860s with his comments about 'soaped poles in bear gardens', returned to the fray in 1874 with a furious rebuttal of Stephen's thesis. Ruskin was ostensibly responding not to *The Playground* but to Stephen's review in the *Alpine Journal* of Edward Whymper's best-selling memoir *Scrambles Amongst the Alps* (1871), in which he claimed, 'If the Alpine Club has done nothing else, it has taught us for the first time to really see mountains'.[107]

It was this claim Ruskin aimed to refute by sarcastically reassuring Stephen and his fellow Alpine Club members that mountains had been seen 'by several people before the nineteenth century', including Hesiod, Pindar, Virgil, and Scott. However, in his next paragraph he seemed to be responding directly to the argument in *The Playground* that without having undertaken the 'appropriate service of climbing [ . . . ] no man has really seen the Alps'.[108] For Ruskin, this was precisely the opposite of the truth. 'Believe me, gentlemen', he thundered, 'your power of seeing mountains cannot be developed either by your vanity, your curiosity, or your love of muscular exercise. It depends on the instrument of sight itself, and of the soul that uses it'.[109]

As his insistence on the development and correct use of the 'instrument of sight' indicates, Ruskin believed in the centrality of vision. For Ruskin the only proper way to view a mountain was with an eye educated not by its embodiment in a climbing body that had experienced the cold, vertigo, and exhaustion of a high Alpine ascent, but by its owner's sensitivity and humility in recognizing that human beings must be content with a partial view of any scene. As Roger Cardinal notes, using the example of Ruskin's own drawings, his aesthetic was one 'which thrives on fragmentariness and delivers a lesson or a pleasure though pregnant ellipsis'.[110] Such an aesthetic was never going to be amenable to the claims of the Victorian mountaineers to completeness and superiority.[111]

For all his immense influence as an art critic and cultural commentator, it seems clear that Ruskin had little or no effect on the actual praxis of engagement with mountains in the period under discussion. His most important single statement of mountain aesthetics, the fourth volume of *Modern Painters*, had been published in 1856, before the new ethos in mountaineering emerged, and those Victorian mountaineers who wrote about their sport in the latter part of the century mention him surprisingly rarely. A survey of the various club journals of the period, from *Peaks, Passes, and Glaciers* through to the *Climbers' Club Journal* at the end of the century throws up only occasional mentions of him. When mountaineers do discuss him in print, it is often to contradict his dictum that the real beauty of the Alps was available to 'the old man, the woman or the cripple'.[112] Despite Ruskin's apparent ubiquity and the respect he commanded in artistic circles, his influence on the Victorian mountaineers seems to have been relatively marginal; for the most part, the assumptions that Stephen set out in *The Playground* seem to have been widely shared by subsequent mountaineering writers.

These assumptions may not have been repeated with the same degree of clarity or insistence but they are clearly discernible in many later accounts of climbing. In particular, the notion that only physical experience could guarantee visual accuracy became an article of faith for mountaineering writers. Donkin (who, as a mountain photographer, might have been expected to emphasize the faculty of sight) commented in 1882 on what he regarded as the general inaccuracy and exaggeration of Alpine art. He claimed that 'if we look at the list of celebrated Alpine artists we find that those who best combine accuracy of form with beauty of colouring unite also with these the crowning virtue of being good climbers as well',[113] and significantly he used a physical rather than a visual analogy to explain why so much inaccurate art was produced by non-climbers:

> This tendency to exaggeration is only natural; did we not estimate the steepness of our first snow-slope as being much greater than the reality, and feel decidedly hurt when a scientific companion with a clinometer declared it was only forty degrees, though we thought it nearly perpendicular?[114]

Willink similarly claimed that the climber had an advantage when it came to producing mountain art: 'In the first place he has, in the exercise of his profession, a practical acquaintance with what he is drawing, which ought to save him from many ludicrous errors'.[115] Like Donkin, he used physical rather than visual examples to support this claim:

> A climber knows from experience that, by nature, rocks are hard and snow soft: also that rocks protrude through, or are partially covered by snow, and do not rest upon it. He is more or less acquainted with the habits of a glacier, and knows, at any rate, that it is a plastic mass, travelling slowly down an inclined trough, taking (like snow) its general shape from the configuration of the ground beneath. Couloirs and crevasses, séracs and moraines, are his beloved friends, and are not likely to stray into wrong parts of his paper. In a word, he knows what he is about. Again, it is no small gain that he can, and habitually does, get into places from which he sees his mountain upon more equal terms, and more as it really is.[116]

Such assumptions were by no means limited to discussions of mountain art. Mummery, too, seemed to take it for granted that the climber's impressions of mountain features would be as much physical as visual, as in this telling passage where he records his sensations on the Grepon, shortly after his ascent of the Charmoz: 'It was certainly one of the most forbidding rocks I have ever set eyes on. Unlike the rest of the peak, it was smooth to the touch, and its square-cut edges offered no hold or grip of any sort'.[117] Here an ostensibly visual experience – having set eyes on a mountain feature – is actually transformed into something tactile, and arguably even haptic. While the touch of the rock is a tactile sensation, its failure to afford any grip means that the climber's ability to move up it is frustrated.

In these accounts, purely visual evidence is unreliable until supplemented by direct physical confirmation. Mountaineers were increasingly prone to imply that the experiences that constituted human consciousness in their own field of expertise were primarily embodied, physical experiences, gained through the act of climbing. What Parisi calls the 'distinctively modern formation' of the haptic, with its new understanding of the importance of the physical in the constitution of experience and consciousness, lent support to the Victorian climbers' insistence that the visual alone was unreliable until supplemented by the evidence of physical experience.[118]

Dent, too, argued that the inexperienced climber 'will find it difficult at first, even with the map spread before him, to understand the broad features of the scene he is gazing at' until he has sufficient experience of moving through the scene to put each feature in perspective:

> It is not enough to identify landmarks such as an ice-fall or a huge buttress of rock. Their position and relation to other landmarks have to be grasped, so that any point may be recognised when looked at from an altered distant point of view, or, still more difficult, recognised when actually reached.[119]

Only contact and practice, hard-won experience and physical effort could generate the ability to do this. The ideal mountaineer would have an acute sense of proportion, in the literal sense of the phrase: 'Constant practice alone gives the mountaineer the ability to appreciate minutely the scale of the surrounding scenery, a matter of no slight difficulty [ ... ] and an acute sense of proportion in this respect is indeed a rare gift'.[120]

Writing in 1895, Conway illustrated how deeply Stephen's assumptions had become ingrained in the culture of mountaineering by the end of the century. 'It is a well-recognised fact that the size of mountains can only be appreciated by an experienced eye', declared Conway:

Newcomers to the hills always under-estimate, sometimes absurdly under-estimate, magnitudes and distances. It is only when a man has climbed peaks, and learned by close inspection the actual dimensions of such details as bergschrunds, couloirs, cornices, and the like, that he is enabled to see them from afar off for what they are. The beginner has to learn size by disappointment and fatigue.[121]

This kind of claim for the elevated level of access enjoyed by mountaineers would continue to be made well into the twentieth century.[122] It also reflected a degree of anxiety and insecurity on the part of mountaineers, as the growth of tourism threatened to undermine this privileged quality of experience by allowing tourists access to the mountains without the need for 'disappointment and fatigue'.

## Notes

1. Ernest A. Baker, 'Buachaille Etive Mor and the Crowberry Ridge', *Climbers' Club Journal*, 3 (1900–01), 3–16 (p. 13).
2. Samuel H. Monk, *The Sublime: A Study of Critical Theories in Eighteenth-Century England* (Ann Arbor: University of Michigan Press, 1960), p. 7.
3. Timothy Costelloe, *The Sublime: From Antiquity to the Present* (Cambridge: Cambridge University Press, 2012), p. 5.
4. Baker, 'Buachaille Etive Mor', p. 13.
5. Mark Paterson, *The Senses of Touch: Haptics, Affects and Technologies* (Oxford and New York: Berg, 2007), p. 85; Grunwald, *Haptic Perception*, p. 22; Aloïs Riegl, *Late Roman Art Industry*, trans. by Rolfe Winke (Rome: Giorgio Bretschneider, 1985), p. 25.
6. In Dessoir's case, the term has even older origins, since he was using it to discuss work carried out by Weber in the 1820s: see Parisi, 'Tactile Modernity', p. 191.
7. Lucretius, *De Rerum Natura*, trans. by W.H.D. Rouse, Loeb Classical Library, 3rd edn. (London: Heinemann; Cambridge, MA: Harvard University Press, 1937), p. 85.
8. Edmund Burke, *A Philosophical Enquiry into the Origin of Our Ideas of the Sublime and Beautiful*, ed. by Adam Phillips (1757; Oxford: Oxford University Press, 1990), p. 42.
9. Ruskin, *Modern Painters*, IV, 55, emphasis in original.
10. Ruskin, *Modern Painters*, IV, 65.
11. Schama, *Landscape and Memory*, p. 509, emphasis in original.
12. Ruskin, *Modern Painters*, IV, 113.
13. Ruskin, *Modern Painters*, IV, 335.

14. Ruskin, *Modern Painters*, IV, 337.
15. Baker, 'Buachaille Etive Mor', p. 13.
16. John Hill Burton, *The Cairngorm Mountains* (Edinburgh: William Blackwood, 1864), p. 18.
17. Wordsworth, *Prelude*, XIII. 42–51, pp. 489–536.
18. Burke, *Philosophical Enquiry*, p. 36, emphasis in original.
19. Whymper, *Scrambles*, p. 258.
20. Whymper, *Scrambles*, p. 258.
21. Dent, 'Rothhorn from Zermatt', p. 271
22. Immanuel Kant, *The Critique of Judgement* (Oxford: Clarendon Press, 1952), p. 106.
23. Dent, *Above the Snow Line*, p. 194.
24. Dent, *Above the Snow Line*, p. 195.
25. Mummery, 'Charmoz and de Grepon', p. 163.
26. Mummery, 'Charmoz and de Grepon', p. 164.
27. Jones, *Rock Climbing*, p. xviii.
28. Google Labs N-gram viewer, for example, records a steady decline in usage of the word 'sublime' in English books from around 1850: http://books.google.com/ngrams
29. Ellis, *Vertical Margins*, p. 12.
30. Tyndall, *Glaciers of the Alps*, p. 67.
31. A. Ernest Maylard, 'Ben Lomond', *Scottish Mountaineering Club Journal*, 3 (1894–95), 140–50 (p. 141).
32. Kant, for example, had been careful to distinguish between what he called the '*restful* contemplation' of the mind when apprehending beauty and the way in which 'the mind feels itself *set in motion*' when faced with sublime nature: Kant, *Critique of Judgement*, p. 107.
33. The view until relatively recently was that theories of the sublime underwent two shifts in the course of the eighteenth century: one, from being concerned with art, literature, and rhetoric to being concerned with natural objects; and the second, from being associated with the sublime object to being located in the perceiving subject. The latter shift has conventionally been attributed to Kant, with his insistence that 'all we can say is that the object lends itself to the presentation of a sublimity discoverable in the mind': Kant, *Critique of Judgement*, p. 92. See Monk, *The Sublime*, p. 4; Robert C. Clewis, *The Kantian Sublime and the Revelation of Freedom* (Cambridge: Cambridge University Press, 2009), p. 13.
34. Andrew Ashfield and Peter de Bolla, eds. *The Sublime: A Reader in British Eighteenth-Century Aesthetic Theory* (Cambridge: Cambridge University Press, 1996), p. 14.
35. Ashfield and de Bolla, *The Sublime*, p. 14.
36. Philip Shaw, *The Sublime* (London: Routledge, 2006), p. 96.

37. Burke, *Philosophical Enquiry*, p. 124.
38. Burke, *Philosophical Enquiry*, p. 79.
39. Kant, *Critique of Judgement*, p. 92.
40. Kant, *Critique of Judgement*, p. 111.
41. Douglas Freshfield, 'The Pelmo', *Alpine Journal*, 6 (1872–74), 257–67 (p. 262).
42. Freshfield, 'The Pelmo', p. 263.
43. Freshfield, 'The Pelmo', p. 265.
44. 'New Expeditions in 1877', *Alpine Journal*, 8 (1876–78), 328–41 (p. 339).
45. Rev. W.S. Green, 'A Journey into the Glacier Regions of New Zealand', *Alpine Journal*, 11 (1882–84), 57–63 (p. 63).
46. Ellis Carr, 'Two Days on an Ice Slope', *Alpine Journal*, 16 (1892–93), 422–46 (p. 444).
47. Geoffrey Hastings, 'Over Mont Blanc by the Brenva Route, Without Guides', *Alpine Journal*, 17 (1894–95), 537–51 (p. 545).
48. Hastings, 'Over Mont Blanc' p. 547.
49. Hastings, 'Over Mont Blanc', p. 548.
50. Hastings, 'Over Mont Blanc', p. 549.
51. Hastings, 'Over Mont Blanc', p. 551.
52. Dent, 'Address to the Alpine Club', p. 15; Freshfield, 'Solitude of Abkhazia', p. 238.
53. Ruth Devine, 'McCormick, Arthur David', in *Dictionary of Irish Biography*, 9 vols (Cambridge: Cambridge University Press, 2009) V, 867–68.
54. 'Mr. A. D. McCormick's Caucasian Sketches', *Alpine Journal*, 18 (1896–97), 181–83 (p. 181).
55. 'McCormick's Caucasian Sketches', p. 181.
56. Alfred Tennyson, 'The Lady of Shallot', 91, in *The Poems of Tennyson*, ed. by Christopher Ricks, Longmans Annotated English Poets (London: Longmans, 1969), pp. 354–61.
57. Byron, *Childe Harold*, I. 104, pp. 19–206.
58. Wordsworth, *Prelude*, VIII. 47, pp. 297–345.
59. The allusion is probably to William Shakespeare, *Measure for Measure*, II. 2.
60. Jennifer Daryl Slack and John Macgregor Wise, *Culture and Technology: A Primer* (London: Peter Lang, 2005), p. 18.
61. Colley, *Victorians in the Mountains*, p. 99.
62. H.G. Willink, 'Exhibition of Mr. Donkin's Photographs', *Alpine Journal*, 14 (1888–89), 309–10 (p. 309).
63. Steve Vine, 'Blake's Material Sublime', *Studies in Romanticism*, 41 (2002), 237–57 (p. 239).
64. John Keats, 'To J. H. Reynolds Esq.', in *John Keats: The Major Works*, ed. by Elizabeth Cook (Oxford: Oxford University Press, 2008), pp. 182–85 (p. 184).

65. Onno Oerlemans, *Romanticism and the Materiality of Nature* (Toronto: University of Toronto Press, 2002), p. 4.
66. Conway, *Alps from End to End*, p. 174.
67. L. Norman-Neruda, 'Some New Ascents in the Bernina Group', *Alpine Journal*, 15 (1890–91), 461–71 (p. 470).
68. Norman-Neruda, 'Some New Ascents', p. 470.
69. Willink, 'Snowdon at Christmas', p. 41.
70. Girdlestone, *High Alps*, p. 12.
71. Wordsworth, *Prelude*, I. 360–400, pp. 36–72.
72. Dent, *Above the Snow Line*, p. 217.
73. Wordsworth, *Prelude*, I. 392–93, pp. 36–72.
74. Abraham, *Rock Climbing*, p. 70.
75. Abraham, *Rock Climbing*, p. 71.
76. Clinton T. Dent, 'The History of an Ascent of the Aiguille du Dru', *Alpine Journal*, 9 (1878–80), 185–200.
77. The Aiguille du Dru, according to the reviewer of *Above the Snow-Line*, was for Dent 'the centre and crown of all things Alpine, which has so fascinated him, that he is ever hovering around it, whether he has already conquered it, or whether he is still besieging it': 'Reviews', *Alpine Journal*, 12 (1884–86), 129–36 (p. 130).
78. John Stoddard, *John Stoddard's Lectures* (New York, Chicago and London: Belford, Middlebrook, 1897).
79. Stoddard, *Stoddard's Lectures*, p. 224.
80. Frederic W.H. Myers, 'On a Grave at Grindelwald', 1–10, in *Frederic William Henry Myers: Collected Poems*, ed. by Eveleen Myers (London: Macmillan, 1921), p. 213.
81. Wherry also quoted this poem in connection with the death of Richard Lewis Nettleship on Mont Blanc in 1892. Myers' lines 'seem to have been made for such an event', he wrote: Wherry, *Alpine Notes*, p. 85.
82. My use of the word 'him' in this context is not coincidental: this was a strongly gendered assumption, in which the sense of agency and self-confidence is assumed to be a male prerogative.
83. Hevly, 'Heroic Science', p. 68.
84. Girdlestone, *High Alps*, p. 12.
85. Byron, *Childe Harold*, II. 225.
86. Girdlestone, *High Alps*, p. 54.
87. F. Vaughan Hawkins, 'The Matterhorn – First Assault', in John Tyndall, *Hours of Exercise in the Alps* (London: Longman, Green, 1871), pp. 27–52 (p. 36), emphasis in original.
88. Hawkins, 'The Matterhorn', p. 39.
89. Schama, *Landscape and Memory*, p. 505, emphasis in original.

90. Leslie Stephen, 'The Allelein-horn', in *Vacation Tourists*, ed. by Francis Galton (London: Macmillan, 1861), pp. 264–81 (p. 275).
91. Stephen, 'The Allelein-horn', p. 275.
92. Stephen, *Playground*, p. 276.
93. Stephen, *Playground*, p. 273.
94. Stephen, *Playground*, p. 274.
95. Stephen, *Playground*, p. 277.
96. Bernard Semmel, *The Methodist Revolution* (London: Heinemann, 1974), p. 43.
97. Stephen, *Playground*, p. 281.
98. Stephen, *Playground*, p. 277.
99. Stephen, *Playground*, p. 278.
100. Stephen, *Playground*, p. 279.
101. Stephen, *Playground*, p. 287.
102. Crary, *Suspensions of Perception*, p. 12.
103. Crary, *Suspensions of Perception*, p. 12.
104. Stephen, *Playground*, p. 278.
105. Crary, *Suspensions of Perception*, p. 155, emphasis in original.
106. Stephen, *Playground*, p. 282.
107. Leslie Stephen, 'Mr. Whymper's Scrambles Amongst the Alps', *Alpine Journal*, 5 (1870–72), 234–40 (p. 235).
108. Stephen, *Playground*, p. 287.
109. John Ruskin, *Deucalion: Collected Studies of the Lapse of Waves, and Life of Stones* (Kent: George Allen, 1879), p. 11. Ruskin's comments were made in a lecture at the Museum of Oxford in October 1874, but later published in *Deucalion*.
110. Roger Cardinal, 'Ruskin and the Alpine Ideal', in *Ruskin in Perspective*, ed. by Carmen Casaliggi and Paul March-Russell (Newcastle upon Tyne: Cambridge Scholars Publishing, 2010), pp. 157–76 (p. 169).
111. Ann Colley reclaims Ruskin's 'physical and kinetic relationship to the mountains' and shows how his 'strenuous experiences influenced his way of seeing the mountain landscape he admired, and how, in turn, they helped shape his concept of imperfect vision'. However, her argument focuses largely on his personal record of mountain ascents between 1844 and 1849 – well before the period discussed here – and on ekphrasis of his own mountain drawings, rather than on his later prose and published speeches: Colley, 'Ruskin', p. 43.
112. See, for example, J. Oakley Maund, 'The Gross Lauteraarhorn from the West, and an Attempt on the Eastern Ridge of the Eiger', *Alpine Journal*, 11 (1882–84), 27–39 (p. 27); 'Address by Prof. T. G. Bonney, President', *Alpine Journal*, 11 (1882–84), 373–82 (p. 379).
113. Donkin, 'Photography', p. 65.

114. Donkin, 'Photography', p. 65.
115. H.G. Willink, 'Alpine Sketching', *Alpine Journal*, 12 (1884–86), 361–80 (p. 363).
116. Willink, 'Alpine Sketching', p. 363.
117. Mummery, 'Charmoz and de Grepon', p. 170.
118. Parisi, 'Tactile Modernity', p. 191.
119. Clinton T. Dent, ed., 'The Principles of Mountaineering', in *Badminton Library of Sports and Pastimes: Mountaineering* (London: Longmans, Green, 1892), pp. 95–136 (p. 132).
120. Dent, 'Principles of Mountaineering', p. 133.
121. Conway, *Alps from End to End*, p. 11.
122. See for example Freshfield, writing in 1923 about the view from a summit in the Maritime Alps: 'I despair of conveying by any words of my own an adequate impression of the feeling of such moments, when the climber's body is at rest, and his mind at leisure to drink in and add to its memories the glories of another vast landscape': Douglas Freshfield, *Below the Snow Line* (London: Constable, 1923), p. 37.

CHAPTER 6

# 'Trippers' and the New Mountain Landscape

## INTRODUCTION

The late-Victorian mountaineers did not have the mountains to themselves. A growing number of tourists were also attracted to the Alps and to the mountainous areas of Britain. Tourists had long visited the Alps, the Scottish Highlands, and the English Lake District, drawn in part by the legacy of Romantic literature. However, accelerating social and economic change meant that by the late nineteenth century far more Britons enjoyed the financial means and leisure time to travel to these areas. The new phenomenon of mass tourism considerably altered the physical appearance of mountain landscapes, with a growing rail network, the construction of funicular railways, and the development of infrastructure for visitors. Social and even psychological changes in the mountain experience mirrored these physical transformations.

Climbers, meanwhile, developed new strategies to distinguish themselves from tourists and to insist on the antithesis of mountaineering and tourism. The very stridency of anti-touristic rhetoric among mountaineering writers indicates a level of anxiety, and this in turn illustrates a contradiction in the attitudes of mountaineers towards tourists. While the aesthetic of the haptic sublime and the insistence on their privileged viewpoint allowed climbers to feel superior to the 'trippers' who congregated in the valleys or were transported up mountains by funicular railways, there

© The Author(s) 2016
A. McNee, *The New Mountaineer in Late Victorian Britain*,
Palgrave Studies in Nineteenth-Century Writing and Culture,
DOI 10.1007/978-3-319-33440-0_6

is also a sense in which this superiority was threatened by the influx of visitors and by the very different values they brought with them.

## 'Tormented by Cockneys'

Contributing the chapter on Alpine climbing to Anthony Trollope's *British Sports and Pastimes* (1868), Stephen set out the position he was to return to so often in his subsequent writing. The true mountaineer who ascends the high Alps, he wrote, 'bears away indelible impressions such as are hidden from the traveller confined to the valleys, and tormented by cockneys and inn-keepers'.[1]

This comment encapsulates some of the assumptions examined in the preceding chapters: that the climber has access to a privileged level of experience not available to the purely visual observer; that such an experience is incommunicable to those who have not shared it; and that the climber is in some sense transformed by the experience. As we have seen, these positions would be asserted by a wide variety of mountaineering writers from around this time onwards. Stephen's casual assumption that the valley-bound traveller would be 'tormented by cockneys' was to become an equally widespread assertion – one that was arguably just as important to the history of late-Victorian mountaineering.

Stephen and his peers and successors felt compelled to comment on the 'cockney' visitors to mountain regions as a result of changes that had transformed the social and physical profile of these areas. Indeed, it could even be argued that a new mountain topography emerged in the second half of the nineteenth century, in which the exclusivity and sense of being pioneering explorers that the first generation of mountaineers had enjoyed were supplanted by much wider access to mountainous regions and a new infrastructure to support increased visitor numbers. This in turn represented a threat to the climbers' claim to a uniquely authentic and immersive experience of the mountains.

Even before Thomas Cook led his first tour group to Switzerland in the early 1860s, writers were complaining about the downward social mobility of the mountain experience, with the figure of the 'cockney' tripper an increasingly common bugbear as the century went on. Stephen was particularly exercised by the spectre of the cockney tourist. In a paper read to the Alpine Club in 1871 he described a favourite Chamonix inn as 'an oasis in a desert of cockneyism',[2] while in *The Playground of Europe*, published the same year, he claims: 'The bases of the mountains are immersed in a deluge of cockneyism – fortunately a shallow deluge – while their summits rise high into the bracing air, where everything is pure and poetical'.[3] Another paper given to the Alpine Club in 1874 included a reference to the Montenvers as one of 'the most cockney-ridden of all the well-known points of view' in the Alps, and there are plenty of other references to cockneys in his writing about mountains and mountaineering.[4]

This was far from a solitary obsession of Stephen's. The archetype of the 'cockney tourist' had been around for decades before he used it.[5] However, the occasional mentions of cockneys in travel writing from around the 1830s turn into a surge of disparaging references from the 1870s onwards. Not only the frequency but the bitterness and class enmity involved seem to intensify as the century proceeds, suggesting that the figure of the lower middle-class tourist – variously characterized as a 'cockney traveller', as the metonymic 'Arry or 'Arriet, as the much-derided 'tripper', and the despised 'Cookite' – created considerable anxiety and resentment among the mountaineers of the late-Victorian period.

The cockneys that Stephen and others complained of were not members of the urban proletariat such as costermongers and cabmen whom the word came to connote in the twentieth century, but rather members of the lower middle classes, often clerks or shop assistants.[6] It was this group – and in particular, the clerks – who were primarily being described when writers mentioned 'cockneys' or referred to someone as 'Arry. The figure of 'Arry began life in a series of *Punch* sketches beginning in 1877: 'Arry, according to his creator, was a "cockney cad," "loud, slangy and vulgar," with a taste for "smart patter and snide phrases".'[7] He was 'a commercial clerk earning around £2 a week and could expect a fortnight's holiday together with whatever came his way from the turf'.[8] 'Arry clearly took on a life of his own outside the pages of *Punch* (George Gissing, for example, used the name for a character in his 1886 novel, *Demos*), and mountaineering writers often use the soubriquet to describe a particularly vulgar type of tripper. John Barrow, writing in 1886 about the English Lake District, describes the tall summit cairn of Thornthwaite Crag on the High Street ridge as 'being little visited by the irrepressible tripper ('Arry, as he is now generally called) whose delight is to pull down cairns, and cut, scratch, or scribble his name wherever he can do so with impunity',[9] while Charles Edward Mathews told the inaugural dinner of the Climbers' Club in 1898 that climbing was 'a sport that for some mysterious cause appeals mainly to the cultivated intellect. 'Arry or 'Arriet would never climb a hill'.[10]

It would be misleading, however, to suggest that objections to mass tourism were made purely on class grounds. Even the relatively respectable and sober clients of Thomas Cook, who began operating pleasure trips within Britain as early as 1845 and led the first escorted group to Switzerland in 1863, were frequently the object of disdain in the pages of mountaineering literature.[11] Cook's tours were often blamed by subsequent writers for accelerating the growth of cockney tourism, but in fact the tenor of his business reflected his early background transporting groups by rail to Temperance meetings, and his clientele tended to be associated with an ethos of sobriety, self-improvement, and Nonconformist religion that was far removed from the behaviour associated with 'Arry and his ilk.[12] One of the participants on his first Swiss trip, Jemima Morrell, wrote up her diary for private publication in 1863, and included encounters with cockney visitors which suggested that such tourists were actually frowned upon by Cook's group. Morrell records a meeting with 'an Englishman who was "Doing Switzerland jolly" and who had "done" the Rigi and had had "horrid weather" and was going to "do" the Faulhorn opposite'.[13] The slang used and the attitudes displayed by this character are typical of the way cockney tourists were portrayed, suggesting that Morrell and her fellow Cook's tourists were well aware of such social gradations, and that their own self-image was solidly respectable, albeit still lower middle-class.

This complicates the notion of a simple class antithesis between the usually upper middle-class mountaineers and the lower middle classes they looked down upon. Nonetheless, accounts by climbers typically elide the distinction between cockney clerks carving their names into trees and Cook's tourists attempting to acquire culture and experience on an organized tour; they tend to employ the term 'Cookite' indiscriminately to denote any group of tourists, whether conducted by Thomas Cook or not. As we have seen, Victorian mountaineers were typically members of the professional classes, who valued what Collini describes as the 'ethic of work and the ethos of strenuousness', and set great store by the exercise of skill and competence – not only in their business lives but also in their hobby of mountaineering.[14] A sense of self-reliance and agency, and the purposive use of leisure time, were defining features of this class. They were also unusual in their appetite for physical discomfort, even danger, and their sense that value lay in overcoming those discomforts and dangers through the exercise of skill, judgement, and physical and mental tenacity. Seen from this perspective, the real objection to the 'Cookites' was not so much that they were irreverent cockneys (which in fact they were generally not) but that they had chosen a mode of travel that was safe, predictable, and dependent upon the direction of Cook as guide.

It was this very safeness and predictability that attracted so many of Cook's clients. Elizabeth Tuckett, sister of Francis Fox Tuckett and an Alpine traveller herself, recalled meeting one of his groups in Florence in the 1860s. The party she met were 'a gentleman, his wife and two daughters, worthy Londoners'. Not having 'much experience in the mysteries of "foreign travel"', they had been advised to apply to Cook.[15] This group was spending a month travelling through Italy and Switzerland, at a cost of twenty-five pounds per person. The cost of the trip suggests a reasonable disposable income, while the reason for taking it as part of one of Thomas Cook's groups – their dearth of travel experience – indicates a lack of confidence in their own ability to negotiate the challenges of overseas travel. This, of course, stands in direct contrast to the approach of the New Mountaineers, with their emphasis on experiences of mountain landscapes that were rendered authentic and meaningful by physical contact and by the exercise of technical skill. Cook's tours in particular and the phenomenon of mass tourism in general threatened to subvert this approach by providing a mountain experience that was packaged and in which the tourist relied not on his or her own training but on the services of a professional guide.

Ironically, there was a sense in which the tourists' reliance on their guide was not so dissimilar from that of the early days of mountaineering. In the first couple of decades of the Alpine Club, even the most adventurous members routinely climbed with local guides. It was not until the 1870s that British climbers felt confident enough to climb without guides, and even then the practice remained controversial.[16] Nonetheless, even before guideless climbing became the norm, the dependence of trippers upon the services of guides was presented as part of a wider antithesis between the scripted experience of tourists and the unscripted experience of mountaineers. The former was portrayed as certain of outcome, shallow, and prosaic; the latter as contingent, physically immersive, and in some cases even poetic. The touristic experience was mediated by tour guides and funicular railways, while the mountaineers' experience was unmediated and thus more authentic. Seen from this perspective, even Stephen's remarks about cockneys, while superficially concerned with class distinction, are in fact primarily concerned to contrast the debased experience of the tourist in the valleys with the elevated sensibility of the mountaineer who has expended the effort and acquired the skills needed to reach the summits, 'where everything is pure and poetical'. This antithesis was arguably as important to the mountaineering critics of Cook and his clients as the more obvious consideration of social class, and it allowed many mountaineering writers to collapse the subtle distinction between Cook's respectable clients and the more rambunctious clerks. As Buzard puts it, Cook's tourists 'were seen as surrendering their own initiative to an organized power that directed and propelled them on their way; their presumed passivity, obtrusiveness, and obeisance before steam and cicerone threatened both the places and the paradigm of independent travel'.[17] Neither the Cookite nor the cockney clerk welcomed or even understood the harsh pleasures of mountain climbing, in which cold, pain, and fatigue allowed the climber to achieve sublime experiences and enhanced understanding of the mountain landscape.

This contrast between the authentic traveller, who brings home original and valuable impressions of places visited, and the tourist who is ignorant, incurious, and lacking the education or sensitivity to benefit from the experience of foreign travel, already had a long pedigree by the time it was made by mountaineering writers.[18] Travel writers had posited distinctions between travellers and tourists for decades. These were based not only on class but on what Walton calls 'a kind of moral superiority, founded in a search for authenticity and cultural understanding, taking in the hidden and esoteric [ ... ] and entailing a willingness to endure discomforts and take risks in pursuit of a special kind of experience'.[19]

The idea of a 'pursuit of a special kind of experience' that necessitates danger and discomfort could almost serve as a manifesto for the claims made by late nineteenth-century mountaineers, and in this sense they represent a degree of continuity with earlier critics of tourism. However, mountaineering literature in this period also constitutes a specific discourse about tourism with its own unique features. Specifically, mountaineering writers who criticize tourists display a concern with the degraded or superficial nature of touristic experience and also an anxiety about how tourists potentially threaten the connection between aesthetic appreciation and physical experience. They frequently insist upon the difference between the work of the mountain climber and the casual, ultimately worthless play of the tourist. The notion of an inseparable link between the embodied experience of the climber who scales a mountain and the visual impression the mountain makes was a consistent theme of mountaineering prose, and since the tourist could not hope to have such an embodied experience, his or her impressions of mountain regions were necessarily partial or superficial.

At the same time, there is also a sense that this superiority is challenged by the ubiquity of tourists and by the facilities created for their benefit. As the experience of visiting mountains became less exclusive and less physically challenging, there was inevitably a suspicion that the whole point of mountaineering – using the machinery of the human motor to reach the summit of a mountain peak, and in the process acquiring an enhanced understanding of the mountain landscape – was undermined by the existence of easier, less dangerous mountain experiences. This was articulated by Mummery when he complained in 1895 about the 'vulgarisation of Zermatt, the cheap trippers and their trumpery fashions', and the 'pious worshippers of the great god "Cook" who enjoy ascending mountains in funicular railways'.[20] Referring to a proposed scheme to build a funicular railway to the summit of the Matterhorn, he predicted: 'To ascend the Matterhorn in a steam lift, and all the time remember that brave men have been killed by mere stress of difficulty on its gaunt ice-bound cliffs, will be to the Cockney and his congeners unmixed delight'.[21]

Mummery himself was a man of relatively humble origins, who had originally been blackballed from membership of the Alpine Club because of his trade background in the family tanning business.[22] His own class position, along with his generally liberal and progressive views, makes it unlikely that he was complaining about tourists from simple snobbery. Instead, he is contrasting the authentic experience of the mountaineer who climbs the Matterhorn using only muscle, skill, and courage, with that of the tourist who obviates the need for all three by taking a funicular railway to the summit. This antithesis was rendered all the more real, and the need to confront it more pressing, by the perception that tourism had altered the physical nature of mountain regions and threatened to alter it still further.

## The New Mountain Landscape

Mummery's comment underlines the paradoxical nature of mountaineering responses to tourism; writers mocked the tourists and at the same time perceived them as a threat to the authenticity and exclusivity of the climber's experience. As Mummery's reference to funicular railways suggest, this threat was not only to do with the sheer number of new visitors, but also the structural changes to the topography of mountain regions that they brought about. The second half of the nineteenth century saw a newly constructed overlay of buildings and machinery on the surface of mountains, and a creeping urbanization of the Alps, in particular. Railways capable of carrying passengers up the steep slope of a mountain were just one manifestation of this change.

The first Alpine funicular opened in 1871, from Vitznau to the summit of the Rigi, a Swiss range that had already become synonymous with mass tourism by this stage.[23] Another branch to the summit of the Gotthard Pass opened shortly afterwards, and a railway to the top of Mount Pilatus was completed in 1889.[24] Further lines to the summits of Wengern Alp and Gornergrat opened in 1893 and 1898 respectively. A scheme to build a railway to the summit of the Jungfrau was widely criticized but nonetheless began construction in 1896.[25]

Mountaineers reacted with predictable hostility. One writer despairingly likened the Jungfrau to a sacrificial victim to 'that modern Minotaur, the Circular Tourist'.[26] Writing in 1889 about proposed railways over the Col Ferrex, the Great Saint Bernard Pass, and from Annecy to Albertville, another anonymous contributor to the *Alpine Journal* wrote: 'Railways are indeed convenient, but in some places one does not want them, and the cry soon will be not that there are too few, but too many of these iron roads in the Alps, whither men resort for quiet'.[27] Charles Edward Mathews complained in 1892 of how 'the means of reaching the great Playground are getting easier year by year', and bemoaned the numbers of tourists who were 'turned out of railway carriages every summer day'.[28] Mathews' characterization of this mode of transport was telling. The steam engine, he wrote, 'drags the now luxurious tourists to our old familiar home of Zermatt – home no more!'[29]

Similar concerns had been voiced in Britain for some time. Proposals to extend the railway network into the centre of the Lake District had been controversial as far back as 1845, when Wordsworth wrote to the *Morning Post* to oppose the scheme.[30] Wordsworth couched his opposition to the railway extension in terms that recalled his earlier description of the Lake District as 'a sort of national property' that deserved to be left unspoilt.[31] However, there was also a strain of elitism in Wordsworth's protests, with their implication that this national property could not be enjoyed or appreciated by everyone – only by those 'persons of pure tastes' with the discernment to appreciate it. Wordsworth's concerns that the railway would bring 'swarms of pleasure-hunters, most of them thinking that they do not fly fast enough through the country which they have come to see', seem to prefigure the complaints of later generations of mountain lovers, who felt that making it too easy for tourists to reach mountainous areas not only risked spoiling those landscapes but also threatened the status of their own experiences.[32] Responses to the proposed extension of the Lake District line in the latter part of the century were couched in broadly similar terms. A scheme to extend the railway to Ambleside, Grasmere, and even further into the region re-emerged in 1876, and as Stephen Gill points out, its opponents (Ruskin foremost among them) essentially reiterated Wordsworth's argument about the sanctity of the area and its vulnerability to mass tourism.[33]

Concerns about the impact of tourism thus continued to be couched in terms of a binary opposition between the educated and sensitive elite who were able to appreciate the mountain landscape and the plebeian masses who threatened that landscape by their presence. Writing one of the earliest articles about rock climbing in the Lake District, in *All the Year Round* in 1884, G.N. Williamson noted that Ambleside was already 'vulgarised beyond hope' by 'crowds of thirsty "trippers" from the Staffordshire potteries', bringing with them 'greasy sandwich-papers and porter-bottles', and warned, 'Let the railway be brought there from Windermere, and this ruin will be complete'.[34]

Others were even more explicit about the threat to the climber's exclusivity that the railway would pose. Specifically, they presented the ability of tourists to easily reach what had hitherto been remote and inaccessible regions as a decadent and retrograde development. So, for example, in a letter to the *Pall Mall Gazette* protesting against the Ambleside Railway Bill, which had passed a second reading in 1887, George Meredith denounced the proposal in the strongest terms:

> The project smells of all that is vilest in English middle class Philistinism, suggestive of stale beer-bars, where the adulterated draught precipitates the reckless excursionist, who has had his healthy exercise done for him by the steam-engine, into scarlet pugilism, and his holiday, after laying its curse on the valley, closes its prancings under the sentences of the magistrates.[35]

Meredith's focus on the way that the mechanical power of the railway usurps the physical effort required to reach mountainous terrain is central here, echoing as it does the complaints of Alpine mountaineers that the trippers had not expended the necessary effort to fully appreciate the mountain landscape into which they were transported.

The protests in the Lake District were not about funicular railways, but rather about the extension of the existing rail network into the heart of a mountainous region. However this concern with the greater ease the railways made possible was essentially the same as the misgivings expressed about funiculars in the Alps. Scotland and Wales, too, were perceived as threatened and potentially diminished by the spread of tourist railways and by tourist facilities in general. The railway line to the summit of Snowdon did not open until 1896, but by 1886 mountaineering writer Mark Paterson remarked that Snowdon was

> the only real mountain in Britain which, I think, as yet boasts of its hotel or hotels; and long may it retain so peculiar a title to esteem. Content with a crust to satisfy hunger, I have no sympathy for the average Cockney who cannot tolerate a few hours' separation from his beloved beer.[36]

Paterson went on to condemn the taste for restaurants at the top of mountains as a foreign fad:

> Wantonness of wealth and luxury will find many objects for depletion, but few of them at once so silly and so costly as this of carrying lazy tourists by steam up a mountain to drink beer and champagne, where the purest of waters flows on every side. Of all the curiosities of civilization, a railway up a mountain-side to a 'shebeen' on the top is certainly the oddest.[37]

The contrast between the ascetic mountaineer, his Spartan appetites satisfied by a crust of bread and a drink of stream water, and the voluptuous tourist who has gained the summit without the appropriate physical effort, once again reflects the preoccupation with the physical and with ideas about fatigue and effort. The true mountaineer takes pleasure in ascetic denial and his experience of the mountain is actually enhanced and intensified by having only bread and stream water to fortify his body.[38] Writing about the same mountain, Snowdon, in 1894, John Fleming complained in the *Cairngorm Club Journal*: 'The summit of this fine mountain is desecrated with three small restaurants; sleeping accommodation can even be had [ ... ] Photographs and all sorts of trifles are also on sale'. Fleming 'felt glad that the Cairngorms had not yet been, nor were likely to be, "tripper-ised" to this extent'.[39] Scotland, however, was far from immune from the threat of railways and their associated lack of effort. Writing in 1893 about proposals to extend the West Highland line into Glencoe, Almond reflected:

> It was almost sad to look at the serried mass of the Glencoe hills, and think that one more wilderness was being vulgarised by a railway. It is more sad to think that they may soon make some of their funicular devilments up some of our greater hills. To ignore manly sentiment, and discourage the use of legs, is to impair two of the most important factors in the greatness of a nation.[40]

Funicular railways were a relatively minor offshoot of the massive expansion of the British and Continental European rail network that had begun in the first half of the century and would continue to improve access to both the Alps and British mountain areas. The British network had undergone extraordinary growth in the years leading up to the period under discussion. In 1835, there were just 471 miles of track in England and Ireland; this had risen to 13,411 miles by the middle of the century and to 30,843 miles of track by 1885, according to James Walvin, who points out: 'Whenever a new line was opened to the coast or into the country, it generated an abundance of excursion travel among low income groups'.[41] The railway line to Windermere in the southern Lake District, for example, had opened in 1847, immediately allowing a much wider social range of visitors access to the Lakes, and was extended to Keswick in 1864.[42] Similarly rapid growth took place on the European mainland, making travel to and within the Swiss Alps easier than ever before. From 1848 onwards, a huge expansion of the Swiss railway network saw extensions into some of the main Alpine valleys followed by connections between Alpine countries such as the St. Gotthard tunnel, which opened in 1881 to connect Zurich and Germany with Italy.[43]

It was primarily this phenomenal growth in the rail network, coupled with growing demand from the lower middle classes with their relative prosperity and rising aspirations for leisure activities, that had allowed Cook's business to grow. However, it had also helped Alpine mountaineering to take off as a sport, and the mountaineers themselves had a much more ambivalent response to the railway network as a whole than to the rise of the funicular. Many welcomed the ability that the railways gave them to get to mountainous regions, and acknowledged the debt they owed to the expanded network, even if it meant that other, less welcome visitors were able to join them. Thus, we find this rather surprising note in an otherwise scathing 1873 *Alpine Journal* review of 'Pocket Guide-books' to the Alps (probably written by Freshfield, the then editor), which describes the tone of one guidebook as that of 'a cockney humourist, whose wit, unrepressed among the noblest scenes of nature, fits exactly with that of the tourist abroad for the first time, and ignorant of any foreign tongue'.[44] A few sentences later, in an overview of how much mountaineering and mountain tourism has progressed since the early days of Murray's guidebooks, the writer notes:

> The completion of railroads to the very foot of the Alps gave an immense impulse to Alpine adventure. Englishmen realised for the first time that in central Europe, and within forty-eight hours of London, there was a region almost as unknown, and in parts quite as badly mapped, as the interior of Africa. The luxury of discovery, the excitement of treading on virgin ground and encountering and overcoming strange and at first sight insurmountable obstacles, was brought suddenly within reach of men of moderate means and leisure.[45]

This relatively welcoming tone continued alongside a strand of criticism that simply dismissed the railway as the engine for bringing unwelcome tourist visitors to formerly wild regions. Scottish mountaineers appeared particularly ambivalent in their responses to construction of the West Highland Railway from Glasgow to Fort William, which began in 1889. Writing in the *Scottish Mountaineering Club Journal* in 1890, Gilbert Thomson enthusiastically predicted: 'With the construction of the West Highland Railway, Arrochar will become one of the most accessible parts of the Highlands'.[46] Yet an 1894 review of a book entitled *Mountain, Moor and Loch on the Route of the West Highland Railway*, a guide to the scenery to be seen on the train route, describes it as

> avowedly for the railway tourist, and he, doubtless, will think that he knows [Rannoch] moor well when he has been trundled over it, and will check off the mountains he has seen with as much satisfaction as the climber does those he has climbed.[47]

The following year the same journal carried an article by Robertson (later to become the first Munroist) in which he notes that the 'wild summits that lie between Fort William and Loch Treig' had been inaccessible until the recent extension of the West Highland Railway to Corrour. Robertson predicted enthusiastically that, thanks to the railway, these summits would now 'echo to the sound of hobnailers and ice axes, and a new and fruitful district [...] will thus be added to the rapidly increasing list of good "climbing centres"'.[48] Scottish mountaineers seemed undecided whether the railways were a good thing because they allowed climbers easier access to the Highlands, or a bad thing because that access was also extended to tourists.

A similar ambivalence is evident in accounts of Alpine railways. Writing about the Alps in the same year Robertson was discussing the Highlands, Conway, despite decrying the number of tourists who have 'made parts of the country unpleasant to travel in', has little sympathy for those who criticize the extension of the rail network to Zermatt: 'It is the fashion to abuse these improved mountain high-ways, a foolish fashion to my thinking', he writes, noting that the crowds of people visiting Zermatt now have an efficient way of getting there, rather than clogging up the old mule path.[49]

The growth of the rail network was only one aspect of the wider development of a tourist infrastructure that seemed to threaten the exclusivity of the mountains. Virtually every aspect of the Alpine experience was changed for the generation of Victorians who travelled there from around the later 1860s onwards. From the journey out to the Continent, which was now likely to involve sharing a ferry to Boulogne or Dieppe with a group of Cook's tourists, to the accommodation options in Swiss resorts, where the mountaineer might find himself sharing the table d'hôte dinner with 'cockney tourists brought out in bands at so much a head',[50] to the arrival on the summit of a mountain after a challenging climb, only to find oneself joined by a group of fellow countrymen transported there by a new funicular railway, the mountaineer was faced by a transformed – and much less exclusive – experience of the mountains.

## WRITING OUT THE TOURISTS

One reaction of mountaineers to this transformation was to condemn the depredations of the cockney tourists who had invaded their territory. Another was to find new strategies for maintaining the prestige and exclusivity of their own activity. Above all, the mountaineers were concerned to maintain the distinction between the sense of agency and authenticity in their pursuit of climbing, and what they characterized as the aimless, bovine docility that allowed tourists to be led by guides or carried by trains through the mountain landscape.

They maintained this distinction both by some fairly straightforward physical strategies – travelling to new areas, climbing mountains by new routes, climbing in winter, dispensing with guides, and generally being careful to do things that the casual tourist could not emulate – and by a range of narrative, textual, and social strategies with the same aim. This was partly a matter of changing vocabulary. So, for example, the word 'tourists' is used in the first volume of *Peaks, Passes, and Glaciers,* in 1859, in a non-pejorative sense; the mountaineers whose exploits are recorded in this journal are themselves 'tourists', an appellation which no self-respecting mountaineer of the 1870s onwards would ever use about him or herself.[51] By 1882, in an *Alpine Journal* review of a Barcelona mountaineering club's journal, *Lo Anuario de la Associacio d'Excursiones, Catalana*, the reviewer could remark without fear of contradiction from his presumed readership that the meaning of words in foreign languages can subtly change when translated into English: '"Tourists" with us implies folk whose tours are controlled by external forces, not by their own free will. "Excursionists" suggests irresistibly sandwich papers and eight hours at the seaside'.[52] The word tourist, which had only been in existence since the late eighteenth century, began to be used pejoratively quite early in the nineteenth century, but up until around the late 1860s it could still be used in a neutral way, or as a synonym for 'traveller'.[53] This relatively benign use of the word did not last long, at least in mountaineering circles, and by the end of the century Ramsay could blithely define the 'average Tourist' as

> that strange compound of curiosity without intelligence, of money without manners, of modest attainments and immoderate self-satisfaction, that has taken such a craze for locomotion during the last half-century, and done so much to deform those fair parts of the earth which have been opened up – almost created – for its benefit.[54]

Subtle changes also emerged in the structure of mountaineering narratives. The difference between the account Tyndall gave in his *Mountaineering in 1861* (published in 1862) and later mountaineering narratives is instructive in this regard. He described in some detail his steamer journey out to Boulogne, and then his onward train journey to the Alps, where he was later joined by a friend at their 'bivouac' – in fact, a hotel in the Swiss town of Meiringen.[55] A few days after arriving, he records: 'In the afternoon I strolled up to the Siedelhorn; a mountain often climbed by tourists for the sake of the prospects it commands'.[56] This narrative, in which Tyndall travels to the Alps in the same way as any other tourist (even recording his companions' experiences with seasickness and the disappointing meal they ate at Boulogne), stays in a hotel in an Alpine resort, and climbs a mountain popular with tourists for the sake of the view, seems rather gauche when compared to accounts even a decade or so later, in which mountaineers typically elide any experiences – such as those of travel or accommodation – which might overlap with those of ordinary trippers. Written accounts of Alpine climbing from the 1870s onwards rarely go into detail about the journey out to the Alps, preferring to concentrate instead on the activities of the mountaineer once arrived there.

Many accounts also supplemented this shift in focus with a kind of studied nonchalance, which the more self-aware of mountaineers were sometimes honest enough to admit was a pose. Dent, writing in 1885, described the 'proper attitude' to be adopted by the English mountaineer when 'watching the evening incursion of tourists' to Chamonix: this involved the climber 'leaning against the wall on the south side of the street, and so to pose himself as to indicate independence of the proceedings and to wear an expression of indifference tinged with a suggestion of cynical humour'.[57] Dent was tacitly acknowledging that there was a degree of pleasure on the part of the mountaineer at feeling superior to the tourists.

A similar situation obtained in Britain, where hotel visitors' books provide ample evidence of a cultural clash between mountaineers and tourists, and of attempts by mountaineers to safeguard the exclusivity of their hobby in the face of touristic incursions. Climbers mostly stayed at a handful of well-known hotels in Scotland, the Lake District, and north Wales, but they did not enjoy exclusive use of these establishments. The most remote of the British climbing centres was the Sligachan Hotel on Skye; by the end of the century, it still took as long to travel there from London as to get to Switzerland.[58] Yet by this stage even it had acquired the reputation of being 'the headquarters of the Circular Tourist', as Brown put it:

> It is a place to which he rushes from the steamboat and rushes back again next day, having discharged his double obligation of tasting a little real Talisker and seeing the Coolins through a mist darkly from a seat in a retreating waggonette.[59]

The mixing of social classes that took place in these centres, the enforced proximity of climbers and trippers, and the opportunities which arose for open or coded displays of irreverence towards middle-class conventions, all seem to have created a particularly febrile environment in which social scorn was exhibited not only by mountaineers towards the tourists but also back in the other direction.

The earliest surviving visitors' book from the Wasdale Head Inn – the main centre of Lake District climbing in this period – opens in 1879, and almost immediately these tensions and anxieties are apparent. These documents are less mediated, more unofficial and spontaneous, and have more potential for subversive or contradictory comments to be appended to existing entries than in any formal book or journal. As a result, it is in these books that we can mostly clearly observe the complex relationship between class, anxiety, and cultural capital that underlay debates about mountaineering and tourism. Some of the entries are in Greek, an indicator not just of a certain level of education but also of assumptions about who will be reading the book, while at the other extreme many visitors display an irreverence and insouciance generally absent from more formal published texts of this period. So, for example, a J. Maysop from Manchester wrote in August 1879:

> Arrived here on a bright spring morning, took particular care to order grub for four at 12.30 on the nail.
> We had a precious cup of tea
> And ham and eggs you see.
> We were a hungry lot,
> And we did not care a jot,
> For we had come on a spree, spree, spree.[60]

It might be rash to make assumptions about Maysop's social class based on this entry, but what is certain is that published accounts by climbers, whether in book form or in mountaineering club journals, rarely if ever use words like 'spree' or 'grub'. Similarly, the doggerel attributed to Maggie Taylor and Isaac Morris of Liverpool in July 1880 expresses an attitude and uses vocabulary rarely if ever encountered in published mountaineering writing of this time:

> This weather is awful,
> I think it's not lawful
> To rain on a Sunday like this.
> We drove up for a spree,

The mountains to see.
So that pleasure we're fated to miss.[61]

The *Punch* character 'Arry was prone to using the word 'spree' to denote an exciting and vaguely disreputable pleasure outing: 'wen a spree's on, 'Arry's there'.[62] This was the kind of clerk's slang that John Carey suggests 'annoyed intellectuals partly because it was flippant and philistine and trivialised "serious" subjects'.[63]

Some of the entries are openly irreverent (for example, this anonymous 1880 comment apparently aimed at the proprietor: 'You old bugger, give me change out of that one shilling'),[64] and contributors to the Wasdale Head books frequently scrawl epithets like 'rot', 'bosh', and 'idiot!' beside entries they disapprove of. This attitude is by no means restricted to 'lower-class' visitors: the Reverend William Dosworth, of St Olave's Vicarage in York, visiting in 1894 with a genteel-sounding party that included 'the Misses Slade' and five other young ladies, wrote that his party 'crossed the perilous bridge over the torrent just below the hotel, passed by the cottage chimney to the arête higher up where they roped, and lay in the field reading *Tit-Bits*'.[65] Given how seriously many Victorian mountaineers took their sport and themselves, this parody of a climbing anecdote reads like a piece of calculated mockery, emphasized by the bathetic reference to *Tit-Bits* magazine.[66]

Other entries are harder to interpret, such as the comment by A. P. of Kendal and I. Campbell Baines of Wanstead: 'We got to the top [of Scafell Pike] after displaying the Bull dog tenacity for which the Britisher is famous – although very much disgusted by not finding a pub on the top'.[67] This could well be ironic, as could the 1882 comment by I.R. Bleakley of Bolton that his party had 'arrived last night by the most fearful passes and don't know how to get hence – fear we shall have to cross Scafell Pikes – a dismal prospect'.[68] The suspicion that Bleakley is parodying the overblown style of eighteenth-century travel writing – what Chloe Chard, writing about travel literature in the period 1750 to around 1830, calls 'the rhetoric of hyperbole'[69] – is reinforced by his addendum to this entry: 'P.S. Ham and eggs good'.

The informal and potentially anonymous genre of the visitor's book seemed to encourage this kind of irreverence not only for older literary and aesthetic conventions but also for what had by now become the accepted norms of mountaineering literature. This often took the form of cheerful contempt for entries written by those who identified themselves as climbers or hill walkers. So when the Reverend C. Baker of Bath recorded in the Wasdale Head visitors' book, 'After an enchanting journey over the Pass of

Scafell Pikes, must especially remark the kindness shown to him by the hostess – his condition was deplorable, he having been lost in the descent', other visitors took the opportunity to mock his earnestness. 'His senses were lost before he went', one person commented under this entry, while another wrote above it: '£10 reward is offered for the apprehension of the undermentioned individual'.[70] The visitors' book served as an outlet for this sort of cross-class impertinence and for the expression of the attitudes that mountaineering writers had been deploring in the more formal genre of books and articles. By 1894, it comes as little surprise to find an anonymous writer admit in the logbook of Glencoe's Clachaig Hotel: 'We don't know where we are, and don't care as long as we enjoy ourselves. Beer is alright'.[71]

This reads like the archetypal 'cockney' attitude that Victorian climbers found so distressing, and the mountaineering visitors fought a rearguard action against this approach in the pages of the same visitors' books. Sometimes this simply took the form of scrawled comments beside or underneath the entries written by those considered to be trippers. Under the 1881 signatures of four men from Macclesfield, someone has written the following complaint:

> If the gentlemen whose names appear above when they come again would kindly remember that most respectable people like to sleep at 5 o'clock in the morning, and that whistling, shouting, etc etc are not generally calculated to make the aforementioned class of people enjoy their slumbers, things would be better.[72]

An 1884 entry by four visitors to the Wasdale Head Inn recounts how 'the four above gentlemen ascended the Scawfell from the Woolpack, leaving that place at 11.45'. Someone else has added 'query' above the word 'gentlemen' and the same hand has written underneath this entry: 'It is a pity that the gentleman (?) who wrote (?) this did not study his hand-writing a little more'[73] This kind of policing, both of the unacceptable behaviour of trippers and of the way in which their experiences were recorded, was widespread. Beside a long poem by G.R. Shaw in the Wasdale Head book someone has written: 'Why should the space of a Visitors' Book be wasted by this trash? The writer might at least spell correctly!'[74]

Pen-y-Gwryd, the small hotel at the foot of Snowdonia's Llanberis Pass, had a visitors' book from 1853 onwards. By the 1880s, however, the tensions inherent in having tourists and climbers accommodated under the same roof led one mountaineering visitor, Hugo J. Young, to present the landlord with a new volume to supplement the existing visitors' book. The 'Locked Book', inscribed on the cover with the title 'Not the Visitors' Book', was explicitly intended to distinguish between mountaineers and tourists, and to exclude the latter. It opens in 1884 with a revealing entry by Young himself:

> On my visit to Pen-y-Gwryd I have noticed that your Visitors' Book has become the receptacle for all sorts of nonsense scribbled by the casual passer-by. On the other hand many notes are recorded of lasting use and interest to many who delight to stay weeks with you. It would I think be an advantage to keep the two distinct.[75]

Young's determination that mountaineering visitors should retain the power to control and choose which accounts of visits to this locale are recorded gains added symbolism by his decision to provide the book with a lock so that 'by exercising control over the key you may prevent its pages from abuse'.[76]

Contributors strictly policed the Locked Book to ensure that the accounts of serious visitors to the hotel were not undermined by the comments of 'the casual passer-by'. As noted in Chap. 2, one visitor made a proposal for a comparable logbook at the Wasdale Head Inn in 1880, recommending the landlord to open a book only to be used by 'bona fide walkers', as entries by renowned Lakeland climbers including Walter Parry Haskett Smith and Cecil Slingsby were being adulterated by frivolous comments and were sometimes 'blotched' by the ink of other writers.[77] This suggestion was not taken up, and climbing entries continued to be made in the normal Wasdale visitors' book. The Sligachan did, however, introduce a book specifically for climbing entries in 1893.

Entries considered legitimate for inclusion in the Locked Book were not simply confined to mountaineering anecdotes, although these did predominate in the years up to the end of the century. Botanical notes, geological observations, and even some poetry all found their way into the book and were evidently approved of by its guardians. Any comments deemed more appropriate for the normal visitors' book were ruthlessly expunged, however. So for example, an entry for July 1890 reading simply, 'I have stayed at this hotel with my brother and his wife for the past week, and have been more than satisfied with our treatment in every way', has been crossed out with the comment, 'Clearly meant for the Visitors' Book'.[78] An entry by Mr. and Mrs. Bernard Drake for Easter 1893 recording that they had 'spent a very pleasant week. Can strongly recommend this hotel to all in search of health' was crossed through on the same grounds.[79]

Yet at the same time, from the early days of the Locked Book relatively banal accounts of excursions during which, as Frederic Wilkins of Birmingham conceded in his May 1885 entry, 'Nothing very extraordinary [was] attempted', remain extant in the book, while lists of ferns, birds, and flowers observed in the area, as well as poems and songs, also generally escaped censure or censorship.[80] The difference between these entries and, for example, the doggerel that was often written in the Wasdale visitors' book is partly one of class. Poems in the Locked Book include light-hearted but skilful pastiches of Walt Whitman and W.S. Gilbert, including one called 'Cragwork' in the style of the song 'As Some Day it May Happen' from *The Mikado*.[81] Similarly, the entry by H. Dixon of Northampton recording finding a type of moss 'previously recorded only from two localities in Ireland and from Lyn-y-groes, near Dalgelly',[82] or the list of ferns 'still to be found, to the writer's knowledge, in the neighbourhood of Pen-y-Gwryd',[83] suggest a degree of specialist knowledge that was in keeping with the tone and ethos of the Locked Book – and, for that matter, with the wider concern about access to specialist skills and knowledge that was discussed in Chap. 2 as important to late-Victorian mountaineering. The level of culture required to produce a parody of a Gilbert lyric or the degree of scientific knowledge involved in producing a comprehensive list of flora were accomplishments limited to a relatively small middle-class coterie. However, as well as this straightforward class element, they are also analogous to the mountaineering entries in that they share a tone of serious intent and an elevation of hobbies into something that might be termed work.

If the exclusivity of Pen-y-Gwryd's Locked Book was partly due to concerns about class it was also at least partly a reflection of this concern with work, in both its physical sense and in the sense of a meaningful, purposeful activity. The entries that were permitted in the Locked Book, whether about climbing, botany, or other subjects, display a kind of seriousness of purpose and a level of expertise which is missing from the more off-the-cuff and irreverent entries written by the 'casual passer-by'. It is this seriousness and skill that gives mountaineering its cultural capital and its air of authenticity, and the whole purpose of the Locked Book (and the suggestion for its equivalent at Wasdale) was to reinforce the authenticity and the privileged status of the mountaineer. The lengths to which mountaineering visitors went in order to protect this prestige suggest that the presence of tourists in domains such as Llanberis, Wasdale, or Skye represented a threat – not simply a class threat, but a challenge by the forces of casual dilettantism to the privileged nature of the activity of mountain climbing.

## Maintaining Exclusivity

Textual strategies alone were not sufficient to maintain the boundary between mountaineer and tourist. Over the same period, there were a number of changes to the practice of climbing. Some of these took place in response to material changes, such as the development of new equipment, but others were directly aimed at maintaining the exclusivity of mountaineering.

From the 1870s onwards the pioneering of new, more challenging routes and winter ascents of Alpine mountains, and the growth of guideless climbing, were intended at least in part 'to differentiate the climber from the ordinary tourist', as Peter Hansen points out.[84] These new challenges were, to some degree, part of the natural development of what was still a relatively young pursuit by the end of the century. However, it is no coincidence that they were taking place at almost the precise historical moment when mass tourism to the Alps threatened to usurp the privileged position of mountaineers, and there is plenty of evidence from mountaineering literature of the time to suggest that the climbers were consciously responding to this threat. John Hill Burton's 1867 suggestion that mountaineers turn their attention to British mountains as an arena where they could climb independently of the 'iron rule of the professional guide' was soon followed not only by a turn towards climbing in Scotland and the Lake District, but also by the practice – which remained controversial for some years – of guideless climbing in the Alps. Girdlestone's *High Alps Without Guides* was a seminal text in this regard, as was an 1877 *Alpine Journal* article by A.C. Cust on the first ascent, the previous year, of 'The Matterhorn Without Guides'.[85] Cust's article contains this telling passage:

> In view of the present shoals of professing climbers, it was once suggested to me by a distinguished authority that it would come about that the only way real mountaineers would be able to differentiate themselves would be by banding together to go without guides.[86]

The suggestion that 'real' mountaineers felt the need to 'differentiate themselves' from those who aped their status is typical of the way mountaineers responded to mass tourism at this time, and while guideless climbing was probably an inevitable outcome of the greater experience and proficiency of British mountaineers as the century wore on, it was also at least partly motivated by the desire to differentiate oneself from the tourist who is hauled up mountains by a local guide. The strategies for such differentiation were more varied than simply climbing guideless, or attempting new routes or winter ascents. Travelling to areas where tourists were less likely to visit was another common strategy – ironically, one which was frequently written about in mountaineering books, thus paradoxically increasing the attraction of hitherto unspoilt regions. So in *The Playground of Europe* Stephen describes in familiar terms how Zermatt has become 'the centre of attraction for thousands of tourists' but goes on to note:

> So feeble is the curiosity of mankind, and so sheeplike are the habits of the ordinary traveller, that these remote fastnesses still retain much of their primitive seclusion. Evelona, Zinal, and the head of the Turmanntal, are still visited only by a few enthusiasts. Even the Sass valley, easily accessible as it is, and leading to one of the most justly celebrated of Alpine passes, attracts scarcely one in a hundred of the many visitors to the twin valley of Zermatt.[87]

Four years later, Freshfield recommended to his readers the pleasures of the southern Italian Alps, still unsullied by the attentions of cockney tourists, and predicted that there was little cause to worry that these areas would soon be overrun:

> In truth the unequivocal warmth of the valleys of the southern Alps in August, the English travelling season, will check the incursions of cockneydom; for the modern British tourist professes himself incapable of enjoying life, much less exercise, under even a moderate degree of heat.[88]

Mountaineers were still pursuing and writing about this fairly obvious strategy – of leaving the better-known regions to the tourists and looking instead to more obscure corners of the Alps for authentic mountaineering experiences – up to the end of the century. In his 1898 paper on 'Progress in the Alps', George deplored the ongoing construction of the Jungfrau railway, which meant that the region 'is thus going to be turned into an Alpine Clapham Junction', but pointed out that there were still areas not far from the funicular route 'where one may spend the whole day without seeing a human being, or hearing a sound save the distant cowbells and the occasional thunder of an avalanche'. But he went on to warn: 'Cart ropes shall not draw from me a hint as to where it is situated, lest the tribes of Cook and Lunn should descend on it, and destroy it utterly'.[89]

In some cases, the desire to escape from well-trodden mountains and their increasingly organized and regimented tourist infrastructure encouraged mountaineers to look farther afield. By the late 1860s, the first British expedition to the Caucasus had taken place, then Whymper led an expedition to the Andes in 1879.[90] British climbers explored the Alps of New Zealand's South Island in the early 1880s,[91] while Freshfield led the first climbing expedition to Corsica in 1880.[92] In the Himalayas, what little climbing and exploration that had taken place prior to the 1880s had been carried out for scientific motives or under the auspices of the Great Trigonometrical Survey. From the 1880s, various teams of British climbers started to explore the region, starting with William Woodman Graham, who claimed to have climbed the 23,000 feet Kabru, a claim later disputed by Conway, who led a notable expedition to the Karakoram region in 1892.[93] Mummery made the first ascent of Dych-Tau, the second-highest peak in the Caucasus, in 1888, and would die attempting the Himalayan peak of Nanga Parbat in 1895, the same year his *My Climbs in the Alps and Caucasus* was published.

Himalayan mountaineering was closely bound up with imperialism and with the exigencies of the Great Game, and it would be misleading to suggest that these forays into new mountain ranges were simply part of a strategy to maintain the mountaineers' distinction from tourists. However, the urge to climb in new regions was also at least partly motivated by the need to carve out territory that had not been colonized by tourists, and some climbers were explicit about this. Reviewing a book about the German explorers Adolph, Hermann, and Robert Schlagintweit and their Himalayan travels for the *Alpine Journal* in 1872, John Stogdon

> laid it down with a kind of regret that I was not to be born some thirty years hence, when it is to be hoped railways will have made the Himalayas almost as accessible to us as the Alps have been before.[94]

Stogdon went on to claim that, 'adventure and exploration have set up their prizes elsewhere' now that the Alps have been conquered, thus managing the neat rhetorical trick of bemoaning the domestication of the Alps while hoping for comparable levels of infrastructure in the Himalayas so that they could become more accessible to climbers.[95]

If the Himalayas and other distant mountain ranges could provide a potential version of the Alps not yet colonized by cockneys, conversely domestic mountain landscapes were also pressed into service for a similar purpose. The remoter parts of Scotland, in particular, provided new challenges and a renewed sense of exclusivity for climbers. As the accounts in visitors' books illustrate, however, many climbers felt the need to protect the cultural capital of mountaineering from the more casual trippers.

The Cairngorm Club was founded in 1887 (see Chap. 2). By 1890, the Club had become so popular that its May meeting at Mount Keen, near Glen Esk, advertised as 'an easy day for a lady', attracted 162 participants, of whom 45 were women. As the Club's official history put it, 'it was realised that this "picnic mountaineering" attended by such large numbers was neither desirable or practicable', and the club's committee raised the membership qualifications to require 'the ascent of a Scottish mountain of at least 3,500 feet, plus the ascent of one of the four highest Cairngorms'.[96] They also raised membership fees, and were relieved to find that the next meet attracted only twenty-one people.[97] This emphasis on the potential of Scotland's landscape – wilder and on a larger scale than the Lake District or Wales – for solitude and exclusivity was to be an ongoing feature of Scottish climbing literature. Writing about Ben Nevis in 1896, William Brown commented on the relative freedom from dilettante tourists of even the most popular Scottish peaks. 'In Switzerland', he wrote, 'you see persons crossing glaciers with galoshes and umbrellas. In this country a more healthy respect for steep places keeps Mr Tripper from emulating such feats'.[98]

Even in the more crowded Lake District, serious climbers found ways to distinguish themselves from the tourist hordes. As Walter Parry Haskett Smith's 1894 guide to *Climbing in the British Isles* makes clear, this was largely a question of being discerning enough to choose the right location or of visiting at the right time. Writing about Buttermere, for example, he notes: 'Once a day the Keswick waggonettes swoop upon the place, bringing trippers by the score, but at other times it is a quiet and enjoyable spot'.[99] He also set out the advantages of winter climbing in terms that not only condemned the shallow experience of touristic visitors but also stressed the serious intent of the true mountaineer and alluded to the heightened reality to which the climber supposedly has access. The climber who visits the Lake District out of season, according to Smith, enjoys purer and more exclusive ownership of the landscape:

> You stride cheerily along, freed for a time from the din of toiling cities, and are not harassed at every turn by howling herds of unappreciative 'trippers'. The few who do meet on mountains are all bent on the same errand and 'mean business'; half-hearted folk who have not quite made up their minds whether they care for the mountains or not, people who come to the Lakes for fashion's sake, or just to be able to say that they have been there, are snugly at home coddling themselves before the fire [ . . . ] How different are the firm outlines of those distant peaks from the hazy indistinctness which usually falls to the lot of the summer tourist![100]

This passage exemplifies some of the tropes of mountaineering writing discussed in this and earlier chapters: the dismissal of 'trippers'; the claim that the mountaineer's perspective is clearer and more accurate than the 'hazy indistinctness' of other observers; the contrast between vigorous physical engagement and the 'coddling' of comfortable modernity; the antithesis of the dilettante and the committed mountaineer; and above all, the image of the climber as someone who 'means business'. In both their writing and their material practices, the mountaineers of this period were acutely aware that they were doing something that was inherently more serious and had more value than simple tourism. Even if the period from the 1870s onwards witnessed tensions between the old guard and the New Mountaineers, climbers of both persuasions generally agreed that their hobby was somehow more aesthetically, spiritually, and perhaps even morally elevated than the activities of the 'trippers'.

Ultimately, the discourse about tourism in mountaineering literature involves a central paradox. The mountaineers unquestionably looked down on the tourists and regarded their own experiences as more valuable and authentic. It is also clear that they tended to collapse the distinction between 'old' and 'new' mountaineers when tourism was discussed, presenting mountaineering per se as inherently superior to tourism. Yet this confident belief in their own superiority seems simultaneously undercut by anxiety on the part of mountaineering writers; the value of mountain climbing seemed to be threatened by the incursion of mass tourism, in turn causing climbers to insist all the more strongly on that value.

This anxiety engendered a range of responses and strategies. Responses to tourism – as with attitudes to the rise of the New Mountaineer – were neither monolithic nor static, and even where they appeared to be class-based they often expressed a more complex and nuanced anxiety. Nonetheless, there is clearly a consistent thread running through much commentary on tourism – a sense that the mountain world is changing and that the frontiers of exploration and discovery are moving elsewhere. The closing years of the nineteenth century would see mass tourism give birth to the rise of winter sports such as tobogganing and skiing, which would in turn give rise to even greater commercialization of the Alps. The mountaineers' world had changed irrevocably.

## Notes

1. Leslie Stephen, 'Alpine Climbing', in *British Sports and Pastimes*, ed. by Anthony Trollope (London: Virtue, Spalding, 1868), pp. 257–89 (p. 287).
2. Leslie Stephen, 'Round Mont Blanc', *Alpine Journal*, 5 (1870–72), 289–305 (p. 295).
3. Stephen, *Playground*, p. 289.
4. Leslie Stephen, 'A New Pass in the Chain of Mont Blanc', *Alpine Journal*, 6 (1872–74), 351–64 (p. 352).
5. See, for example, William Brockedon, *Journal of Excursions in the Alps: The Pennine, Graian, Cottian, Rhetian, Lepontian, and Bernese* (London: James Duncan, 1833), p. 169; Ruskin, *Complete Works*, XXXVI, 117; Herman Merivale, 'Alpine Travelers', *Edinburgh Review*, October 1856, pp. 433–53 (p. 446).
6. John Carey points out that the 'section of the middle and lower middle classes employed in commerce, banks, insurance and real estate increased markedly' in the period from 1860 to 1910, not just in Britain but throughout western Europe: John Carey, *The Intellectuals and the Masses: Pride and Prejudice among the Literary Intelligentsia, 1880–1939* (London: Faber & Faber, 1992), p. 58.
7. Gareth Stedman Jones, 'The 'Cockney' and the Nation, 1780–1988', in *Metropolis London: Histories and Representations Since 1800*, ed. by David Feldman and Gareth Stedman Jones (London and New York: Routledge, 1989), pp. 271–324 (p. 290).
8. Stedman Jones, 'The "Cockney" and the Nation', p. 291.
9. John Barrow, *Mountain Ascents in Westmoreland and Cumberland* (London: Sampson Low, Marston, Searle, and Rivington, 1868), p. 81.
10. The remarks were made by Mathews, but reported in the Club's journal by George Bryant: George R. Bryant, 'The Formation of the Climbers' Club', *Climbers' Club Journal*, 1 (1898–99), 1–7 (p. 7).

11. Cook took between 130 and 150 tourists on this first trip, and soon established regular visits to Interlaken and Lucerne: Jill Hamilton, *Thomas Cook: The Holiday-Maker* (Stroud: Sutton, 2005), p. 146.
12. John Pudney, *The Thomas Cook Story* (London: Michael Joseph, 1953), p. 54. Hoppen also notes that Cook's tours often followed identical itineraries to their Grand Tour predecessors, and describes his clients as 'deeply serious' travellers: Hoppen, p. 369.
13. Jemima Morrell, *Miss Jemima's Swiss Journal: The First Conducted Tour of Switzerland* (1863; London: Putnam, repr. 1963), p. 66.
14. Collini, *Public Moralists*, p. 32.
15. Elizabeth Tuckett, *Beaten Tracks: Pen and Pencil Sketches in Italy* (London: Longmans, Green, 1866), p. 181.
16. See, for example, Craufurd Grove, 'Comparative Skill'.
17. Buzard, *Beaten Track*, p. 60.
18. Buzard dates the perceived conflict between authenticity and 'spurious' experience back to roughly around the end of the Napoleonic wars, when British travellers could once again undertake the Grand Tour. He suggests that the wider availability of a formerly exclusive travel experience 'gave rise to new formulations about what constituted "authentic" cultural experience [...] and new representations aimed at distinguishing authentic from spurious or merely repetitive experience': Buzard, *Beaten Track*, p. 6.
19. Walton, 'British Tourism Between Industrialisation', p. 113.
20. Mummery, 'Der Teufelsgrat', p. 116.
21. Mummery, 'Der Teufelsgrat', p. 116.
22. Peter H. Hansen, 'Mummery, Albert Frederick (1855–1895)', *Oxford Dictionary of National Biography* (Oxford University Press, 2004) doi:10.1093/ref:odnb/19526.
23. Andrew Beattie, *The Alps: A Cultural History* (Oxford: Signal Books, 2006), p. 177.
24. Hansen, 'British Mountaineering', p. 259.
25. Hansen, 'British Mountaineering', p. 262.
26. 'The Proposed Jungfrau Railway', *Alpine Journal*, 18 (1896–97), 405–08 (p. 408).
27. 'Reviews and Notices', *Alpine Journal*, 14 (1888–89), 255–74 (p. 274).
28. C.E. Mathews, 'New Experiences in the Old Playground', *Alpine Journal*, 16 (1892–93), 19–30 (p. 26).
29. Mathews, 'New Experiences', p. 26.
30. Gill, *Wordsworth*, p. 248.
31. William Wordsworth, *Guide to the Lakes* (1810; London: Frances Lincoln, repr. 2004), p. 93.
32. Thompson, *English Lakes*, p. 186.

33. The members of what would from 1883 become the Lake District Defence Society were drawn almost wholly from the ranks of the Wordsworth Society, and echoed his attitudes and arguments: Gill, *Wordsworth*, p. 257.
34. G.N. Williamson, 'The Climbs of the English Lake District', *All the Year Round*, November 1884, Part 1, pp. 77–82 (p. 77).
35. *Letters*, ed. by Cline, p. 853.
36. M. Paterson, *Mountaineering Below the Snow-Line: The Solitary Pedestrian in Snowdonia and Elsewhere* (London: George Redway, 1886), p. 48.
37. Paterson, *Mountaineering Below the Snow-Line*, p. 49.
38. E.R.G., 'Reviews', p. 43.
39. John Fleming, 'Snowdon', *Cairngorm Club Journal*, 1 (1893–96), 90–95 (p. 93).
40. Almond, 'Ben-y-Gloe', p. 239.
41. James Walvin, *Leisure and Society, 1830–1950* (London: Longman, 1978), p. 21.
42. John Towner, *An Historical Geography of Recreation and Tourism in the Western World, 1540–1940* (Chichester: John Wiley, 1996), p. 153.
43. Hansen, 'British Mountaineering', p. 258.
44. 'Pocket Guide-Books', *Alpine Journal*, 6 (1872–74), 153–58 (p. 153).
45. 'Pocket Guide-Books', p. 155.
46. Gilbert Thomson, 'The Arrochar Mountains', *Scottish Mountaineering Club Journal*, 1 (1890–91), 63–69 (p. 63).
47. 'Mountain, Moor and Loch on the Route of the West Highland Railway', *Scottish Mountaineering Club Journal*, 3 (1894–95), 174–75 (p. 174).
48. A.E. Robertson, 'Two Days in Lochaber', *Scottish Mountaineering Club Journal*, 3 (1894–95), 267–71 (p. 267).
49. Conway, *Alps from End to End*, p. 159.
50. Wills, 'Fenêtre de Salena', p. 31.
51. A rare exception to this rule can be found in Elizabeth Le Blond's 1883 memoir of winter Alpinism, in which she uses the word to describe a putative climber of the Grandes Jorasses: Burnaby, *High Alps in Winter*, p. 2.
52. 'Reviews and Notices', *Alpine Journal*, 11 (1882–84), 48–55 (p. 55).
53. Thompson, *Suffering Traveller*, p. 40. Buzard also notes an early pejorative use of the term in Wordsworth's 1800 poem 'The Brothers': Buzard, *Beaten Track*, p. 20.
54. Ramsay, 'Rise and Progress', p. 11.
55. John Tyndall, *Mountaineering in 1861: A Vacation Tour* (London: Longman, Green, 1862), p. 9.
56. Tyndall, *Mountaineering in 1861*, p. 20.
57. Dent, *Above the Snow Line*, p. 99.
58. Abraham, *Rock Climbing*, p. x.

59. Brown, 'Coolins', p. 208.
60. Kendal, Cumbria County Archive (CCA), WDSO163 Fell and Rock Climbing Club, A1525.3, 'Wasdale Head Hotel Visitors' Book, 1879–1885', Vol. 1, 3 August 1879.
61. Kendal, CCA, A1525.3, Vol. 1, 18 July 1880.
62. Stedman Jones, 'The "Cockney" and the Nation', p. 291.
63. Carey, *Intellectuals*, p. 59.
64. Kendal, CCA, A1525.3, Vol. 1, August 1880.
65. Kendal, CCA, WDSO163 Fell and Rock Climbing Club (FRCC) archives, A1525.3, 'Wasdale Head Visitors' Book, 1894', Vol. 4, August 1898.
66. *Tit-Bits* magazine, which began publishing in 1881, was popular with lower middle-class readers, and was at least partly responsible for introducing many of them to the possibility of taking rural holidays. A special edition – reprinted in book form in 1883 – included a guide to the Lake District, as well as to various British seaside resorts, 'with particulars of Railway Fares, and full, reliable, and interesting information, as to scenery, climate and attractions': *Where to Go: Reprinted (by Special Request) from Tit-Bits* (Manchester: Guardian, 1883), pp. 63–88.
67. Kendal, CCA, A1525.3, Vol. 1, 9 June 1880.
68. Kendal, CCA, A1525.3, Vol. 1, 9 August 1882.
69. Chloe Chard, 'From the Sublime to the Ridiculous: The Anxieties of Sightseeing', in *The Making of Modern Tourism: The Cultural History of the British Experience, 1600–2000*, ed. by Hartmut Berghoff, Barbara Korte, Ralph Schneider, and Christopher Harvie (Basingstoke: Palgrave, 2002), pp. 47–68 (p. 48).
70. Kendal, CCA, A1525.3, Vol. 1, undated.
71. Edinburgh, NLS, Acc. 11538 item 14, 'Clachaig Hotel, Glencoe logbook, 1889–1904', 28 August 1894.
72. Kendal, CCA, A1525.3, Vol. 1, 5 June 1881.
73. Kendal, CCA, A1525.3, Vol. 1, 26 May 1884.
74. Kendal, CCA, WDSO163 FRCC archives, A1525.3 'Wasdale Head Visitors' Book, 1885–1891', Vol. 2, 21 August 1889.
75. Pen-y-Gwryd, 10 April 1884, p. 1.
76. Pen-y-Gwryd, 10 April 1884, p. 1.
77. Kendal, CCA, A1525.3, Vol. 2, 14 September 1889.
78. Pen-y-Gwryd, July 1890, p. 30.
79. Pen-y-Gwryd, Easter 1893, p. 68.
80. Pen-y-Gwryd, 4 May 1885, p. 6.
81. Pen-y-Gwryd, July 1893, pp. 73–74.
82. Pen-y-Gwryd, 27 July 1888, p. 20.
83. Pen-y-Gwryd, September 1885, p. 10.
84. Hansen, 'British Mountaineering', p. 356.

85. A.C. Cust, 'The Matterhorn Without Guides', *Alpine Journal*, 8 (1876–78), 242–56.
86. Cust, 'Matterhorn', p. 246.
87. Stephen, *Playground*, p. 89.
88. Freshfield, *Italian Alps*, p. 2.
89. H.B. George, '"Progress" in the Alps', *Alpine Journal*, 19 (1898–99), 10.
90. R.L.G. Irving, *A History of British Mountaineering* (London: B. T. Batsford, 1955), p. 96.
91. Irving, *British Mountaineering*, p. 134.
92. Irving, *British Mountaineering*, p. 114.
93. Ronald Clark, *The Victorian Mountaineers* (London: B. T. Batsford, 1953), p. 214.
94. J. Stogdon, 'Schlagintweit's Himalayan Travels', *Alpine Journal*, 6 (1872–74), 43–50 (p. 43).
95. Stogdon, 'Himalayan Travels', p. 43.
96. Murray, *Cairngorm Club*, p. 17.
97. The Club was, however, unique in this period in continuing to accept female members.
98. Brown, 'Climbing in Scotland', p. 2.
99. Smith, *Climbing in the British Isles*, I, 16.
100. Smith, *Climbing in the British Isles*, I, 159.

CHAPTER 7

# Conclusion

By the beginning of the twentieth century, the changes described in this book had consolidated into a fairly consistent approach to writing about mountaineering. A set of assumptions became widespread, many of which have proven extremely durable. The centrality of the climber's physical contact with the material reality of the mountain environment; the belief that this gave the mountaineer a heightened understanding or appreciation of that environment; the claims made for the physical, mental, and spiritual benefits of the sport; a concern with technique, skill, and competence; and the privileging of such attributes as hardiness, tenacity, stoicism, and manliness – all these were widely if not universally accepted. Some of these assumptions would perish, like many cherished beliefs of the Victorian and Edwardian periods, in the slaughter of the First World War. Others continue to be held by many mountaineers to this day.

The process of change in the mountain environment accelerated in the twentieth century. In Scotland, Wales, and the Lake District, there were further improvements to transport links and other infrastructure, and from 1896 a tourist railway to the summit of Snowdon. In the Alps even more dramatic changes were taking place. In addition to the funicular railways and other developments described in Chap. 6, the Alps were the setting for the emergence of what became known as winter sports. Although British climbers had led the way in opening up the Alps during the Golden Age, there had long been active mountaineers in many other countries. The first foreign Alpine Club was formed in the United States as early as 1863, and by the end of the century national mountaineering clubs had been set up in Austria, Switzerland, Italy, Norway, Germany, France, Spain, Belgium, Sweden, New Zealand, and South Africa.[1] All these developments would soon lead to even greater interest in and touristic travel to the Alps and other mountain ranges. This did not precisely translate into a more democratic or egalitarian mountain culture – travel to the Alps and participation in winter sports remained the prerogative of the relatively wealthy, and skiing is a predominantly middle-class phenomenon even today – but it did further undermine the exclusivity that mountaineers had enjoyed as recently as the 1850s and early 1860s.

Mountaineering itself remained very much the preserve of a privileged elite for a long time, but it had changed from being the odd, eccentric, even disreputable activity that it seemed in the wake of the 1865 Matterhorn tragedy to something respectable and relatively familiar. Working-class participation in mountaineering would not become widespread until the late 1940s, although countryside walking (including hill-walking) was a more egalitarian activity.[2] Working-class rambling clubs had been in existence since at least the 1870s to encourage and facilitate this, often in the face of strong resistance from landowners.[3] Groups such as the West of Scotland Ramblers Alliance, formed in 1892, supplemented the more elite Scottish mountaineering clubs.[4] But in the early part of the twentieth century, British mountaineering continued to develop along the lines established in the late nineteenth century, and of course many climbers of the 1880s and 1890s were still active in the first decade or so of the new century. The Scottish Highlands, and in particular Ben Nevis, were the focus of a great deal of activity in this period; a total of thirty new routes were forged on Ben Nevis between 1896 and 1920.[5] The years following the Armistice saw a renewed interest in Himalayan mountaineering, with a series of attempts to climb Everest. These attempts continued to be linked to British imperial attitudes (indeed, it is possible to argue that the struggle to conquer Everest in the twentieth century was a much more direct expression of imperial sentiment than most mountaineering in the nineteenth) and to the automatic, though increasingly uncertain assumption of British national superiority.[6]

At the same time, mountaineering became just one of a number of reasons to travel to the mountains. Winter sports, and the health benefits of high mountain air for those suffering from tuberculosis, also drew more and more visitors.[7] Skiing was introduced to the Alps by Scandinavian visitors in the 1860s, but a former Indian Army officer, Colonel C.C. Napier, is credited with popularizing the sport after skiing at Davos in 1888.[8] Skiing, tobogganing, and other winter sports soon caught on, and quickly became a mainstay of the winter economy in many parts of the Alps. The first decade of the twentieth century saw a massive increase in tourism to Switzerland, in particular, and this trend continued – with wartime interruptions – through most of the twentieth century.

The rise of winter sports and the continued growth in tourist numbers inevitably changed the experience of mountaineering still further. Yet the values and attitudes formulated by late nineteenth-century mountaineers continued to inform and influence attitudes to mountains. Even today, attitudes to mountain landscapes – arguably to wild nature in general – can be traced back in part to the ethos developed in this period. The huge popularity of hill-walking, mountaineering, and outdoor activities in general, owes at least as much to the legacy of the New Mountaineers as to Wordsworth or Coleridge.

A couple of examples, one from the late twentieth century and one from the twenty-first, will suffice to illustrate this. In his account of the disastrous climbing season of 1996, which saw twelve climbers killed on Mount Everest in just a few days and several others horribly maimed, the American writer Jon Krakauer draws an unsparing portrait of the rampant commercialism, egotism, and ruthlessness that characterize modern Himalayan mountaineering, and the consequences for the mountain environment and the Nepalese people who live and work there. Nonetheless, in the course of his narrative Krakauer – himself a member of one of the ill-fated commercial climbing expeditions that attempted to reach the summit of Everest that year – steps back to examine his own motivations and those of his fellow climbers, and concludes that while they may superficially seem to be mere 'adrenaline junkies', they are in fact driven by something rather more exalted.[9] He claims that 'in subjecting ourselves to week after week of toil, tedium, and suffering, it struck me that most of us were probably seeking, above all else, something like a state of grace'.[10] This sounds remarkably similar to the claims made by late nineteenth-century climbers for the 'moral invigoration of enduring value' to be gained from 'contact with cold stony reality'.[11] It is not difficult to imagine Stephen, Freshfield, Conway, or Mummery using the phrase 'state of grace' to describe their own feelings in the mountains.

An even more recent example of this continuity comes in a letter published in November 2012 in the *London Review of Books* (*LRB*). Referring to the 'discarded oxygen bottles and dead bodies despoiling what was once a pristine landscape held sacred by the peoples of the high Himalaya', Janet Crook complains that 'no corner of the world, highest mountain or deepest ocean, Arctic or Antarctic, rainforest or desert, is now safe from corporate exploitation, either for its natural resources or its cachet as a tourist destination'.[12] She goes on to claim that, 'the spiritual aspect of mountaineering is disappearing', and to argue that banning the use of supplementary oxygen 'may be the only way of preventing the Himalaya going the way of the Alps, now largely a giant adventure playground for well-off thrill-seekers'.[13]

The parallels and resonances with some of the mountaineering texts discussed in this study are striking. We have the lament that the 'spiritual aspect' of climbing, located in some unspecified time in the past, has been lost. There is the familiar warning that tourism and its related commercial pressures threaten a delicate environment, and the dismay at the ugly detritus of tourism (in the case of the nineteenth-century Alps, funiculars and other facilities for 'trippers'; in the twenty-first century, empty oxygen tanks and the corpses that climbers now routinely step across on their way to the summit of Everest). There is also the assumption that mountain landscapes closer to home have already been spoilt beyond redemption, necessitating a focus on farther horizons. Crook's concerns at the loss of the 'spiritual aspect' of climbing bring to mind Maylard's 1899 worries about 'the too greater infusion of the purely physical element', encountered in Chap. 3.[14] Even her use of the word 'playground' echoes the title of Stephen's 1871 book, although the connotations of the word are here pejorative rather than celebratory.

This is not to suggest that any of the *LRB* correspondent's complaints are unjustified or needlessly alarmist. Indeed, much of her diagnosis is borne out by other accounts, and her prescription for preventing further damage in the Himalayas is shared by many authoritative observers. It does, however, illustrate how present-day assumptions about the value and ethics of mountaineering, and about the problematic nature of widespread participation in mountain climbing, continue to be underpinned by a set of notions developed in the late nineteenth century. The idea that the person who immerses him or herself in the landscape necessarily has a superior view of it; that the experience of mass tourism is by definition ersatz and unrewarding; the belief that the more people who come to visit a landscape the more it will become spoiled and diminished; and the vague but persistent belief that something akin to a 'state of grace' can be achieved through physical effort in the mountains; all these have their origins in this period.

The late nineteenth century, then, sets the template for mountaineering in its twentieth and twenty-first century forms. *Fin-de-siècle* climbers would probably feel disoriented in today's very changed context, but they might also be surprised to find that they share some beliefs with their twenty-first century counterparts. The New Mountaineer, so novel, contentious, and alarming in his day, has had a lasting effect on the way we approach mountains today.

## Notes

1. Unsworth, *Hold the Heights*, p. 384.
2. For the emergence of working-class climbers in post-Second World War Britain, see Thompson, *Unjustifiable Risk*, pp. 189–260.
3. Thompson, *Unjustifiable Risk*, p. 134.
4. Harvey Taylor, *A Claim on the Countryside: A History of the British Outdoor Movement* (Edinburgh: Keele University Press, 1997), p. 81.
5. Crocket and Richardson, *Ben Nevis*, p. 85.
6. The early Everest expeditions also inspired probably the most famous and succinct explanation for climbing ever given, when George Mallory – who would die trying to reach the summit in 1924 – was asked why he wanted to climb the mountain, and replied, 'Because it's there.' See Wade Davis, *Into the Silence: The Great War, Mallory and the Conquest of Everest* (London: The Bodley Head, 2011), p. 465.
7. Tuberculosis sufferers started to arrive in the Swiss town of Davos from the 1860s, and 'health tourism' there was booming by the late 1880s. See Ring, *English Made the Alps*, p. 134; Fleming, *Killing Dragons*, p. 327.
8. Ring, *English Made the Alps*, p. 135. The travel agent Henry Lunn also played an important role in the 1890s, and is sometimes referred to as the father of Alpine skiing. See Fleming, *Killing Dragons*, p. 329.
9. Jon Krakauer, *Into Thin Air: A Personal Account of the Everest Disaster* (New York: Villard, 1997) p. 135.
10. Krakauer, *Into Thin Air*, p. 136.
11. Conway, *Alps from End to End*, p. 174.
12. Janet Crook, 'Damnable Heresies', Letter, *London Review of Books*, 8 November 2012, p. 4.
13. Crook, 'Damnable Heresies', p. 4.
14. Maylard, 'Scottish Mountaineering', p. 312.

# Glossary

**Aiguille** A sharply pointed mountain summit or rock pinnacle.
**Arête** A thin, knife-edged ridge separating two valleys.
**Bergschrund** A deep crevasse formed by moving glacier ice, usually at the top of a glacier. Often a formidable obstacle for mountaineers to cross.
**Brocken spectre** An optical illusion sometimes witnessed in mountains, when the sun shines from behind an observer looking into mist, causing the observer's own shadow to appear in greatly magnified form.
**Col** The lowest point on a ridge connecting two peaks, forming a pass.
**Cornice** An overhanging ridge of snow on the edge of a mountain, usually on the leeward side. Cornices present a danger to walkers and climbers, as they can appear solid but collapse when any weight is placed upon them.
**Corrie** A large amphitheatre formed at the head of a valley by glacial erosion. Known in the Francophone Alps as a cirque and in Wales as a Cwm.
**Couloir** A steep and narrow gully on a mountain side, often filled with ice and snow in winter. Used by climbers as a route of ascent, but often prone to rock and ice falls.
**Gabbro** Type of coarse igneous rock, particularly associated with the Cuillin hills on the Isle of Skye but also found in some parts of the Alps.

© The Author(s) 2016
A. McNee, *The New Mountaineer in Late Victorian Britain*,
Palgrave Studies in Nineteenth-Century Writing and Culture,
DOI 10.1007/978-3-319-33440-0

**Glissading** Rapid but controlled descent of a scree or snow slope, using an ice-axe in the latter case to control speed and direction.

**Ice-fall** Part of a glacier characterized by fast-moving ice and frequent crevasses and **séracs**.

**Moraine** Rock and soil debris caused by glacial action.

**Scrambling** In contemporary parlance, climbing relatively easy routes that do not require a rope for protection, but in the nineteenth century often used for any kind of climbing on rock, whether with or without ropes.

**Sérac** Large block of ice formed by intersecting crevasses on a glacier, prone to falling and therefore considered a dangerous obstacle.

# BIBLIOGRAPHY

The Digital Object Identifier (DOI) has been given for online resources. Anonymous items have been placed at the beginning of the relevant section, arranged in alphabetical order of title, disregarding the initial definite or indefinite article. Climbing club publications have all been cited as journals rather than magazines.

## PRIMARY TEXTS

### *Archive Material*

Edinburgh, National Library of Scotland, Acc. 11538, Item 16, Sligachan Hotel Visitors' Book, 'For Climbing Remarks Only. 1893–1921'
Edinburgh, National Library of Scotland, Acc. 11538, Item 14, 'Clachaig Hotel, Glencoe Logbook, 1889–1904'
Kendal, Cumbria County Archive, WDSO163, Fell and Rock Climbing Club archive, A1525.3, 'Wasdale Head Visitors' Book, 1879–1885'
Kendal, Cumbria County Archive, WDSO163, Fell and Rock Climbing Club archive, A1525.3, 'Wasdale Head Visitors' Book, 1885–1891'
Kendal, Cumbria County Archive, WDSO163, Fell and Rock Climbing Club archive, A1525.3, 'Wasdale Head Visitors' Book, 1894'
London, Alpine Club archive, ACM7000 Book 2, 'Catalogue of Maps'
Pen-y-Gwryd Hotel, Nant Gwynant, Wales, 'Not the Visitors' Book: Contributions on Mountain Rambles, Botany, Geology, and Other Subjects of Interest Connected with Pen-y-Gwryd. 1884–n.d.

## Journals, Newspapers, and Magazines

'The Alpine Club Exhibition of Pictures and Photographs', *Alpine Journal*, 16 (1892–93), 342–47
'Alpine Notes', *Alpine Journal*, 11 (1882–84), 238–43
'Alpine Notes', *Alpine Journal*, 12 (1884–86), 128–29
'Alpine Notes', *Alpine Journal*, 12 (1884–86), 167–78
'Alpine Notes', *Alpine Journal*, 12 (1884–86), 462–71
'Alpine Notes', *Alpine Journal*, 15 (1890–91), 440–48
'Alpine Notes', *Alpine Journal*, 17 (1894–95), 196–201
'Alpine Notes', *Alpine Journal*, 17 (1894–95), 451–61
'Editorial', *The Times*, 27 July 1865, p. 8
'In Memoriam, Francis Maitland Balfour', *Alpine Journal*, 11 (1882–84), 101–03
'Mountain Climbers and Mountain Gymnasts', *Alpine Journal*, 15 (1890–91), 224–25
'Mountain, Moor and Loch on the Route of the West Highland Railway', *Scottish Mountaineering Club Journal*, 3 (1894–95), 174–75
'Mountaineering Made Easy', *Alpine Journal*, 14 (1888–89), 326–27
'Mr A. D. McCormick's Caucasian Sketches', *Alpine Journal*, 18 (1896–97), 181–83
'New Expeditions in 1877', *Alpine Journal*, 8 (1876–78), 328–41
'New Expeditions in 1894', *Alpine Journal*, 17 (1894–95), 250–66
'A New Map of the Adamello', *Alpine Journal*, 7 (1874–76), 277–78
'New Maps of the Caucasus', *Alpine Journal*, 14 (1888–89), 57
'Ordinary Members of the Cairngorm Club', *Cairngorm Club Journal*, 1 (1893–96), unpaginated
'The Passage of the Sesia-Joch from Zermatt to Alagna by English Ladies', *Alpine Journal*, 5 (1870–72), 367–72
'Pocket Guide-Books', *Alpine Journal*, 6 (1872–74), 153–58
'Proceedings of the Alpine Club', *Alpine Journal*, 15 (1890–91), 457–60
'Proceedings of the Alpine Club', *Alpine Journal*, 17 (1894–95), 85–98
'The Proposed Jungfrau Railway', *Alpine Journal*, 18 (1896–97), 405–08
'Records Left on Mountain Tops', *Alpine Journal*, 14 (1888–89), 323
'Reviews', *Alpine Journal*, 12 (1884–86) 129–36
'Reviews', *Cairngorm Club Journal*, 2 (1896–99), 69
'Reviews and Notices', *Alpine Journal*, 11 (1882–84), 183–91
'Reviews and Notices', *Alpine Journal*, 11 (1882–84), 305–07
'Reviews and Notices', *Alpine Journal*, 14 (1888–89), 255–74
'Reviews and Notices', *Alpine Journal*, 16 (1892–93), 327–42
'Reviews and Notices', *Alpine Journal*, 17 (1894–95), 527–34
Adamson, Robert, 'Hill Climbing in Skye', *Cairngorm Club Journal*, 1 (1893–96), 181–91

Allbutt, T. Clifford, 'On the Effect of Exercise upon the Bodily Temperature', *Alpine Journal*, 5 (1870–72), 212–18
———, 'On the Health and Training of Mountaineers', *Alpine Journal*, 8 (1876–78), 30–40
Almond, Hely H., 'Ben-y-Gloe on Christmas Day', *Scottish Mountaineering Club Journal*, 2 (1892–93), 235–39
Baker, Ernest A., 'Buachaille Etive Mor and the Crowberry Ridge', *Climbers Club Journal*, 3 (1900–01), 3–16
———, 'Practice Scrambles in Derbyshire', *Climbers' Club Journal*, 1 (1898–99), 53–65
Bonney, T.G., 'Address by Prof. T. G. Bonney, President', *Alpine Journal*, 11 (1882–84), 373–82
———, 'The Alpine Club Map of Switzerland', *Alpine Journal*, 7 (1874–76), 218–23
Bowles, R.L., 'Sunburn', *Alpine Journal*, 14 (1888–89), 122–27
Boyd, H.C., 'Ben A'an', *Scottish Mountaineering Club Journal*, 4 (1896–97), 155–58
Brown, William, 'Ascent of Ben Nevis by the N. E. Buttress', *Scottish Mountaineering Club Journal*, 3 (1894–95), 323–31
———, 'Climbing in Scotland: Ben Nevis', *Cairngorm Club Journal*, 2 (1896–99), 1–8
———, 'The Coolins in '96', *Scottish Mountaineering Club Journal*, 4 (1896–97), 193–208
Bryant, George R., 'The Formation of the Climbers' Club', *Climbers' Club Journal*, 1 (1898–99), 1–7
Bryce, James, 'Some Stray Thoughts on Mountaineering', *Cairngorm Club Journal*, 1 (1893–96), 1–6
Bullock, H. Somerset, 'Chalk Climbing on Beachy Head', *Climbers' Club Journal*, 1 (1898–99), 91–97
Campbell, Thomas Fraser S., 'Ben Lui', *Scottish Mountaineering Club Journal*, 1 (1890–91), 207–14
———, 'The Glen Sannox Hills', *Scottish Mountaineering Club Journal*, 1 (1890–91), 31–36
Carr, Ellis, 'Two Days on an Ice Slope', *Alpine Journal*, 16 (1892–93), 422–46
Cash, C.G., 'The Ordnance Survey and the Cairngorms', *Cairngorm Club Journal*, 3 (1899–1902), 85–88
Collie, John Norman, 'Climbing Near Wastdale Head', *Scottish Mountaineering Club Journal*, 3 (1894–95), 1–9
———, 'A Reverie', *Scottish Mountaineering Club Journal*, 5 (1898–99), 93–102
Conway, Martin, 'Centrists and Excentrists', *Alpine Journal*, 15 (1890–91), 397–403
———, 'The Dom from Domjoch', *Alpine Journal*, 15 (1890–91), 104–11
———, 'Exhausted Districts', *Alpine Journal*, 15 (1890–91), 255–67

Corner, Edred M., 'The Loch Treig Hills and Ben Na Lap', *Scottish Mountaineering Club Journal*, 5 (1898–99), 66–69

Cornish, Theodore, 'An Ascent of the Weisshorn from Zinal; and Some Notes on Winter Climbing', *Alpine Journal*, 15 (1890–91), 195–205

Craufurd Grove, F., 'Address to the Alpine Club', *Alpine Journal*, 13 (1886–88), 213–20

———, 'Alpine Training Diet', *Alpine Journal*, 12 (1884–86), 149–56

———, 'The Comparative Skill of Travellers and Guides', *Alpine Journal*, 5 (1870–72), 87–96

Cust, A.C., 'The Matterhorn Without Guides', *Alpine Journal*, 8 (1876–78), 242–56

Daniel, E.C., 'First Aid to the Injured in Climbing Accidents', *Climbers' Club Journal*, 1 (1898–99), 43–49

Dent, Clinton T., 'Address to the Alpine Club', *Alpine Journal*, 15 (1890–91), 3–16

———, 'Alpine Climbing – Past, Present and Future', *Alpine Journal*, 9 (1878–80), 65–72

———, 'The History of an Ascent of the Aiguille du Dru', *Alpine Journal*, 9 (1878–80), 185–200

———, 'The Rocky Mountains of Skye', *Alpine Journal*, 15 (1890–91), 422–36

———, 'The Rothhorn from Zermatt', *Alpine Journal*, 6 (1872–74), 268–74

Dewar, Francis J., 'Beinn Mhic Mhonaidh', *Scottish Mountaineering Club Journal*, 3 (1894–95), 70–72

Dickens, Charles, 'Hardihood and Foolhardihood', *All the Year Round*, August 1865, p. 86

Donkin, W.F., 'Photography in the High Alps', *Alpine Journal*, 11 (1882–84), 63–71

Downes Law, Edward, 'Alpine Notes: Cotton versus India Rubber', *Alpine Journal*, 10 (1880–82), 41–42

———, 'Alpine Notes: India Rubber versus Paper as a Material for Alpine Maps', *Alpine Journal*, 10 (1880–82), 40–41

E.R.G., 'Reviews', *Climbers' Club Journal*, 3 (1900–01), 42–46

Fleming, John, 'Snowdon', *Cairngorm Club Journal*, 1 (1893–96), 90–95

Freshfield, Douglas, 'An Address to the Alpine Club', *Alpine Journal*, 18 (1896–97), 1–17

———, 'The Club Map Cupboard', *Alpine Journal*, 10 (1880–82) 42–44

———, 'The Dolomites of Val Rendena', *Alpine Journal*, 5 (1870–72), 249–59

———, 'The Pelmo', *Alpine Journal*, 6 (1872–74), 257–67

———, 'The Solitude of Abkhazia', *Alpine Journal*, 15 (1890–91), 237–55

George, Hereford Brooke, 'Axe versus Alpenstock', *Alpine Journal*, 4 (1868–70), 126–29

———, 'Photography in the High Alps', *Alpine Journal*, 4 (1868–70), 402–10

———, '"Progress" in the Alps', *Alpine Journal*, 19 (1898–99), 4–13

Gibson, J.H., 'Snowcraft in Scotland', *Scottish Mountaineering Club Journal*, 2 (1892–93), 322–24
Gordon, John, 'An Arctic Summer Day on Cairn Toul', *Cairngorm Club Journal*, 1 (1893–96), 157–63
Green, Rev. W.S., 'A Journey Into the Glacier Regions of New Zealand', *Alpine Journal*, 11 (1882–84), 57–63
Hastings, Geoffrey, 'Over Mont Blanc by the Brenva Route, Without Guides', *Alpine Journal*, 17 (1894–95), 537–51
Hinxman, Lionel W., 'Ben Eighe and the Torridon Hills', *Scottish Mountaineering Club Journal*, 1 (1890–91), 187–94
Jackson, E.P., 'A Winter Quartette', *Alpine Journal*, 14 (1888–89), 200–10
Kennedy, Edward Shirley, 'The Ascent of Monte della Disgrazia', *Alpine Journal*, 1 (1863–64), 3–20
Kennedy, Thomas, 'Zermatt and the Matterhorn in Winter', *Alpine Journal*, 1 (1863–64), 77–82
Leaf, Walter, 'Climbing with a Hand-Camera', *Alpine Journal*, 15 (1890–91), 472–79
Llewelyn Davies, Rev. J., 'Ascent of one of the Mischabel-Hörner, called the Dom', *Peaks, Passes, and Glaciers*, 1 (1859), 194–206
Macauley, James, 'Some Grampian and Sutherland Recollections', *Cairngorm Club Journal*, 2 (1896–99), 28–33
Mathews, Charles Edward, 'The Alpine Obituary', *Alpine Journal*, 11 (1882–84), 78–89
———, 'New Experiences in the Old Playground', *Alpine Journal*, 16 (1892–93), 19–30
Mathews, William, 'The Mountains of Bagnes', *Peaks, Passes, and Glaciers*, 1 (1859), 76–125
———, 'On the Determination of Heights by Means of the Barometer', *Alpine Journal*, 2 (1865–66), Part 1, 33–41
———, 'On the Determination of Heights by Means of the Barometer', *Alpine Journal*, 2 (1865–66), Part 2, 63–67
———, 'The Sympiezometer and Aneroid Barometer', *Alpine Journal*, 2 (1865–66), 397–404
Maund, J. Oakley, 'The Gross Lauteraarhorn from the West, and an Attempt on the Eastern Ridge of the Eiger', *Alpine Journal*, 11 (1882–84), 27–39
Maylard, Alfred Ernest, 'Ben Lomond', *Scottish Mountaineering Club Journal*, 3 (1894–95), 140–50
———, 'Climbing Considered in its Physiological Aspects', *Scottish Mountaineering Club Journal*, 4 (1896–97), Part 1, 267–75
———, 'Climbing Considered in its Physiological Aspects', *Scottish Mountaineering Club Journal*, 5 (1898–99), Part 2, 17–23
———, 'Scottish Mountaineering: Retrospective and Prospective', *Scottish Mountaineering Club Journal*, 5 (1898–99), 308–14

——, 'Winter Ascents: Ben Vorlich and Stuc-a-Chroin on the 1st January 1891', *Scottish Mountaineering Club Journal*, 1 (1890–91), 222–34

Merivale, Herman, 'Alpine Travelers', *Edinburgh Review*, October 1856, pp. 433–53

Monro, C.G., 'Mountain Sickness', *Alpine Journal*, 16 (1892–93), 446–55

Moore, A.W., 'On Some Winter Expeditions in the Alps', *Alpine Journal*, 5 (1870–72), 62–76

Mummery, A.F., 'The Aiguilles des Charmoz and de Grepon', *Alpine Journal*, 16 (1892–93), 159–73

Munro, Hugh, 'An Teallach: Ross-shire', *Scottish Mountaineering Club Journal*, 3 (1894–95), 10–18

——, 'Reduced Ordnance Survey Maps', *Scottish Mountaineering Club Journal*, 1 (1890–91), 180–83

Naismith, William, 'Ben Nevis in 1880 and 1889', *Scottish Mountaineering Club Journal*, 1 (1890–91), 215–21

——, 'Snowcraft in Scotland', *Scottish Mountaineering Club Journal*, 2 (1892–93), 157–67

——, 'Three Days Among the Cuchulins', *Scottish Mountaineering Club Journal*, 1 (1890–91), 56–62

Nichols, R.C., 'Excursions in the Graian Alps: The Ascent of the Ste. Helene', *Alpine Journal*, 2 (1865–66), 387–97

Nicolson, Alexander, 'Skye and Sgur-nan-Gillean in 1865', *Scottish Mountaineering Club Journal*, 2 (1892–93), 99–108

Norman-Neruda, L., 'Some New Ascents in the Bernina Group', *Alpine Journal*, 15 (1890–91), 461–71

P.W.T., 'Alpine Implements, etc', *Alpine Journal*, 15 (1890–91), 98

Ramsay, George Gilbert, 'Ascent of Suilven by the Grey Castle', *Scottish Mountaineering Club Journal*, 4 (1896–97), 23–34

——, 'In Memoriam: Professor John Veitch', *Scottish Mountaineering Club Journal*, 3 (1894–95), 175–82

——, 'The President's Address at the First Annual Dinner, December 12, 1889', *Scottish Mountaineering Club Journal*, 1 (1890–91), 1–11

——, 'Rise and Progress of Mountaineering in Scotland', *Scottish Mountaineering Club Journal*, 4 (1896–97), 1–15

Robertson, A.E., 'Two Days in Lochaber', *Scottish Mountaineering Club Journal*, 3 (1894–95), 267–71

Slingsby, William Cecil, 'A Night Adventure on the Dent Blanche', *Alpine Journal*, 15 (1890–91), 404–17

Smith, William C., 'The Cairngorms', *Cairngorm Club Journal*, 3 (1899–1902), 8–14

Stafford Anderson, J., 'The Dent Blanche from Zinal', *Alpine Journal*, 11 (1882–84), 158–72

Stephen, Leslie, 'Ascent of the Rothhorn', *Alpine Journal*, 2 (1865–66), 67–79
———, 'Alpine Dangers', *Alpine Journal*, 2 (1865–66), 273–85
———, 'Mr. Whymper's Scrambles Amongst the Alps', *Alpine Journal*, 5 (1870–72), 234–40
———, 'A New Pass in the Chain of Mont Blanc', *Alpine Journal*, 6 (1872–74), 351–364
———, 'The Peaks of Primiero', *Alpine Journal*, 4 (1868–70), 385–402
———, 'Recent Accidents in the Alps', *Alpine Journal*, 4 (1868–70), 373–79
———, 'Round Mont Blanc', *Alpine Journal*, 5 (1870–72), 289–305
———, 'Sunset on Mont Blanc', *Cornhill Magazine*, October 1873, pp. 457–67
Stogdon, J., 'The Late Accident on Mont Blanc', *Alpine Journal*, 5 (1870–72), 194–99
———, 'Schlagintweit's Himalayan Travels', *Alpine Journal*, 6 (1872–74), 43–50
Stott, J.G., 'Mountain Memories', *Scottish Mountaineering Club Journal*, 4 (1896–97), 224–37
Thomas, Percy W., 'Rocky Mountain Sickness', *Alpine Journal*, 17 (1894–95), 140–41
Thomson, Gilbert, 'The Arrochar Mountains', *Scottish Mountaineering Club Journal*, 1 (1890–91), 63–69
———, 'Practice Scrambles', *Scottish Mountaineering Club Journal*, 2 (1892–93), 8–12
Tuckett, F.F., 'Amounts of Ozone at Different Altitudes', *Peaks, Passes, and Glaciers*, 2 (1862), 445–54
———, 'The Col Vicentino, Bosco del Consiglio, and Monte Cavallo', *Alpine Journal*, 6 (1872–74), 124–44
Vansittart, G.N., Letter, 'Mr. Vansittart's Ascent of Mont Blanc', *The Daily News*, 26 August 1851
Watts, Theodore, 'Aspects of Tennyson: Tennyson as Nature-Poet', *The Nineteenth Century*, 33 (1893), 836–856
Whymper, Edward, 'The Ascent of Mont Pelvoux', *Peaks, Passes, and Glaciers*, 2 (1862), 233–56
Williamson, G.N., 'The Climbs of the English Lake District', *All The Year Round*, November 1884, Part 1, pp. 77–82
Willink, H.G., 'Alpine Sketching', *Alpine Journal*, 12 (1884–86), 361–80
———, 'Exhibition of Mr Donkin's Photographs', *Alpine Journal*, 14 (1888–89), 309–10
———, 'Snowdon at Christmas, 1878', *Alpine Journal*, 16 (1892–93), 33–42
Wills, Alfred, 'The Passage of the Fenêtre de Salena', *Peaks, Passes, and Glaciers*, 1 (1859), 1–38
Wilson, Claude, 'The Corno Bianco', *Alpine Journal*, 17 (1894–95), 475–92
Woolley, Hermann, 'The Ascent of Dych-tau', *Alpine Journal*, 15 (1890–91), 173–91

## Books

Anon, *Where to Go: Reprinted (By Special Request) from Tit-Bits* (Manchester: Guardian, 1883).

Abraham, Ashley, *Rock Climbing in Skye* (London: Longmans, Green, 1908)

d'Angeville, Henriette, *My Ascent of Mont Blanc* (1838; London: HarperCollins, 1992)

Barrow, John, *Mountain Ascents in Westmoreland and Cumberland* (London: Sampson Low, Marston, Searle, and Rivington, 1868)

Berenson, Bernard, *The Florentine Painters of the Renaissance*, 3rd edn. (New York and London: G. P. Putnam and Sons, 1908)

Bicknell, John W., ed., *Selected Letters of Leslie Stephen, 1864–1882*, 2 vols. (Basingstoke: Macmillan, 1996)

Brockedon, William, *Journals of Excursions in the Alps: the Pennine, Graian, Cottian, Rhetian, Lepontian, and Bernese* (London: James Duncan, 1833)

Burke, Edmund, *A Philosophical Enquiry into the Origins of our Ideas of the Sublime and Beautiful*, ed. by Adam Phillips (1757; Oxford: Oxford University Press, 1990)

Burnaby, Mrs Fred (Elizabeth Le Blond), *The High Alps in Winter: or, Mountaineering in Search of Health* (London: Sampson Low, Marston, Searle, and Rivington, 1883)

———, (as Mrs. Aubrey Le Blond), *Day In, Day Out* (London: The Bodley Head, 1928)

Burton, John Hill, *The Cairngorm Mountains* (Edinburgh: William Blackwood and Sons, 1864)

Cline, C.L., ed., *The Letters of George Meredith*, 2 vols. (Oxford: Clarendon Press, 1970)

Conway, Martin, *The Alps from End to End* (London: Archibald Constable, 1895)

Coolidge, W.A.B., *Alpine Studies* (London: Longmans, Green, 1912)

———, *The Alps in Nature and History* (London: Methuen, 1908)

———, and Eliot Howard, eds., *A Pioneer in the High Alps: Alpine Diaries and Letters of F. F. Tuckett, 1856–1874* (London: Edward Arnold, 1920)

Cowell, J.J., 'The Graian Alps and Mount Iseran', in *Vacation Tourists*, ed. by Francis Galton (London: Macmillan, 1861), pp. 239–63

Dent, Clinton T., *Above the Snow Line* (London: Longmans, Green, 1885)

———, ed., *Badminton Library of Sports and Pastimes: Mountaineering* (London: Longmans, Green, 1892)

———, 'Equipment and Outfit', in *Badminton Library of Sports and Pastimes: Mountaineering* (London: Longmans, Green, 1892)

———, 'Mountaineering and Health', in *Badminton Library of Sports and Pastimes: Mountaineering* (London: Longmans, Green, 1892), pp. 77–94

——, 'The Principles of Mountaineering', in *Badminton Library of Sports and Pastimes: Mountaineering* (London: Longmans, Green, 1892), pp. 95–136

——, 'Reconnoitring', in *Badminton Library of Sports and Pastimes: Mountaineering* (London: Longmans, Green, 1892), pp. 137–56

Freshfield, Douglas, *Below the Snow Line* (London: Constable, 1923)

——, *Italian Alps: Sketches in the Mountains of Ticino, Lombardy, the Trentino, and Venetia* (1875; Oxford: Basil Blackwell, repr. 1937)

George Gordon, and Lord Byron, 'Childe Harold's Pilgrimage', in *Lord Byron: The Major Works*, ed. by Jerome J. McGann (Oxford: Oxford University Press, 2008), pp. 19–206

Girdlestone, A.G., *The High Alps Without Guides, Being a Narrative of Adventures in Switzerland* (London: Longmans, Green, 1870)

Gribble, Francis, *The Early Mountaineers* (London: T. Fisher Unwin, 1899)

Harrison, Frederic, *My Alpine Jubilee* (London: Smith, Elder, 1908)

Hawes, Benjamin, *A Narrative of an Ascent to the Summit of Mont Blanc Made During the Summer of 1827 by Mr. William Hawes and Mr. Charles Fellowes* (privately printed, 1828)

Hawkins, F. Vaughan, 'The Matterhorn – First Assault', in *Hours of Exercise in the Alps*, ed. by John Tyndall (London: Longman, Green, 1871), pp. 27–52

Hudson, Charles, and Edward Shirley Kennedy, *Where There's a Will There's a Way: An Ascent of Mont Blanc by a New Route and Without Guides* (London: Longmans, Brown, Green and Longmans, 1856)

James, William, *Principles of Psychology*, 2 vols. (London: Macmillan, 1890)

Jones, Owen Glynne, *Rock Climbing in the English Lake District* (London: Longmans, Green, 1897)

Kant, Immanuel, *The Critique of Judgement* (1790; Oxford: Clarendon Press, 1952)

Keats, John, 'To J. H. Reynolds Esq.', in *John Keats: The Major Works*, ed. by Elizabeth Cook (Oxford: Oxford University Press, 2008), pp. 182–85

Kilgour, William T., *Observers at the Highest Meteorological Station in the British Isles* (Paisley: Alexander Gardner, 1905)

Lucretius, *De Rerum Natura*, trans. W.H.D. Rouse, Loeb Classical Library, 3rd edn. (London: Heinemann; Cambridge, MA: Harvard University Press, 1937)

Mathews, Charles Edward, *The Annals of Mont Blanc* (London: T. Fisher Unwin, 1898)

——, 'The Recollections of a Mountaineer', in *Badminton Library of Sports and Pastimes: Mountaineering*, ed. by Clinton T. Dent (London: Longmans, Green, 1892), pp. 348–79

Morrell, Jemima, *Miss Jemima's Swiss Journal: The First Conducted Tour of Switzerland* (1863; London: Putnam, repr. 1963)

Mosso, Angelo, *Fatigue*, trans. Margaret and W.B. Drummond (London: Swan Sonnenschein, 1904)

Mummery, Albert, *My Climbs in the Alps and Caucasus* (London: T. Fisher Unwin, 1895)

Mummery, Mary, 'Der Teufelsgat', in *My Climbs in the Alps and Caucasus*, ed. Albert Mummery (London: T. Unwin Fisher, 1895), pp. 66–95

Myers, Frederic W.H., 'On a Grave at Grindelwald', in *Frederic William Henry Myers: Collected Poems*, ed. by Eveleen Myers (London: Macmillan, 1912), p. 213

Oppenheimer, Lehmann J., *The Heart of Lakeland* (London: Sherratt and Hughes, 1908)

Pater, Walter, *The Renaissance: Studies in Art and Poetry*, ed. by Kenneth Clark (London: Fontana/Collins, 1961)

Paterson, M., *Mountaineering Below the Snow-Line: The Solitary Pedestrian in Snowdonia and Elsewhere* (London: George Redway, 1886)

Pilkington, Charles, 'Climbing Without Guides', in *Badminton Library of Sports and Pastimes: Mountaineering*, ed. by Clinton T. Dent (London: Longmans, Green, 1892), pp. 307–24

Rey, Guido, *The Matterhorn*, trans. J.E.C. Eaton (London: T. Fisher Unwin, 1907)

Richards, I.A., 'The Lure of High Mountaineering', in *Complementarities: Uncollected Essays*, ed. by John Paul Russo (Manchester: Carcanet New Press, 1977), pp. 235–245

Riegl, Aloïs, *Late Roman Art Industry*, trans. Rolfe Winke (Rome: Giorgio Bretschneider, 1985)

———, *Historical Grammar of the Visual Arts*, trans. Jacqueline E. Jung (New York: Zone Books, 2004)

Ruskin, John, *Complete Works*, ed. by E.T. Cook and Alexander Wedderburn, 39 vols. (London: George Allen, 1903–12)

———, *Deucalion: Collected Studies of the Lapse of Waves, and Life of Stones* (Kent: George Allen, 1879)

———, *Modern Painters*, 5 vols. (London: J. M. Dent, 1843–60), IV (1856)

———, *Praeterita*, ed. by Tim Hilton. (London: Alfred A. Knopf, 2005)

———, *Sesame* and *Lilies* (London and New Haven: Yale University Press, 2002)

Scott, Sir Walter, *Rob Roy* (Edinburgh: Edinburgh University Press, 2008)

Smith, Albert, *The Story of Mont Blanc* (London: David Bogue, 1853)

Smith, Walter Parry Haskett, *Climbing in the British Isles*, 2 vols. (London: Longmans, Green, 1894)

Spencer, Herbert, *An Autobiography*, 2 vols. (London: Williams and Norgate, 1904)

Stephen, Leslie, 'The Allelein-Horn', in *Vacation Tourists*, ed. by Francis Galton (London: Macmillan, 1861), pp. 264–81

———, Alpine Climbing. In *British Sports and Pastimes*, ed. Anthony Trollope (London: Virtue, Spalding, 1868), pp. 257–89

———, *The Playground of Europe* (London: Longmans, Green, 1871)
———, 'A Substitute for the Alps', in *Men, Books and Mountains* (London: The Hogarth Press, 1956), pp. 203–12
Stoddard, John, *John Stoddard's Lectures* (New York, Chicago, and London: Belford, Middlebrook, 1897)
Tennyson, Alfred, 'Morte d'Arthur', in *The Poems of Tennyson*, ed. by Christopher Ricks, Longmans Annotated English Poets (London: Longmans, 1969), pp. 585–98
———, 'The Lady of Shallot', in *The Poems of Tennyson*, ed. by Christopher Ricks (London: Longmans, 1969), pp. 354–61
Trollope, Anthony, *Travelling Sketches* (London: Chapman and Hall, 1866)
Tuckett, Elizabeth, *Beaten Tracks: Pen and Pencil Sketches in Italy* (London: Longmans, Green, 1866)
Tyndall, John, *Glaciers of the Alps* (London: John Murray, 1860)
———, *Hours of Exercise in the Alps* (London: Longman, Green, 1871)
———, *Mountaineering in 1861: A Vacation Tour* (London: Longman, Green, 1862)
Wherry, George, *Alpine Notes and the Climbing Foot* (Cambridge: Macmillan & Bowes, 1896)
Whymper, Edward, *Scrambles Amongst the Alps in the Years 1860–1869* (London: John Murray, 1871)
Wills, Alfred, *Wanderings Among the High Alps* (London: Richard Bentley, 1856)
Wilson, Henry Schütz, *Alpine Ascents and Adventures* (London: Sampson Low, Marston, Searle, and Rivington, 1878)
Wordsworth, William, *Guide to the Lakes* (1810; London: Frances Lincoln, repr. 2004)
———, *The Prelude: The Four Texts*, ed. by Jonathan Wordsworth (London: Penguin, 1995)

## Secondary Texts

### Theses

Hansen, Peter Holger, 'British Mountaineering, 1850–1914', (unpublished doctoral dissertation, Harvard University, 1991)

### *Journals, Newspapers, and Magazines*

Bainbridge, Simon, 'Romantic Writers and Mountaineering', *Romanticism*, 18 (2012), 1–15
Blakeney, T.S., and D.F.O. Dangar, 'Oscar Eckenstein', *Alpine Journal*, 65 (1960), 62–79

Bristow, Joseph, 'Whether "Victorian" Poetry: A Genre and its Period', *Victorian Poetry*, 42 (2004), 81–109

Campbell, Robin N., 'My Dear Douglas', *Scottish Mountaineering Club Journal*, 34 (1990), 388–99

Colley, Ann C., 'John Ruskin: Climbing and the Vulnerable Eye', *Victorian Literature and Culture*, 37 (2009), 43–66

Crook, Janet, 'Letter, Damnable Heresies', *London Review of Books*, 8 November 2012, p. 4

Daniele, France, Camillo di Giulio, and Charles M. Tipton, 'Angelo Mosso and Muscular Fatigue: 116 years After the First Congress of Physiologists', *Advances in Physical Education*, 30 (2006), 51–57

Dierig, Sven, 'Engines for Experiment: Laboratory Revolution and Industrial Labour in the Nineteenth-Century City', *Osiris*, 2nd ser., 18, 'Science and the City' (2003), 116–34

Eaton, R.D., 'In the "World of Death and Beauty": Risk, Control, and John Tyndall as Alpinist', *Victorian Literature and Culture*, 41 (2013), 55–73

Hansen, Peter Holger, 'Albert Smith, the Alpine Club, and the Invention of Mountaineering in mid-Victorian Britain', *The Journal of British Studies*, 34 (1995), 300–24

———, 'Review', *Victorian Studies*, 54 (2012), 334–36

Hevly, Bruce, 'The Heroic Science of Glacier Motion', *Osiris*, 2 (1996), 66–86

Kember, Joe, 'The View from the Top of Mont Blanc: The Alpine Entertainment in Victorian Britain', *Living Pictures*, 2 (2003), 21–45

Morrison, Kevin A., 'Embodiment and Modernity: Ruskin, Stephen, Merleau-Ponty and the Alps', *Comparative Literature Studies*, 46 (2009), 498–511

Robbins, David, 'Sport, Hegemony and the Middle Classes: The Victorian Mountaineers', *Theory, Culture and Society*, 4 (1987), 579–601

Roche, Clare, 'Women Climbers 1850–1900: A Challenge to Male Hegemony', *Sport in History* (2013), doi: 10.1080/17460263.2013.826437

Vine, Steve, 'Blake's Material Sublime', *Studies in Romanticism*, 41 (2002), 237–57

## *Books*

Adams, James Eli, *Dandies and Desert Saints: Styles of Victorian Masculinity* (Ithaca and London: Cornell University Press, 1995)

Ardito, Stefano, *Mont Blanc: Discovery and Conquest of the Giant of the Alps*, trans. by A.B.A. Milan (Shrewsbury: Swan Hill Press, 1996)

Ashfield, Andrew and Peter de Bolla, eds., *The Sublime: A Reader in British Eighteenth-Century Aesthetic Theory* (Cambridge: Cambridge University Press, 1996)

Bailey, Peter, *Leisure and Class in Victorian England: Rational Recreation and the Contest for Control, 1830–1885* (London: Routledge, 1978)

Bates, Robert H., *Mystery, Beauty, and Danger: The Literature of the Mountains and Mountain Climbing Published in English Before 1946* (Portsmouth, NH: Peter E. Randall, 2000)

Beattie, Andrew, *The Alps: A Cultural History* (Oxford: Signal Books, 2006)

Beer, Gavin de, *Early Travellers in the Alps* (New York: October House, 1930)

Beer, Gillian, *Darwin's Plots: Evolutionary Narrative in* Darwin, George Eliot *and Nineteenth-Century Fiction*, 3rd edn. (Cambridge: Cambridge University Press, 2009)

Bernal, J.D., *Science and Industry in the Nineteenth Century* (New York: Routledge, 1953)

Bevin, Darren, *Cultural Climbs: John Ruskin, Albert Smith and the Alpine Aesthetic* (Berlin: VDM, 2010)

Braham, Trevor, *When the Alps Cast their Spell: Mountaineers of the Alpine Golden Age* (Glasgow: Neil Wilson, 2004)

Brown, Rebecca A., *Women on High: Pioneers of Mountaineering* (Boston: Appalachian Mountain Club Books, 2002)

Buzard, James, *The Beaten Track: European Tourism, Literature, and the Ways to Culture, 1800–1918* (Oxford: Clarendon Press, 1993)

Cardinal, Roger, 'Ruskin and the Alpine Ideal', in *Ruskin in Perspective*, ed. by Carmen Casaliggi and Paul March-Russell (Newcastle upon Tyne: Cambridge Scholars, 2010), pp. 157–76

Carey, John, *The Intellectuals and the Masses: Pride and Prejudice among the Literary Intelligentsia, 1880–1939* (London: Faber and Faber, 1992)

Chard, Chloe, 'From the Sublime to the Ridiculous: The Anxieties of Sightseeing', in *The Making of Modern Tourism: The Cultural History of the British Experience, 1600–2000*, ed. by Hartmut Berghoff, Barbara Korte, Ralph Schneider, and Christopher Harvie (Basingstoke: Palgrave, 2002), pp. 47–68

Clark, Ronald, *An Eccentric in the Alps* (London: Museum Press, 1969)

———, *The Victorian Mountaineers* (London: B. T. Batsford, 1953)

Clarke, Edwin and L.S. Jacyna, *Nineteenth-Century Origins of Neuroscientific Concepts* (Berkeley, Los Angeles, and London: University of California Press, 1987)

Clewis, Robert R., *The Kantian Sublime and the Revelation of Freedom* (Cambridge: Cambridge University Press, 2009)

Colley, Ann C., *Victorians in the Mountains: Sinking the Sublime* (Farnham: Ashgate, 2010)

Collini, Stefan, *Public Moralists: Political Thought and Intellectual Life in Britain, 1850–1930* (Oxford: Clarendon Press, 1991)

Costelloe, Timothy, *The Sublime: From Antiquity to the Present* (Cambridge: Cambridge University Press, 2012)

Crary, Jonathan, *Suspensions of Perception: Attention, Spectacle, and Modern Culture* (Cambridge, MA: MIT Press, 2001)

———, *Techniques of the Observer: On Vision and Modernity in the Nineteenth Century* (Cambridge, MA: MIT Press, 1992)

Crocket, Ken, and Simon Richardson, *Ben Nevis: Britain's Highest Mountain* ([n.p.]: Scottish Mountaineering Trust, 1986)

Crowley, Aleister, *The Confessions of Aleister Crowley*, ed. by John Symonds and Kenneth Grant (London: Penguin, 1989)

Cunningham, Frank F, *James David Forbes: Pioneer Scottish Glaciologist* (Edinburgh: Scottish Academic Press, 1990)

Davis, Wade, *Into the Silence: The Great War, Mallory and the Conquest of Everest* (London: The Bodley Head, 2011)

Dempster, Andrew, *The Munro Phenomenon* (Edinburgh: Mainstream Publishing, 1995)

Devine, Ruth, 'McCormick, Arthur David', in *Dictionary of Irish Biography*, 9 vols. (Cambridge: Cambridge University Press, 2009), V, pp. 867–68

Donnan, F.G., 'Collie, John Norman (1859–1942)', in *Oxford Dictionary of National Biography* (Oxford: Oxford University Press, 2004), doi:10.1093/ref:odnb/32498

Douglas, ed., *Mountaineers: Great Tales of Bravery and Conquest* (London: Royal Geographical Society, 2011)

Drummond, Peter, *The First Munroist* (Glasgow: Ernest Press, 1993)

Ellis, Reuben, *Vertical Margins: Mountaineering and the Landscapes of Neo-Imperialism* (Madison: University of Wisconsin Press, 2001)

Fitzsimons, Raymund, *The Baron of Piccadilly: The Travels and Entertainments of Albert Smith, 1816–1860* (London: Geoffrey Bles, 1967)

Fleming Fergus, *Killing Dragons* (London: Granta, 2001)

Flint, Kate, *The Victorians and the Visual Imagination* (Cambridge: Cambridge University Press, 2000)

Forman, Ross, 'Empire', in *The Cambridge Companion to the Fin de Siècle*, ed. by Gail Marshall (Cambridge: Cambridge University Press, 2007), pp. 91–111

Frank, Robert G., 'The Telltale Heart: Physiological Instruments, Graphic Methods, and Clinical Hopes', in *The Investigative Enterprise: Experimental Physiology in the Nineteenth Century*, ed. by William Coleman and Frederic L. Holmes (Berkeley, Los Angeles, and London: University of California Press, 1988), pp. 211–90

Fraser, Hilary, 'Foreword', in *Illustrations, Optics and Objects in Nineteenth-Century Literary and Visual Cultures*, ed. by Luisa Calè and Patrizia Di Bello (Basingstoke: Palgrave Macmillan, 2010), pp. ix–xv

Freedgood, Elaine, *Victorian Writing about Risk: Imagining a Safe England in a Dangerous World* (Cambridge: Cambridge University Press, 2000)

Gill, Stephen, *Wordsworth and the Victorians* (Oxford: Clarendon Press, 1998)

Grunwald, Martin, *Human Haptic Perception: Basics and Applications* (Basel: Birkhäuser, 2008)

Hamilton, Jill, *Thomas Cook: The Holiday-Maker* (Stroud: Sutton Publishing, 2005)

Hankinson, Alan, *The First Tigers: The Early History of Rock Climbing in the Lake District* (London: J. M. Dent, 1972)

——, *The Mountain Men: A History of Rock Climbing in North Wales – From its Beginning to 1914* (Cheshire: Mara Books, 1977)

Hansen, Peter Holger, 'Mummery, Albert Frederick (1855–1895)', in *Oxford Dictionary of National Biography* (Oxford: Oxford University Press, 2004), doi:10.1093/ref:odnb/19526

——, *The Summits of Modern Man: Mountaineering After the Enlightenment* (Cambridge, MA.: Harvard University Press, 2013)

Harrison, John, *Synaesthesia: The Strangest Thing* (Oxford: Oxford University Press, 2001)

Hearle, J.W.S., H.A. McKenna, and N. O'Hear, *Handbook of Fibre Rope Technology* (Cambridge: Woodhead, 2004)

Hewitt, Rachel, *Map of a Nation: A Biography of the Ordnance Survey* (London: Granta, 2010)

Hobsbawm, Eric, and Terence Ranger, eds., *The Invention of Tradition* (Cambridge: Cambridge University Press, 1983)

Hollis, Catherine W., *Leslie Stephen as Mountaineer: 'Where Does Mont Blanc End, and Where Do I Begin?'*, The Bloomsbury Heritage Series (London: Cecil Woolf, 2010)

Holt, Richard, *Sport and the British: A Modern History* (Oxford: Clarendon Press, 1989)

Hoppen, Theodore K., *The Mid-Victorian Generation, 1846–1886* (Oxford: Clarendon Press, 1998)

Irving, R.L.G., *A History of British Mountaineering* (London: B. T. Batsford, 1955)

Keay, John, *The Great Arc: The Dramatic Tale of how India was Mapped and Everest was Named* (London: HarperCollins, 2000)

Krakauer, Jon, *Into Thin Air: A Personal Account of the Everest Disaster* (New York: Villard, 1997)

Kern, Stephen, *The Culture of Space and Time, 1880–1918* (London: Weidenfeld and Nicolson, 1983)

Le Gallienne, Richard, *The Romantic Nineties* (London: Putnam, 1951)

Ledger, Sally, 'The New Woman and the Crisis of Victorianism', in *Cultural Politics at the Fin de Siècle*, ed. by Sally Ledger and Scott McCracken (Cambridge: Cambridge University Press, 1995), pp. 22–44

Lorimer, Hayden, and Katrin Lund, 'Performing Facts: Finding a Way Over Scotland's Mountains', in *Nature Performed: Environment, Culture and Performance*, ed. by Bronislaw Szerszynski, Wallace Heim, and Claire Waterton (London: Blackwell 2003), pp. 130–44

Lunn, Arnold, *A Century of Mountaineering, 1857–1957* (London: George Allen & Unwin, 1957)

Macfarlane, Robert, *Mountains of the Mind* (London: Granta, 2008)

Maitland, William, *Life and Letters of Leslie Stephen* (London: Duckworth, 1906)

Mangan, J. A., and James Walvin, eds., *Manliness and Morality – Middle-class Masculinity in Britain and America, 1800–1914* (Manchester: Manchester University Press, 1987)

Matthews, Samantha, 'After Tennyson: The Presence of the Poet, 1892–1918', in *Tennyson Among the Poets: Bicentenary Essays*, ed. by Robert Douglas-Fairhurst and Seamus Perry (Oxford: Oxford University Press, 2009), pp. 315–335

McNee, Alan, *The Cockney Who Sold the Alps: Albert Smith and the Ascent of Mont Blanc* (Brighton: Victorian Secrets, 2015)

Milner, Douglas, 'The Art and Sport of Rock Climbing in the English Lake District', in *The Lake District: A Sort of National Property* (London: Victoria & Albert Museum, 1984), pp. 105–15

Mitchell, Ian, *Scotland's Mountains Before the Mountaineers* (Edinburgh: Luath Press, 1998)

Mitchell, Richard G., *Mountain Experience: The Psychology and Sociology of Adventure* (Chicago and London: University of Chicago Press, 1983)

Monk, Samuel H., *The Sublime: A Study of Critical Theories in Eighteenth-Century England* (Ann Arbor: University of Michigan Press, 1960)

Murray, Sheila, *The Cairngorm Club, 1887–1897* (Aberdeen: The Cairngorm Club, 1987)

Nicolson, Marjorie Hope, *Mountain Gloom and Mountain Glory: The Development of the Aesthetics of the Infinite* (Seattle: University of Washington Press, 1959)

O'Connor, W. J., *Founders of British Physiology: A Biographical Dictionary, 1820–1885* (Manchester and New York: Manchester University Press, 1988)

O'Gorman, Francis, '"The Mightiest Evangel of the Alpine Club": Masculinity and Agnosticism in the Alpine Writing of John Tyndall', in *Masculinity and Spirituality in Victorian Culture*, ed. by Andrew Bradstock, Sean Gill, Anne Hogan, and Sue Morgan (Basingstoke: Macmillan, 2000), pp. 134–48

Oerlemans, Onno, *Romanticism and the Materiality of Nature* (Toronto: University of Toronto, 2002)

Østermark-Johansen, Lene, *Walter Pater and the Language of Sculpture* (London: Ashgate, 2011)

Parisi, David, 'Tactile Modernity: On the Rationalisation of Touch in the Nineteenth Century', in *Media, Technology and Literature in the Nineteenth Century*, ed. by Collette Colligan and Margaret Linley (Farnham: Ashgate, 2011), pp. 189–215

Park, Roberta J., 'Biological Thought, Athletics and the Formation of a "Man of Character", 1800–1900', in *Manliness and Morality – Middle-class Masculinity in Britain and America, 1800–1914*, ed. by J. A. Mangan and James Walvin (Manchester: Manchester University Press, 1987), pp. 7–34

Paterson, Mark, *The Senses of Touch: Haptics, Affects and Technologies* (Oxford and New York: Berg, 2007)

Perkin, Harold, *The Rise of Professional Society: England since 1880* (London: Routledge, 1989)

Pudney, John, *The Thomas Cook Story* (London: Michael Joseph, 1953)

Rabinbach, Anson, *The Human Motor: Energy, Fatigue and the Origins of Modernity* (Berkeley and Los Angeles: University of California Press, 1992)

Radford, Andrew and Mark Sandy, eds., *Romantic Echoes in the Victorian Era* (Aldershot: Ashgate, 2008)

Richardson, Alan, *British Romanticism and the Science of the Mind* (Cambridge: Cambridge University Press, 2001)

Ring, Jim, *How the English Made the Alps* (London: John Murray, 2000)

Robertson, David, 'Mid-Victorians Amongst the Alps', in *Nature and the Victorian Imagination*, ed. by U. C. Knoepflmacher and G. B. Tennyson (Berkeley: University of California Press, 1977) pp. 113–36

Robinson, Jane, *Wayward Women: A Guide to Women Travellers* (Oxford: Oxford University Press, 1990)

Rylance, Rick, *Victorian Psychology and British Culture, 1850–1880* (Oxford: Oxford University Press, 2000)

Sale, Richard, *Mapping the Himalayas: Michael Ward and the Pundit Legacy* (Ross-on-Wye: Carreg, 2009)

Schama, Simon, *Landscape and Memory* (New York: Alfred A. Knopf, 1995)

Semmel, Bernard, *The Methodist Revolution* (London: Heinemann, 1974)

Shaw, Philip, *The Sublime* (London: Routledge, 2006)

Sherwood, Marion, *Tennyson and the Fabrication of Englishness* (Basingstoke: Palgrave Macmillan, 2013)

Shires, Linda M., *Perspectives: Modes of Viewing and Knowing in Nineteenth-Century England* (Columbus, Ohio: Ohio State University Press, 2009)

Simmel, Georg, 'The Alpine Journey', in *Simmel on Culture*, ed. by David Frisby and Mike Featherstone (London: Sage, 1997), pp. 219–21

Simmons, Clare A., *Popular Medievalism in Romantic-Era Britain* (Basingstoke: Palgrave Macmillan, 2011)

Simon, Jonathan, 'Taking Risks: Extreme Sports and the Embrace of Risk in Advanced Liberal Societies', in *Embracing Risk: The Changing Culture of Insurance and Responsibility*, ed. by Tom Baker and Jonathan Simon (Chicago and London: University of Chicago Press, 2002), pp. 177–208

Slack, Jennifer Daryl and John Macgregor Wise, *Culture and Technology: a primer* (London: Peter Lang, 2005)

Smith, Ian, *Shadow of the Matterhorn: The Life of Edward Whymper* (Ross-on-Wye: Carreg, 2011)

Spufford, Francis, *I May Be Some Time: Ice and the English Imagination* (London: Faber and Faber, 1996)
Stedman Jones, Gareth, 'The 'Cockney' and the Nation, 1780–1988', in *Metropolis London: Histories and Representations since 1800*, ed. by David Feldman and Gareth Stedman Jones (London and New York: Routledge, 1989), pp. 271–324
Steven, Campbell, *The Story of Scotland's Hills* (London: Robert Hale, 1975)
Strange, Greg, *The Cairngorms: 100 Years of Mountaineering* ([n.p.]: Scottish Mountaineering Trust, 2010)
Taylor, Harvey, *A Claim on the Countryside: A History of the British Outdoor Movement* (Edinburgh: Keele University Press, 1997)
Taylor, William C., *The Snows of Yesteryear: J. Norman Collie, Mountaineer* (Toronto: Holt, Rinehart and Winston, 1973)
Thompson, Carl, *The Suffering Traveller and the Romantic Imagination* (Oxford: Clarendon Press, 2007)
Thompson, Ian, *The English Lakes: A History* (London: Bloomsbury, 2010)
Thompson, Simon, *Unjustifiable Risk: The Story of British Climbing* (Milnthorpe, Cumbria: Cicerone, 2010)
———, *A Long Walk with Lord Conway: An Exploration of the Alps and an English Adventurer* (Oxford: Signal Books, 2013)
Tigges, Wim, '"Heir of all the Ages": Tennyson Between Romanticism, Victorianism and Modernism', in *Victorian Keats and Romantic Carlyle: The Fusions and Confusions of Literary Periods*, ed. by C. C. Barfoot (Amsterdam and Atlanta, GA: Rodopi, 1999), pp. 307–22
Towner, John, *An Historical Geography of Recreation and Tourism in the Western World, 1540–1940* (Chichester: John Wiley, 1996)
Unsworth, Walt, *Hold the Heights: The Foundations of Mountaineering* (London: Hodder & Stoughton, 1993)
———, *Savage Snows: The Story of Mont Blanc* (London: Hodder & Stoughton, 1986)
Vance, Norman, *The Sinews of the Spirit: The Ideal of Christian Manliness in Victorian Literature and Religious Thought* (Cambridge: Cambridge University Press, 1985)
Wallace, Anne D., *Walking, Literature and English Culture: The Origins and Uses of the Peripatetic in the Nineteenth Century* (Oxford: Clarendon Press, 1993)
Walton, John K., 'British Tourism Between Industrialization and Globalization', in *The Making of Modern Tourism*, ed. by Korte Berghoff, and Harvie Schneider (Basingstoke: Palgrave, 2002), pp. 109–31
Walvin, James, *Leisure and Society, 1830–1950* (London: Longman, 1978)
Williams, Cicely, *Women on the Rope: The Feminine Share in Mountain Adventure* (London: George Allen & Unwin, 1973)

Yeo, Richard, *Defining Science: William Whewell, Natural Knowledge, and Public Debate in Early Victorian Britain* (Cambridge: Cambridge University Press, 1993)

———, 'Natural Philosophy', in *An Oxford Companion to the Romantic Age: British Culture, 1776–1832*, ed. by Ian McCalman and others (Oxford: Oxford University Press, 1999), pp. 320–28

Young, Paul, *Globalization and the Great Exhibition: The Victorian New World Order* (Basingstoke: Palgrave Macmillan, 2009)

# INDEX

## A

*Above the Snow Line* (Dent), 144n37, 186n77
Abraham, Ashley, 60, 141, 150, 170, 171
Abraham, George, 60, 150
abseiling, 112
accidents, mountaineering, 33, 56, 62–63, 171–172
Adamello range (Alps), 45
  See also Presanella range
Adamson, Robert, 84, 104n44
aesthetics, physiological, 23, 109, 120, 125
Agassiz, Louis, 6
Aletschhorn (Alps), 58, 89
Allbutt, Thomas Clifford, 117, 118, 144n36, 144n39
Allen, Grant, 120, 123
*All The Year Round*, 27n51, 197
Almond, Hely H., 75, 76, 102n7, 199
*Alpine Ascents and Adventures* (Wilson), 91, 105n78
Alpine Club
  *Alpine Club Register*, 36

*Alpine Journal*, 11–13, 17, 33, 39, 40, 42, 45, 46, 48, 52, 54, 55, 56, 58, 61, 62, 63, 64, 84, 87, 118, 129, 164, 166, 179
  disputes, 13, 64, 211
  founded, 32
  membership profile, 10, 11, 36, 41, 195
  overseas Alpine Clubs, 220
  *Peaks, Passes, and Glaciers*, 11, 33, 53, 59, 87, 129, 180
  picture exhibitions, 54, 56, 164
*Alpine Journal*, see Alpine Club
*Alpine Studies* (Coolidge), 68n60
Alpinism, Golden Age of, 9, 14, 15
*Alps from End to End, The* (Conway), 26n28, 86
*Alps in Nature and History, The* (Coolidge), 17, 25n6, 25n16
altitude sickness, 112, 118
Am Basteir (Scotland), 170
d'Angeville, Henriette, 38, 66n23
Anderson, J. Stafford, 124, 145n68
Anstruther-Thomson, Kit (Clementina), 120

Aonach Eagach (Scotland), 46
Archer Thomson, James Merriman, 60
Arnold, Matthew, 11
Ashfield, Andrew, 160–161, 184n34
athleticism, 2, 13, 19, 76, 88, 160, 164, 165
Auldjo, John, 8
avalanches, 89, 121, 155, 156, 174, 210

**B**

*Badminton Library of Sports and Pastimes: Mountaineering* (Dent), 47, 65n3, 69n88, 143n8, 143n10, 143n15, 188n119
Bainbridge, Simon, 25n14
Baker, Ernest A., 150, 151, 154, 155, 157, 170, 183n1
Balfour, Francis Maitland, 115, 117, 143n23
Ball, John, 11
Balmat, Auguste, 10
Balmat, Jacques, 5, 8
Barrow, John, 191, 214n9
Bates, Robert H., 10, 26n27
Beer, Gavin de, 25n6
Beer, Gillian, 97, 106n99
Beinn Mhic Mhonaidh (Scotland), 47
Bel Alp, 16
*Below the Snow Line* (Freshfield), 188n122
Ben A'An (Scotland), 47
Ben Nevis, 5, 71n137, 71n138, 94, 134, 212, 220
Berenson, Bernard, 120, 125–126, 145n73
bergschrunds, *see* glaciers
Bernese Oberland, 55
Bevin, Darren, 22, 29n87
Bietschhorn (Alps), 40

Blake, William, 167
Bolla, Peter de, 160–161
Bonney, Thomas George, 44, 67n59
Boyd, Herbert, 47, 68n73
Bradley, Katharine, *see* Field, Michael
Braham, Trevor, 18, 25n7
Brevoort, Meta, 39, 40
Bristow, Joseph, 81, 103n31
Broad Stand, *see* Scafell
Brocken Spectre, 61
Brown, Rebecca A., 21, 28n81
Brown, William, 94, 95, 98, 106n90, 118, 144n45, 203, 212
Bryce, James, 136, 138, 147n113
Buachaille Etive Mor (Scotland), 150
Burke, Edmund, 150, 152, 155, 157, 160, 161, 162, 183n8
Burnaby, Mrs. Fred, *see* Le Blond, Elizabeth
Burton, John Hill, 154–155, 156, 157, 173, 177, 184n16, 209
Buzard, James, 24, 30n93, 194, 215n18, 216n53

**C**

Cader Idris (Wales), 61
Cairngorm Club
  *Cairngorm Club Journal*, 33, 36, 48, 66n35, 82, 84, 94, 135, 198
  Founded, 32, 212
  membership profile, 36
  women members, 41, 212, 218n97
*Cairngorm Mountains, The* (Burton), 154, 209
Cairngorms, 48, 154, 198, 212
Cardinal, Roger, 180, 187n110
Carey, John, 205, 214n6
Carr, Ellis, 163, 185n46
Cash, C.G., 48, 51, 68n78
Caucasian Survey, Russian, 45

Caucasus mountains, 41, 45, 54, 211
Chamonix, 6, 8, 15, 87, 159, 176, 190, 203
  Compagnie des Guides de Chamonix, 6
Chard, Chloe, 205, 217n69
*Childe Harold's Pilgrimage* (Byron), 7, 50, 68n85, 165, 174
Cir Mhor (Scotland), 1, 24n1, 81, 103n28
Clachaig Inn, *see* visitors' books
Clark, Ronald, 18, 67n49, 218n93
class, social, 36–38, 190–195, 197, 204
climbers, *see* mountaineer, types of
Climbers' Club
  *Climbers' Club Journal*, 33, 56, 70n120, 110, 180, 183n1, 214n10
  membership profile, 33, 191
*Climbing in the British Isles* (Smith), 65n1, 212
*Climbs in the Alps and Caucasus, My* (Mummery), 41, 61, 67n45, 211
cockneys, *see* tourists and tourism
codification, 23, 32, 35, 42–43, 117, 138
Coleridge, Samuel Taylor, 50–51, 81, 93, 167, 221
  climbing on Scafell, 50–51
Colley, Ann C., 21, 22, 28n78, 40, 166, 187n111
Collie, John Norman
  coins phrase 'New Mountaineer', 1, 24n1, 31, 80, 152
  criticises ethos of other climbers, 80, 84
  mountaineering career, 80
  prose style, 97–98

Collini, Stefan, 36, 65n7, 192
Collins, Wilkie, 93
Conway, Martin
  ascent of Dom, 122
  on 'cold stony reality' of climbing, 10, 74, 85, 167, 221
  describes ideal mountaineer, 85
Cook, Thomas, 190, 192–194, 199, 201, 211, 215n11
Coolidge, William Augustus Brevoort
  on climate of opinion after Matterhorn tragedy, 15–16
  climbs with aunt, Meta Brevoort, 39–40
  on guideless climbing, 64
  historian of mountaineering, 7, 17
  on quality of maps, 45
Cooper, Edith, *see* Field, Michael
*Cornhill* magazine, 11, 26n30, 146n98
Cornish, Theodore, 125, 145n70
Crary, Jonathan, 23, 30n91, 116, 120, 178
Craufurd Grove, Florence
  on guideless climbing, 64
  on nutrition, 58, 117
  on qualities required by mountaineers, 64
  on women climbers, 21, 40
crevasses, *see* glaciers
Croz, Michel, 15
Cuillins (Scotland), 1, 46, 101, 170
Cust, A.C., 209, 218n85

D

de Bolla, Peter, 160–161, 184n34
Dennis, John, 127
Dent Blanche (Alps), 124, 145n68, 159

Dent, Clinton
  career in physiology, 115
  on conservation of energy, 110
  multiple attempts on Aiguille du
      Dru., 158, 170, 171, 186n76,
      186n77
  on possibility of climbing
      Everest, 118
  on snow and rock climbing,
      difference between, 135–136
Dessoir, Max, 152, 183n6
Dewar, Francis J., 47, 68n72
Dickens, Charles, 15, 27n51, 93
diet, see nutrition
Dixon, H.B., 60
Dolomites, 121, 124, 145n59,
    162
Donkin, William, 54, 55, 166, 181
Douglas, Lord Francis, 15
Douglas, William, 82
Downes Law, Edward, 52, 69n92,
    69n93
Dru, Aiguille du (Alps), 158, 170,
    186n76, 186n77
Dych-Tau (Caucasus), 71n136, 211

E

*Early Travellers in the Alps* (de
    Beer), 25n6
Eaton, Roger, 19, 20, 21
Eckenstein, Oscar, 60, 61, 71n134,
    143n11
Elliot, Rev. Julius, 62
Ellis, Reuben, 19, 28n64, 160
equipment, climbing
  alpenstock, 53
  camping gear, 51, 57
  clothing, 23, 51, 54, 62, 112
  crampons, 33, 112, 143n11
  ice-axe, 53, 93, 140
  rope, 15, 33, 51, 53–54,
      58, 62, 69n106, 89, 93,
      112, 164
  stoves, 51, 54
Everest, 45, 118, 220–222, 223n6


F

*Fatica, La* (Mosso), 115, 144n25
fatigue, 2, 4, 76, 109, 110, 111,
    114–119, 124, 127–130, 152,
    163, 171, 178, 183, 194, 198
Faulhorn (Alps), 192
Federal Office of Topography,
    Switzerland, 44, 52
Fick, Adolf, 115
Field, Michael (Edith Cooper and
    Katharine Bradley), 120
Fleming, Fergus, 18, 26n26
Fleming, John, 198, 216n39
Flint, Kate, 25n11, 29n89, 43
food, see nutrition
Forbes, James David, 6, 13–15, 25n12
Forman, Ross, 29n88
Franklin, Sir John, 92–94
Fraser, Hilary, 120, 125, 127, 145n54
Freedgood, Elaine, 19, 28n68
Freshfield, Douglas, 65n3, 67n51,
    67n58, 84, 104n45, 121, 141,
    145n59, 148n126, 162, 164,
    185n41, 188n122, 200, 210,
    211, 221
Frey, Max von, 116
Friedrich, Caspar David, 155, 156
frostbite, 112, 118


G

Galton, Francis, 129, 146n92
geology, 6, 12, 18, 42, 60, 71n130,
    97, 154

George, Hereford Brooke, 53, 55, 69n98, 70n109, 210, 218n89
Gesner, Conrad, 5, 17
Gill, Stephen, 79, 103n22, 197
Girdlestone, Reverend Arthur Gilbert, 64, 72n144, 133, 139, 169, 171, 173, 174, 177, 209
Gissing, George, 191
glaciers, 5–7, 14, 54, 132, 133, 156, 1, 212
Glencoe, 46, 49, 60, 70n128, 150, 199, 206, 217n71
Golden Age, *see* Alpinism
Gordon, George, Lord Byron, 7, 50, 68n85
Gordon, John, 135, 147n108
Gornergrat (Alps), 196
Graham, William Woodman, 211
Graian Alps, 12, 26n37, 130, 146n92
Great Trigonometrical Survey, 45, 52, 68n63, 211
Gribble, Francis, 17, 24n4
Gruner, Gottlieb, 5
*Guide to the Lakes* (Wordsworth), 7, 215n31
guideless climbing, 44, 64, 104n39, 146n87, 193, 209
 *See also* Girdlestone; Craufurd Grove; Hudson; Kennedy; Cust; Mont Blanc; Matterhorn
guides, mountain, 6, 10, 15, 39, 41, 53, 64, 118, 209

# H
Hadow, Roger, 15
Hankinson, Alan, 18, 71n134, 142n1
Hansen, Peter, 18, 19, 22, 25n17, 28n61, 28n63, 36, 40, 67n43, 129, 209, 215n22

'haptic sublime', The, *see* sublime
Harrison, Frederic, 138–140, 147n121
Hastings, Geoffrey, 163, 164, 185n47
Hawkins, F. Vaughan, 174, 178, 186n87
*Heart of Lakeland, The* (Oppenheimer), 102n3, 148n129
Helmholtz, Hermann von, 114
Hevly, Bruce, 14, 15, 19, 27n43, 173
Hewitt, Rachel, 20, 22, 28n76, 50
*High Alps Without Guides, The* (Girdlestone), 64, 72n144, 173, 209
High Street (Lake District), 191
Himalayas, 68n64, 71n134, 80, 211, 212, 222
Hinchcliff, Thomas, 11
*History of British Mountaineering, A* (Irving), 18, 218n90
Hobsbawm, Eric, 90–91, 105n76
Hollis, Catherine W., 21, 29n83
Holt, Richard, 29n90, 37
Hoppen, Theodore, 19, 26n31, 215n12
*Hours of Exercise in the Alps* (Tyndall), 16, 27n54, 121, 174, 186n87
Hudson, Reverend Charles, 15, 87, 88 guideless ascent of Mont Blanc, 87–88
Hutton, James, 97

# I
imperialism, 2, 18–19, 22, 24, 29, 45, 211, 220
Irving, R.L.G., 18, 218n90
*Italian Alps* (Freshfield), 148n126, 210

## J

Jackson, E.P., 40, 66n38
James, William, 119, 144n47
Jones, Owen Glynne
   death in climbing accident, 110
   defends aesthetic sensibility of climbers, 95
   obituary, 110
   pioneering rock climber, 42
Jungfrau (Alps), 117, 196, 210, 215n26

## K

Kabru (Himalayas), 211
Kant, Immanuel, 150, 155, 157, 160, 161, 162, 165, 172, 184n22, 184n32, 184n33
Keats, John, 167, 185n64
Kember, Joe, 21, 28n77
Kennedy, Edward Shirley, 11–12, 26n33, 87, 88
   guideless ascent of Mont Blanc, 87, 105n61
Kern, Stephen, 35, 65n5
Kilgour, William, 134, 147n103
Krakauer, Jon, 221, 223n9
Krohn, William D., 116
Kronecher, Hugo, 115

## L

Ladies' Alpine Club, 39, 41
Lake District, English, 2, 42, 60, 95, 110, 189, 191, 196–197, 204–206, 212–213
Leaf, Walter, 55, 70n114
Le Blond, Elizabeth, 39, 55, 70n113, 166, 216n51
Ledger, Sally, 91, 105n77
Lee, Vernon, 120
Le Gallienne, Richard, 90, 105n75
Llewelyn Davies, Reverend J., 129, 146n91
Lochnagar (Scotland), 154, 156, 173
*London Review of Books*, 221
Longinus, Dionysius, 150
Lorimer, Hayden, 82, 104n36
Lucretius (Titus Lucretius Carus), 150, 152, 183n7
Lund, Katrin, 82, 104n36
Lyell, Charles, 97

## M

Macfarlane, Robert, 18, 106n98
*Manchester City News*, 35, 65n4, 81
manliness, 2, 29n90, 37–38, 41, 66n18, 74, 75, 90, 219
mapping, 3, 20–21, 33, 43–48, 50, 51, 52, 76, 82, 88
   See also navigation
masculinity, *see* manliness
Mathews, Charles Edward, 8, 11, 25n19, 63, 65n3, 69n104, 111, 143n8, 191, 196, 214n10, 215n28
Mathews, George Spencer, 11
Mathews, William, 26n41, 89, 105n71, 129, 133, 146n90
Matthews, Samantha, 81, 103n32
Matterhorn
   1865 disaster, 15, 76
   first guideless ascent, 209
Maylard, Albert Ernest
   on enjoyment of climbing, 134, 137, 147n104
   on physiology of mountaineering, 137, 138, 147n116
McCormick, Arthur David, 164, 185n53
Meall Dearg (Scotland), 46
Meredith, George, 39, 197

INDEX    253

Mill, John Stuart, 79
Mitchell, Ian, 18
Mont Aiguille (Alps), 17
Mont Blanc
  accidents on, 63, 186n81
  1827 ascent by Hawes and
    Fellowes, 87, 105n58
  1851 ascent by Albert Smith, 7–8,
    42, 58, 87
  1856 guideless ascent, 87, 105n61
  first ascent, 5
  'Mont Blanc mania', 8
Montenvers (Alps), 133, 191
Monte Rosa (Alps), 25n8, 89,
  115, 163
Mont Velan (Alps), 129
Moore, A.W., 130, 140, 146n93
*Morning Post*, 196
Morrell, Jemima, 192, 215n13
Morrison, Kevin, 22, 29n86
*Morte d'Arthur* (Tennyson), 80–81,
  103n27
Mosso, Angelo, 115, 116, 117, 129,
  137, 143n19, 144n28
*Mountain Ascents in Westmoreland
  and Cumberland*
  (Barrow), 214n9
*Mountaineering in 1861*
  (Tyndall), 202, 216n55
*Mountaineering Below the Snow-Line*
  (Paterson), 216n36
mountaineer, types of
  gymnast, 75, 76, 82, 85, 86, 94, 96,
    102n5, 122, 164
  peak-bagger, 83, 92
  rock acrobat, 75, 76, 87
  Salvationist, 75, 76, 102n7
  Ultramontane, 75, 76, 102n10
*Mountain Gloom and Mountain Glory*
  (Nicolson), 17, 27n58
mountains, see under individual names
Mount Iseran, 130, 146n92

Mount Pilatus, 196
Mummery, Albert
  blackballed from Alpine Club, 195
  on cockney tourists, 195
  death on Nanga Parbat, 80, 211
  defends mountaineering from
    critics, 94
Mummery, Mary, 41, 67n45
Munro, Sir Hugh, 46, 47, 68n67
  creates Munro's Tables, 46, 47, 50,
    51, 117
Munro (category of mountain), 47
Myers, Frederic W.H., 172, 186n80,
  186n81

N
Naismith, William
  criticises Ordnance Survey maps, 45
  formulates Naismith's Rule, 47
  founder member of Scottish
    Mountaineering Club, 37
  on pleasure of climbing, 134, 135
  on use of ice-axe, 53
Nanga Parbat (Himalayas), 80, 211
Napier, Colonel C.C., 221
navigation, 3, 21, 33, 43–52, 76, 82,
  88, 93
  *See also* mapping
Nepal, 56
neurasthenia, 116
New Mountaineer, the, 1–4, 17,
  22–24, 31–33, 35, 38, 41, 43–44,
  51, 52, 54, 56, 58–59, 62–65,
  73–76, 79–81, 85, 89, 90, 91,
  93–96, 99, 101, 111, 127, 149,
  151, 157, 161, 193, 213,
  221, 223
New Zealand, 67n47, 163, 211, 220
Nichols, R.C., 12, 26n37, 105n72
Nicolson, Marjorie Hope, 17, 18,
  27n58

Norman-Neruda, Louis, 167, 186n67
nutrition, 33, 56, 58, 109, 116

## O

Oerlemans, Onno, 167, 186n65
O'Gorman, Francis, 21, 29n82
Oppenheimer, Lehmann J., 60, 74, 102n3, 142
Ordnance Survey, 20, 33, 44–46, 48, 50
Østermark-Johansen, Lene, 123, 145n66

## P

Paccard, Michel-Gabriel, 5, 8
*Pall Mall Gazette*, 197
Paradis, Marie, 38
Parisi, David, 23, 30n92, 119
Pater, Walter, 123, 145n65
Paterson, Mark, 198, 216n36
*Peaks, Passes, and Glaciers*, see Alpine Club
Pelmo (Dolomites), 162
Pen-y-Gwryd Hotel, *see* visitors' books
Perkin, Harold, 37, 61, 65n12
Petrarca, Francesco (Petrarch), 5
photography, 3, 54–56, 166
physiology
    climbers involved in research (
        *see also* Balfour; Dent; Mosso), 115, 117
    experiments in Continental Europe, 114
    influences ethos of mountaineering, 4, 110, 111, 115, 117–123, 137–139
    *Journal of Physiology*, 114
    Physiological Society formed, 114–115
    psycho-physiology, 119, 120
    theories of mountaineering physiology, 115, 118, 135–138
Pigeon, Anna, 39, 40
Pigeon, Ellen, 39, 40
Pilkington, Charles, 46, 112, 143n10
Piz Bernina (Alps), 167
*Playground of Europe, The* (Stephen), 16, 99–101, 106n106, 175–179, 190, 210
*Prelude, The* (Wordsworth), 7, 50, 69n86, 155, 165, 169
Presanella range (Alps), 45
    *See also* Adamello range
professionalism, 36–38, 41, 48, 51
*Punch*, 191, 205

## R

Rabinbach, Anson, 23, 30n92, 110, 119
Radford, Andrew, 79, 90, 103n20
railways
    funicular, 189, 193, 195, 196, 199, 201, 210, 219, 222
    West Highland Railway, 200
Ramsay, George Gilbert, 51, 69n91, 78–79, 83–84, 85, 88, 102n5, 103n23, 104n40, 112, 118, 143n14, 202
    criticisms of fellow mountaineers, 78, 83–84
    on technical nature of mountaineering, 51
Ranger, Terence, 90–91, 105n76
regelation, *see* glaciers
Richards, I.A., 128, 146n85
Richards, Kathleen, 39
Richardson, Alan, 119, 145n49
Riegl, Aloïs, 120, 126, 146n78, 152, 183n5

Rigi (Alps), 192, 196
Ring, Jim, 16, 18, 25n10
risk, 2, 19–20, 63, 91, 151, 152, 155, 156, 159, 166, 194, 195
Robbins, David, 14, 19, 27n42
Robertson, David, 18, 28n60
Robertson, Reverend Archibald Eneas
  becomes 'first Munroist', 46, 200
  on extension of West Highland railway, 200
*Rob Roy* (Scott), 7, 83, 104n38, 104n39
Roche, Clare, 40, 67n44
*Rock Climbing in the English Lake District* (Jones), 66n21, 95, 110
Romantic literature, 6–7, 10, 12, 18, 50, 75, 79–83, 90, 150, 155, 165, 167, 169, 189
rope, *see* equipment, climbing
Rothhorn (Alps), 13
Ruskin, John
  aesthetic theories, 21, 76, 94, 99, 100, 153–154, 180
  criticisms of mountaineering, 76–77, 121, 153, 180
  influence on mountaineers, 17, 180
  religious faith challenged by geology, 97

S
Sandy, Mark, 79, 90, 103n20
de Saussure, Horace Benedict, 5
Scafell (Lake District), 51, 80, 172
Scafell Pike (Lake District), 205
Schama, Simon, 18, 22, 25n6, 38, 153, 175
Schlagintweit brothers (Adolf, Hermann & Robert), 211, 218n94

Schreckhorn (Alps), 27n55, 62, 125
scientism, 13–14, 19
Scotland, 2, 16, 18, 44–50, 53, 56, 69n102, 82–83, 103n23, 104n36, 106n90, 112, 134, 147n107, 150, 198, 203, 209, 212, 219, 220
Scott, Walter, 7, 79, 83, 104n38, 180
Scottish Mountaineering Club
*Scottish Mountaineering Club Journal*, 33, 45, 46–47, 50, 53, 56, 82–83, 84, 96, 137, 200–201
*Scrambles Amongst the Alps in the Years 1860–1869*, 16, 65n14
séracs, 111, 128, 138, 181
Sgurr nan Gillean (Scotland), 1, 24n1, 49, 60, 81, 103n28
Shelley, Percy Bysshe, 7
Shires, Linda M., 126, 146n81
Siedelhorn (Alps), 203
Signalkuppe (Alps), 89
skiing, *see* sports, winter
Skye, Isle of, 1, 24n1, 35, 45, 49, 50, 60, 81, 103n28, 170, 203, 207
Slack, Jennifer Daryl, 166, 185n60
Sligachan Inn, *see* visitors' books
Slingsby, Cecil, 207
Smith, Albert, 7–10, 21, 25n9, 25n17, 25n18, 26n20, 28n62, 29n87, 42, 58, 65n9, 87, 88, 160
Smith, Ian, 22, 29n84
Smith, Walter Parry Haskett, 32, 65n1, 142n4, 207, 212
Smith, William C., 83, 104n37
Simon, Jonathan, 19, 20, 28n70
snow-blindness, 112, 118
Snowdon, 5, 61, 122, 145n63, 155, 176, 198, 216n39, 219
Spencer, Herbert, 4, 44, 67n57
sports, winter, 214, 219–221
Spufford, Francis, 75, 93, 102n4

Stedman, Edmund Clarence, 81
Stephen, Leslie
  on cockney tourists, 190–191, 193, 210
  defends mountaineers from charge of Philistinism, 99–101
  emphasises importance of physical experience, 175–179
  offends Tyndall, 13
  prose style, 16, 99
  on 'sense of superlative sublimity', 99–101
Steven, Campbell, 18
Stogdon, John, 63, 71n141, 211, 218n94
*Story of Mont Blanc, The* (Albert Smith), 8–10, 26n20, 87, 58
Stott, Joseph Gibson, 82, 83, 84, 96, 98, 102n10, 104n35
  criticises state of mountaineering prose, 82–84
sublime, the
  'Empirical Sublime', 21
  'Haptic Sublime', 4, 149–183
  Romantic Sublime, 150, 155, 156, 161, 162, 164, 167, 168, 169
  'superlative sublimity', *see* Stephen, Leslie
Suilven (Scotland), 112, 143n14
sunburn, 112, 118, 132, 144n38

T

Taugwalder, Peter, 15
Tennyson, Alfred Lord, 80, 81, 98, 103n27, 165, 185n56
Thompson, Simon, 18, 22, 24n5, 29n84
Thomson, Gilbert, 56, 70n119, 200, 216n46
Tigges, Wim, 81, 103n30

*Times, The*, 15, 27n50
*Tit-Bits*, 205, 217n66
tourists & tourism
  criticised, 62, 189–203, 206–208
  described as cockneys, 4, 190–192, 195, 201, 210, 212, 214n7
  infrastructure, 189, 190, 195–201, 210–212
  terminology, 190–194, 195, 197, 203, 206, 212–213
  Thomas Cook's tours, 192, 193, 215n12
training, 3, 33, 42, 51, 56, 58, 59, 84, 88, 109, 110, 117, 133, 193
Trollope, Anthony, 77, 103n15
Tryfan (Wales), 60
Tuckett, Elizabeth, 193, 215n15
Tuckett, Francis Fox
  as pioneer of Golden Age, 44
  prose style, 89
Tyndall, John
  on physical exhaustion, 117
  resigns from Alpine Club, 13
  dispute with Forbes, 6, 13

U

Unsworth, Walt, 6, 18, 24n2, 25n8

V

Vance, Norman, 29n90, 37
Vansittart, G.N., 88, 105n65
Veitch, Professor John, 83
vertigo, 162, 169–171, 180
Vine, Steve, 167, 185n63
visitors' books
  Clachaig Inn, 49, 60, 206
  Pen-y-Gwryd, 'Not the Visitors' Book', 59–61, 206–208

Sligachan Hotel, 49, 50, 60, 203
Wasdale Head Inn, 49, 60, 204–206, 207

## W

Wales, 2, 16, 18, 33, 60, 122, 198, 203, 206, 208, 212, 219
Walker, Lucy, 38–39
Wallace, Anne D., 22, 29n85
Walton, John K., 24, 30n93, 194
Walvin, James, 38, 199, 216n41
*Wanderings Among the High Alps* (Wills), 10, 26n25
Wasdale (Lake District), 49, 60, 97, 98, 106n97, 142, 172, 204, 205, 206, 207, 208
Wasdale Head Inn, *see* visitors' books
Watts, Theodore, 81, 103n33
*Waverley* (Scott), 7
weather, 52, 63, 78, 84, 111, 112, 113, 134, 135, 165, 168, 192
Weber, Ernst Heinrich, 114
Weisshorn (Alps), 16, 121
Wengern Alp, 196
West, Thomas, 7
West of Scotland Ramblers Alliance, 220
*Where There's a Will There's a Way* (Hudson and Kennedy), 87, 105n61
White, William Hale (Mark Rutherford), 79
Whymper, Edward
  climbs Matterhorn, 15, 16
  narrow escape from falling sérac, 156
  on manliness, 37
  on sunburn, 132
  publishes *Scrambles Amongst the Alps*, 16
  visits Andes, 211
Williams, Cicely, 21, 28n81
Williamson, G.N., 197, 216n34
Willink, Henry George, 122, 125, 145n63, 168, 178, 181, 185n62, 188n15
Wills, Alfred, 7, 9–11, 26n25, 42, 59, 65n3, 87, 129, 133, 146n89
Wilson, Henry Schütz, 91–93
Wise, John Macgregor, 166
Wislicenus, Johannes, 115, 117
women climbers, 21, 38–41, 173
Wordsworth, William, 7, 50, 79, 81, 142, 155, 156, 165, 169, 170, 196, 197, 215n31

## Y

Yeo, Richard, 25n15, 29n89, 43
Young, Paul, 29n89, 43, 67n55

## Z

Zermatt, 15, 40, 132, 195, 196, 201, 210